Banking and Financial Stability in Central Europe

Banking and Financial Stability in Central Europe

Integrating Transition Economies into the European Union

Edited by

David Green

Professor of Economics and Pro Vice Chancellor, Thames Valley University

and

Karl Petrick

Senior Lecturer in Economics, Leeds Business School, Leeds Metropolitan University

Edward Elgar

Cheltenham, UK • Northampton, MA, USA

Published by
Edward Elgar Publishing Limited
Glensanda House
Montpellier Parade
Cheltenham
Glos GL50 1UA
UK

Edward Elgar Publishing, Inc.
136 West Street
Suite 202
Northampton
Massachusetts 01060
USA

A catalogue record for this book
is available from the British Library

Library of Congress Cataloguing in Publication Data
Banking and financial stability in Central Europe : integrating transition economies into the European Union / edited by David M.A. Green and Karl Petrick.
     p. cm.
  Includes bibliographical references and index.
  1.Banks and banking–Czech Republic. 2.Banking law–Czech Republic.
  3.Banks and banking–Hungary. 4.Banking law–Hungary. 5.Banks and banking–Slovenia. 6.Banking law–Slovenia 7.European Union. I.Green, David M.A., 1952- II.Petrick, Karl, 1970-

  HG3020.3.Z6 B36 2001
  332.1'0943–dc21   2001023594

ISBN 1 84064 512 1

Printed and bound in Great Britain by MPG Books Ltd, Bodmin, Cornwall

Contents

PART IV: CONCLUSION

Figures

Tables

Contributors

István Ábel is Professor of Economics at Budapest University of Economics, and Head of Monetary Planning Section of the Hungarian National Bank. His publications include contributions to books (*Money and Finance in the Transition to a Market Economy*, Edward Elgar, 1998) and academic journals. He currently teaches courses at Budapest University and Central European University.

Yener Altunbas holds a BSc (Economics) degree from the University of Hacettepe, Ankara and a PhD from the University of Wales, Bangor. He has worked as an analyst and economist with Etibank Banking Inc. and as a Research Officer within the Institute of European Finance. Since 1998 Dr Altunbas has been employed as a Research Fellow with the Business School at South Bank University, London. Author of a number of articles on the structure and efficiency of banking markets, his main fields of research interest include the study of European banks, efficiency, stock market analysis, electoral studies, regional economics and urban economics. Some of his recent research is also concerned with marine biology.

Iain Begg is Professor of International Economics at South Bank University, London, and is the joint editor of the *Journal of Common Market Studies*, the leading academic journal dealing with European integration. He served from 1994–97 as the Programme Director of a major research programme on the Single European Market funded by the UK Economic and Social Research Council. He has directed several studies for different directorates of the European Commission and for the European Parliament, the most recent of which was a study of the future of the 'own resources' of the EU. He is currently leading research projects looking at how economies deal with economic problems under EMU and at reform of social protection.

He has published extensively on European policy issues and has been a specialist adviser to the House of Lords European Communities Committee and House of Commons Trade and Industry Select Committee. Recent publications include work on the EU budget, prudential supervision under EMU, the political economy of EMU and economic adjustment under EMU.

Neven Borak is Assistant Professor of quantitative methods for economic analysis at the School of Business and Management and adviser to the CEO of

Autocommerce d.d., Ljubljana. He served as vice-minister of planning and adviser to the Presidency, Government and Parliament of Slovenia. His publications include four books, numerous contributions to books and academic journals. His main research interests are economic policy, transformation processes, financial sector, economic history and modelling. He is one of the editors of newly established academic journal *Economic and Business Review for Central and South-Eastern Europe.*

David Green was formerly Professor of Economics and Dean of the Leeds Business School at Leeds Metropolitan University. He is now Pro Vice-Chancellor at Thames Valley University, London. He was the co-ordinator of the European Commission funded ACE/Phare research project on whose findings this book is principally based. His publications in recent years have focused on developments in and analysis of financial markets and the banking industry. He is well known as an economic commentator and consultant. In recent years he has lectured at Conferences and Universities in Britain, the Czech Republic, France, Germany, Hungary, India, Italy, Mauritius, Pakistan, Poland, Thailand, Slovenia, Spain and the United States.

Vladimir Lavrač is a research fellow at the Institute for Economic Research in Ljubljana and a member of the governing board of the Bank of Slovenia (Slovenian central bank). He co-ordinated two ACE-Phare research projects (Monetary Integration and Disintegration in Europe; Inclusion of Central European Countries in the European monetary integration process). His publications include editing the article 'Introduction of new currencies and national monetary sovereignty' in the *Journal of Development and International Co-operation*, 1995/20–21 and co-editing the book, Paul De Grauwe and Vladimir Lavrač *Inclusion of Central European Countries in the European Monetary Union*, Kluwer Academic Publishers, Boston, 1999.

Roman Matoušek is a Banking Expert in the Czech National Bank (CNB) and Senior Lecture of Finance and Banking at the Charles University. As Head of Research Division in the CNB, he was responsible for supervising and conducting research activities on the Czech financial market. In 1996 he was appointed as an adviser to the Chief Executive Director. He has been involved, as an expert, in a number of international research projects that have been focused on the financial reforms in transition economies. His research outputs have been presented at international conferences and seminars, and published in economic journals. He was a Visiting Fellow at the Birmingham University, London Business School and he was a Visiting Economist in CITICORP, New York, USA. In addition, he received a prestigious Pew Fellowship from the Georgetown University, USA in 1998. He holds a Master's degree in Economics,

Banking and Finance from CORIPE, Turin, Italy and a PhD in Economics from Charles University, Prague.

Karl Petrick is a senior lecturer in economics at Leeds Business School, Leeds Metropolitan University. Previously, he was a Research Fellow with the Business School at South Bank University, London. He holds a BSc degree in Business from Bryant College, USA, as well as a Master's degree in Development Economics and a PhD in Economics, both from the University of Leeds, UK. His research has been focused on the economic and political transition in Eastern and Central European countries. His MA and PhD theses were studies of the transition of the commercial banking sectors in Hungary and the Czech Republic.

Anita Taci started working recently as a financial economist in the Chief Economist office at the European Bank for Reconstruction and Development (EBRD), London, UK. She holds an MSc degree in Mathematics. In the summer of 2000, she is to defend her PhD theses in economics on 'The Efficiency of Bank Lending in Transition Countries and Fiscal Costs of Bank Restructuring' at the Centre for Economics Research and Graduate Education (CERGE), Charles University, the Czech Republic. During 1998–99 she worked as a consultant for the World Bank. She has also been working as a researcher on banking issues at the Economic Institute of the Academy of Sciences in the Czech Republic. Her publications include contributions to books and economic journals. Her main research interests are banking and financial markets, public budget management and transition.

Michel Tison is a lecturer at the Financial Law Institute of Ghent University, where he teaches courses on domestic and European financial and capital markets law and on company law. He obtained his doctoral degree in 1997 at Ghent University with a thesis on the legal aspects of the principle of mutual recognition in European banking and financial law. He has published various articles on Belgian, comparative and European banking and financial law, and on company law.

Preface

This book is the principal outcome of a research project (P96-6009R) funded by the European Union through its Phare/ACE programme.

Thanks are due to participants at conferences in Budapest, London and Prague. These conferences made a substantial contribution to the research programme and the active participation by colleagues from commercial and central banks, supervisory authorities as well as other professional and academic economists was much appreciated. Particular thanks are due to Professor Eddy Wymeersch of the Financial Law Institute at the University of Ghent, Johannes Priesemann of the then European Monetary Institute, Hans Blommestein of the OECD, Ota Kaftan of the Czech National Bank, Edna Young of the UK's Financial Services Authority and David Mayes of the Bank of Finland and South Bank University who spoke at the public conferences in London and Prague. Colleagues in the national banks and supervisory authorities in the Czech Republic, Hungary and Slovenia have all been most helpful. A major aim of the Phare/ACE programme has been to stimulate co-operation between researchers in the European Union and those in Central and Eastern Europe to develop research capacity and skills. The project has certainly enjoyed some success in this regard. During the project's lifetime four participant colleagues have been awarded their doctorates – Karl Petrick, Laszlo Szakadat, Anita Taci and Michel Tison. The project has been blessed in other ways. Roman Matousek and Anita Taci married and Laszlo Szakadát, Michel Tison and David Green have all become fathers.

This book would never have materialised without the able project management of Sarah Plant of the European Institute at South Bank University. Sarah managed the research project from start to finish and was much more than a model of efficiency – her good sense, charm and patience encouraged authors, speakers and researchers to produce the goods on time and in good order. Kate Pegler at Leeds Metropolitan University has played a critical and much appreciated role in getting the manuscript into shape and encouraging the editors to complete the job. Susan Hammant, Katharine O'Riordan and Francine O'Sullivan at Edward Elgar have been most helpful and encouraging throughout. The comments of two anonymous referees were most insightful.

Naturally, this book takes place in a larger context. Our family and personal histories combined with political inclinations lead to our strong support for closer links between peoples and European states with the aim of ensuring democratic, political stability and economic prosperity. We hope that this book will be a small contribution to the achievement of this goal.

Bringing an edited volume together and trying to give it some coherence can be a demanding task. It is a bit like managing an unruly family in which everyone has strong and sometimes conflicting ideas. Moreover, while some produce quickly, others have to be coaxed and blind alleys always seem to be particularly attractive. Throughout this we have been sustained by love and support from our own families and we wish to dedicate our work in bringing this book to life to our respective parents – Diana and Mino Green and Ella and John Petrick.

David Green and Karl Petrick
Leeds
August 2001

1. Introductory Overview

David Green and Karl Petrick

1. INTRODUCTION

Over the past decade, countries in Eastern and Central Europe, the Baltics, and the Commonwealth of Independent States have begun a transition from a centrally planned economy towards a market-based system. As part of this process, a number of these countries have applied to be considered for application into the European Union (EU).[1] It is hoped that inclusion in the EU will help promote democratic rule, as it did in post-fascist Greece, Spain and Portugal, as well as stimulate economic growth and development.

Accession specifically involves adopting EU rules and regulations, involving both political and economic reforms. While the need for political reforms remains, it is fair to say that generally the focus has turned towards the economic prerequisites of EU membership. Within this, the financial sector has assumed central importance, as it is rightly seen as an essential part of the economic infrastructure, as well as an industry of considerable importance in its own right. Major strategic importance is accorded to reforming the financial system by important institutions such as the European Bank for Reconstruction and Development (EBRD), which stated in 1998 that 'building a sound market-oriented financial system is fundamental to the transition from a command to a market system'.[2] Accordingly, the adaptation of EU Banking Directives is a key aspect of the Association Agreement reached between the EU and each transition country that wishes to join the Community.

2. CHARACTERISTICS OF THE BANKING SECTOR WITHIN A CENTRALLY PLANNED ECONOMY

Before discussing the adaptation of EU regulations by the associated countries, it is important to understand the characteristics of a banking sector within a centrally planned economy (CPE). Not only are these characteristics important as distinguishing traits of this sector pre-transition; they also affect the development of this sector during the transition process. This section will discuss both the properties of the banking sector in a CPE and its implications for transition economies.

The starting point for this discussion is the unique role of the monobank, a combination central bank and monopoly commercial bank which was 'simultaneously the financial advisor, the treasurer, the cashier and the auditor of every enterprise'.[3] The monobank has no counterpart in a market economy, and this amalgamation of roles within one institution can only be understood in the context of the centralised character of a CPE, the subsequent central role played by the state in directing economic activities in this system, and the insistence on compliance with targets set by planners. All of these will be discussed further below.

Even in its role as a central bank, the activities of the monobank were different from a central bank in a market economy. As George Garvy stated in 1977, 'the (Mono)bank is an administrative, not a policy making institution'.[4] Its function was to ensure compliance with targets set by planning authorities, and it did not set policy in its own right. It was not a 'bank of banks' as found in a market economy. However, with its monopoly position in providing credit to the productive sector, it was a bank of enterprises.

The origins of the monobank can perhaps be found in what is possibly the most striking property of the centrally planned banking sector as compared to a market economy: the separation of the money supply into two distinct circuits, both serving a different sector in the economy (see Figure 1.1).

In addition, the money supply in either circuit had its own individual set of functions: while the money in a market economy serves as a unit of account, store of value and medium of exchange, the money supply in a given circuit within a centrally planned economy serves only as a subset of these functions, or only functions within a set of given parameters. Enterprise money (the dashed line in Figure 1.1) represented a transfer of money between the banking and productive units of the state sector.

As all industrial sector accounts were held in the monobank, money was simply transferred between accounts. This gives rise to the peculiarities of 'enterprise money':

- It had an accounting identity but no physical component: it was a unit of account only.
- It was non-allocative: an excess/deficit of enterprise money did not equate with an increase/decline in production levels, as these were set separately by the planning authorities.
- It lacked universal purchasing power: it could be utilised only for specific tasks as decided by authorities. Each account in the monobank had a specific purpose (wage payments, accounts payable, etc.), and not only

did a firm need permission from authorities to transfer payments to other firms, it also could not transfer money between its own accounts, nor use money for anything but its stated purpose. Money in enterprise accounts was 'internally non-convertible'.[5]

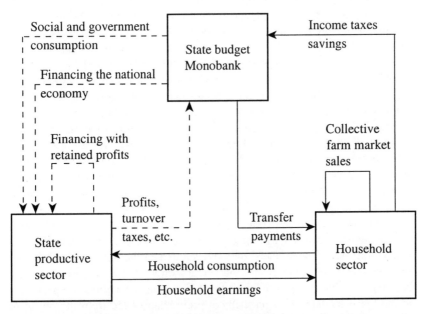

Social and government consumption

State budget Monobank

Income taxes savings

Financing the national economy

Collective farm market sales

Financing with retained profits

Profits, turnover taxes, etc.

Transfer payments

State productive sector

Household consumption

Household sector

Household earnings

- - - - Payments through bank accounts (enterprise money circuit)
———— Cash payments (private money circuit)

Figure 1.1   Monetary flows in a centrally planned economy[6]

'Private money', also called 'household money', was cash: as such it was both a unit of account and a store of value. However, it has been argued that this type of money also lacked universal purchasing power in a CPE, as it was a medium of exchange only within supply limits of consumer goods which were set by authorities.[7]

The separation of the money supply into two distinct circuits affected the methods used by planners to determine the money supply, and affected the development of the banking sector within a centrally planned economy. This was due to the need to keep these two circuits separate, so that an imbalance in one circuit would not disturb the money flows in the other. As a result, there were two large banks, each with a monopoly in their monetary circuit: the monobank serving the productive sector, the state savings bank serving the household sector.

While commercial banks within a market economy may tend to specialise in serving certain markets, the specialisation within a CPE was absolute: the monobank had no experience in providing consumer banking services to households, while the savings bank had no experience in providing services to industrial clients. In the beginning of the transition, the separation of the monetary circuits would be discontinued; that is, the distinction between enterprise money and private money would cease, along with their specialised functions. Money then served as a unit of account, store of value and medium of exchange with no restrictions, just as in a market economy, at least within a given country. It would take longer for currencies to be fully convertible between countries. Once the transition began, however, the specialised nature of various banks, and the subsequent sharp division between industrial and household banking, would remain. This is true even though the banks were free to serve all markets.

Another characteristic of banking within a central planned economy is the underdevelopment of consumer banking (serving the household sector). This stems from the lack of importance, at least in the eyes of planners, of the consumer sector generally. As a result of the monopoly of this sector by the savings bank, there were no specialised banks within the consumer banking sector, as can be found in a market economy. For example, credit unions did not exist. Although co-operative banks served as a rough approximation of this in that they provided banking services for members, they did not extend the full range of banking services that a credit union in a market economy would. Also missing were building societies/savings and loan organisations, which traditionally specialised in mortgage lending. As a result, both pre-transition and from the outset of transition, there were missing or underdeveloped markets within the household banking sector.

Within the enterprise banking market, the monopoly of the monobank on the deposit and lending activity stands out. Just as the state savings bank had no competition within the household market, the monobank had no competition in providing service to firms.

Also very important was the role of production targets in deciding the supply of credit. The monobank had no experience in applying commercial criteria to lending, as it was not concerned with profitability of enterprises or indeed even of the prospect of loan repayment. The 'priorities of payments' by firms were set with payments to suppliers and banks at the bottom of the list.

Ultimately, credit in a CPE was granted in order to fund real production targets and in an attempt to maintain payment discipline among enterprises. This is vastly different to banking behaviour in a market economy, where the ability of a borrower to repay is a key criterion in bank lending. In addition, because planners relied on short-term credit as a monitoring device, the monobank had no little or no experience in providing long-term credits for capital and infrastructure projects ('investment credits' granted by the state were actually subsidies, not loans). Also, due to the lack of financial markets, many specialised financial institutions that can be found in market economies were not present. For example, the 'investment bank' in a CPE was a bank in name only. Thus, there were missing and/or underdeveloped markets in the enterprise sector as well as in the household sector.

And, finally, the ability of enterprises to circumvent restrictive credit policies by non-paying of suppliers is a key issue. This would not be a viable option in a market economy, for suppliers would simply refuse to supply if they were not paid. However, suppliers in a CPE did not have this leeway. Both the level of production and to whom the product was to be supplied were predetermined by planning authorities. In order to fulfil its planning targets, a supplying enterprise had to deliver its goods to other firms, regardless of non-payment. Production concerns were supposed to drive financial ones, although with the supply of goods not being linked to payment, enterprises lacked any incentive to pay suppliers on time.

Overall, enterprises within a CPE operated without strong financial incentives. In fact, without the threat of bankruptcy (all unpaid financial obligations would ultimately be paid by the state) or of non-supply as a result of non-payment, firms had no reason to pay suppliers promptly or to repay bank credit. Furthermore, as production levels determined financial flows, the monobank had little choice but to grant new credits to enterprises during production. This nearly automatic extension of credit resulted in a 'soft budget constraint'[8] for industry. As János Kornai[9] explains, 'this "softening" of the budget constraint appears when the strict relationship between expenditure and earnings has been relaxed, because excess expenditure over earnings will be paid by some other institution, typically by the state. A further conditioning of "softening" is that the decision maker (in the enterprise) expects such financial assistance with high probability, and this probability is firmly built into his behaviour'.

This lack of payments discipline did not bode well for a tightening of the budget constraint of enterprises as market criteria were applied to lending during the transition. In fact, the expectation of a 'soft budget constraint' did not disappear with the ending of the break-up of the monobank into separate central and commercial banking institutions. Throughout the latter half of the 1990s, the issues posed by soft budget constraints were of major concern.

3. AN OVERVIEW OF THIS VOLUME

Three transitional economies, the Czech Republic, Hungary, and Slovenia were studied in depth during the course of this project. This book divides into four parts following this introductory overview.

Part I examines issues regarding banking within the European Union, and also provides an overview of the 'association agreements' reached between the EU and applicant countries. In Chapter 2, Iain Begg and Yener Altunbas investigate developments in the banking sectors of EU member countries, and their impact on regulatory and supervisory issues faced by the EU and more specifically the European Central Bank. In Chapter 3, Michel Tison examines the 'association agreements' that have been entered into by transition countries that wish to join the EU, in particular the adaptation of the *acquis communautaire* by associated countries.

From this starting point, each chapter in Part II investigates the transition of the banking sector in one of the associated countries: Chapter 4 by Roman Matoušek and Anita Taci deals with the Czech Republic; Chapter 5 by Neven Borak and Vladimir Lavrač deals with Slovenia, and Chapter 6 by Karl Petrick deals with Hungary. Although each country has its own particular banking characteristics, several common problems can be identified: a high level of bad debt in the newly formed commercial banks along with an undercapitalisation problem that had to be rectified in order to ensure the stability of the banking sector; a general lack of experience by both banking officials and regulators regarding how to operate in a market system; and missing or underdeveloped markets in both household and industrial banking.

Part III examines a range of policy issues and implications suggested by the analysis. In Chapter 7, István Ábel discusses how problems in the financial sector can lead to crisis in the productive sector of an economy. These spill-over effects of financial crises are one of the reasons that a great deal of importance has been placed on creating a stable financial sector in the transition countries. In Chapter 8, Neven Borak critically examines the developments in the commercial banking sectors of Eastern and Central European countries. At the onset of the transition process, there was much discussion regarding what type of structure the financial sector of a transition economy should assume. There were various proponents of the adoption of a universal banking system,[10] while others advocated an Anglo-Saxon type system with a clear separation of commercial and investment banking activities.[11] This argument has abated, for as Victor Murinde and Andy Mullineaux state, 'the answer is academic in the case of countries joining the EU, which has adopted the "continental model" (universal banking)'.[12] Although, as Murinde and Mullineaux point out, the universal banking model has been widely adopted in transition countries, this model is not a uniform system. Rather, there are a number of differences found in the universal banking systems of Western countries. Likewise, the universal banking system as created in Eastern and Central Europe has its own distinct characteristics, which take into account the features of the commercial banking sector of a transitional economy. Borak labels this 'Eastern Universality'.

In Part IV, Chapter 9, David Green and Karl Petrick discuss the issues raised in the preceding chapters and the policy lessons that can be learned, particularly regarding the role of the state in the financial sector of a transition economy.

NOTES

1. The 10 applicant states are Bulgaria, the Czech Republic, Estonia, Hungary, Latvia, Lithuania, Poland, Romania, the Slovak Republic and Slovenia.
2. EBRD (1998), 'Transition Report 1998: Financial Sector In Transition' EBRD, London, p. 92.
3. P. Dembinski (1988), 'Quality versus Allocation of Money: Monetary Problems of the Centrally Planned Economies Reconsidered', *KYKLOS*, 41:2, p. 290.
4. G. Garvy (1977), *Money, Financial Flows and Credit in the Soviet Union*, Ballinger Publishers, Cambridge, MA, USA.
5. J. Kornai (1992), *The Socialist System: The Political Economy of Communism*, Clarendon Press, Oxford, UK, p. 133.
6. Adapted from K. Haitani (1986), *Comparative Economic Systems: Organisational and Managerial Perspectives*, Prentice-Hall, Englewood Cliffs, NJ, USA, p. 139.
7. G. Garvy (1966), *Money, Banking and Credit in Eastern Europe*, Federal Reserve Bank of New York, New York, USA and A. Zwass (1979), *Money, Banking and Credit in the Soviet Union and Eastern Europe*, Macmillan, London, UK both discuss this aspect of private money.
8. J. Kornai (1986), 'The Soft Budget Constraint', *KYKLOS*, 39:1, pp. 3–30.
9. Ibid. p. 4.
10. For example, J. Corbett and C. Mayer (1991), 'Financial Reform in Eastern Europe: Progress with the Wrong Model', *Oxford Review of Economic Policy*, 7:4, pp. 57–75; C. Niggle (1995), 'The Role of the Financial Sector in the Socialist Economies in Transition – The 2nd Primitive Allocation of Capital', *Review of Social Economy*, 53:3, 311–31.
11. J. Blommestein and S. Spencer (1994), 'The Role of Financial Institutions in the transition to a Market Economy in G. Capiro, D. Folkerts-Landau and T. Lane (eds), *Building Sound Finance in Emerging Market Economies*. (publisher?)
12. V. Murinde and A. Mullineaux 'Introductory Overview: Issues Surrounding Bank and Enterprise Restructuring in Central and Eastern Europe' in A. Mullineaux and C.J. Green (eds), *Economic Performance and Financial Sector Reform in Central and Eastern Europe*, Edward Elgar, Cheltenham, UK, p. 8.

PART I

Regulatory Background

2. Evolution of EU Banking: Supervisory Implications

Iain Begg and Yener Altunbas

The banking industry is at the heart of modern market economies. Banks are crucial, first to transactions, as they provide the backbone of payment systems. Their second fundamental role is as intermediaries between lenders and borrowers, so that they are central to the financing of economic activity. As a key part of any country's 'economic infrastructure' it is no surprise, therefore, that banks are closely monitored by the authorities. Inefficiencies in the banking system can impose significant costs on the 'real' economy, while the ramifications of bank failures can be profound, as the recent experience of several countries shows.

Banks are subject to a range of regulatory and supervisory controls, albeit with substantial differences between countries and market segments. Regulation focuses on issues such as conduct of business, pricing, and market entry, while prudential supervision is concerned more narrowly with assuring the solvency of banks. In the EU, very disparate regulatory and supervisory systems co-exist (Louis et al., 1995). As EMU is consolidated, the coherence of these systems is likely to be subject to scrutiny. Yet there is little sign that either the architecture of the Eurosystem or the authorities implementing it have given much thought to how supervisory and regulatory responsibilities should evolve.

This chapter looks first at the EU banking industry, drawing attention to recent trends. The next section assesses the prospective impact of EMU on the industry, focusing particularly on changes that can be expected to have repercussions for supervision. The subsequent sections of the chapter concentrate on regulatory and supervisory issues.

1. THE EU BANKING INDUSTRY

Banking in the EU has traditionally been segmented into national markets which have evolved along idiosyncratic lines and which have developed institutional forms that are distinctive. Nevertheless, a number of general trends in the structure of EU banking can be discerned, reflecting common competitive factors, regulatory shifts, and the impact of technological and managerial changes that transcend national boundaries.

In nearly all the member states, there has been a marked fall in the number of banks over the last two decades, a trend common to different types of financial intermediaries, including the mutual savings banks, co-operative banks and commercial banks. Nevertheless, the number of banks operating in Europe is still large, suggesting that the EU is still considerably 'over-banked' (see Table 2.1). A second significant trend is that the number of foreign banks has increased in every banking market over the same period. In particular, foreign banks form a significant proportion of the banking sector assets in the UK (260 foreign banks with a 57 per cent assets share in 1996); Belgium (8 banks with 48 per cent of banking sector assets); France (280 banks with 14 per cent of banking sector assets); and Portugal (16 banks with 35 per cent of banking sector assets). In other EU countries, foreign banks generally account for less than 8 per cent of total banking sector assets.

Table 2.1: Number of banks in the European countries, 1984–96

Country	1984	1989	1992	1994	1996
Austria	1257	1240	1104	1053	1019
Belgium	165	157	157	147	141
Denmark	231	233	210	202	197
Finland	644	552	365	356	350
France	358	418	617	607	570
Germany	3025	4089	4200	3872	3674
Italy	1137	1127	1073	1002	937
Netherlands	2079	1058	921	744	658
Norway	248	179	158	153	153
Portugal	18	29	35	44	51
Spain	369	333	319	316	313
Sweden	176	144	119	125	124
Switzerland	581	631	569	494	403
UK	598	551	518	486	478

Sources: OECD (1996, 1994, 1991); British Bankers' Association (1996, 1995); Banca d'Italia (1996); Banco de Portugal (1996); Banque de France (1996, 1990); Bank of Spain (1998); Danish Securities Council (1996, 1994,1992); Deutsche Bundesbank (1997); De Nederlandsche Bank (1996, 1993, 1990); Finnish Bankers' Association (1997, 1996, 1995); Oesterreichische Nationalbank (1998).

Trends in the number of branches are less clear cut (Table 2.2). There was a net increase in Germany, Italy and Spain, but marked declines in Belgium, the Nordic countries and the UK. The reasons for these changes vary: according to Economic Research Europe (1997), the growth in branches in Italy and Spain stems from the removal of branching or territorial restrictions which occurred the late 1980s and early 1990s. By contrast, the increase in Germany is attributed to the expansion of the savings bank sector. In the Nordic countries, the fallout from the crises of the early 1990s was a prime factor in the decrease in the number of bank branches, whereas in Belgium and the UK, mergers and acquisitions have been the main influence.

Table 2.2: Number of branches in the European countries 1984–96

Country	1984	1989	1992	1994	1996
Austria	4005	4378	4667	4683	4694
Belgium	23502	19211	16405	17040	10441
Denmark	3515	3182	2358	2245	2138
Finland	2886	3528	3087	2151	1785
France	25490	25634	25479	25389	25434
Germany	35752	39651	39295	48721	47741
Italy	13045	15683	20914	23120	24406
Netherlands	5475	8006	7518	7269	7219
Norway	1940	1796	1593	1552	1503
Portugal	1469	1741	2852	3401	3842
Spain	31876	34511	35476	35591	37079
Sweden	3083	3302	2910	2998	2527
Switzerland	3874	4245	4169	3821	3543
UK	21853	20419	18218	17362	16192

Sources: As in Table 2.1.

Overall, the number of banks in the EU has fallen, although most countries still have a large number of small local and regional banks in the EU. Despite the large number of banks, there is some evidence of an increase in five-firm concentration ratios (Economic Research Europe, 1997; Danthine et al., 1999), especially in the smaller member states. The growth in entry by foreign banks into many markets offsets any adverse effect of concentration in national markets and it can be argued that banking has in general become more competitive. This is reflected in a narrowing of intermediation margins and has encouraged banks to diversify and to seek complementary income sources. In more mature financial markets, such as the UK, nearly 45 per cent of banking system gross income was generated from non-interest income sources by 1996. The ratio is either above or close to 40 per cent in other member states: Austria (38.7 per cent), France (39.4 per cent), and Sweden (42 per cent). However, much lower ratios elsewhere (Denmark has a ratio of 17.7 per cent and Spain 24.3 per cent, for example) show that there is still scope for diversification.

Table 2.3 shows that the numbers of banks and bank branches differ markedly between member states of the EU. Although these data have to be interpreted with caution because of different definitions of what constitutes a bank, and consequent regulatory restrictions on being so classified, the disparities in bank density (measured in relation to population) are striking. There are huge differences in the numbers of banks per million inhabitants, partly reflecting the historical evolution of countries' financial systems and the nature of bank authorisation procedures.

Table 2.3: Density of banks in the EU

Country	No. of banks 1996	Branches 1996	Change in branches 1992–96 %	Banks per million inhabitants 1996	Branches per million inhabitants 1996	Branch density 1996 EU 12=100
Austria	1019	4 694	0.6	126.4	582.5	113.8
Belgium	141	10 441	−36.4	13.9	1028.0	200.9
Denmark	197	2 138	−9.3	37.4	406.3	79.4
Finland	350	1 785	−42.2	68.3	348.3	68.1
France	570	25 434	−0.2	9.8	435.7	85.2
Germany	3674	47 741	21.5	44.9	583.0	113.9
Italy	937	24 406	16.7	16.3	425.2	83.1
Netherlands	658	7 219	−4.0	42.4	465.1	90.9
Portugal	51	3 842	34.7	5.2	389.4	76.1
Spain	313	37 079	4.5	8.0	944.2	184.5
Sweden	124	2 527	−13.2	13.9	283.9	55.5
UK	478	16 192	−11.1	8.1	275.5	53.8
EU 12 total	8512	183 498	2.4	23.7	511.7	100.0

Source: Authors' calculation based on data from European Commission and tables presented in Economic Research Europe (1997) drawing on various national sources.

As an illustration, Germany, with its large supply of small savings banks, has a density of banks some six times as high as the UK. Two smaller countries, Austria and Finland, have (respectively) over five and three times as many banks as the average for the 12 countries shown, and the Austrians have 15 times as many banks per head as residents of the two countries at the other end of the spectrum, Spain and the UK. From this, the scope for branch rationalisation would also appear to be considerable. The Belgians have nearly four times as many branches per capita as the British and the Swedes, notwithstanding a rapid pace of branch closures which saw over a third of branches close between 1992 and 1996.

In the three Southern countries shown, Italy, Portugal and Spain, the number of banks is comparatively low, reflecting the history of public ownership of much of the banking sector and their relatively less developed financial sectors. In all three countries, however, the number of branches has been increasing in the 1990s, from a low base in Portugal and Italy, but a high one in Spain.

Cost pressures are strong and there is some indication that cost–income ratios – a commonly used measure of efficiency – have been falling across the EU (Table 2.4). Here again, differing factors are at work. In the UK, M&A has been an important explanatory variable. Thus, HSBC's acquisition of Midland generated cost–income ratio falls from over 70 per cent in 1992 to under 60 per cent by the end of 1997, while Lloyds/TSB's cost ratio fell 12 per cent over the period (BankScope, 1998). By contrast, the improved cost performance of many Nordic banks arose largely from the forced reorganisations following the banking crises of the early 1990s. Continental European banks, however, appear to have

Table 2.4: Cost to income ratios in European banking, 1984–96

Country	1984	1989	1992	1994	1996
Austria	–	65.5	64.0	65.1	61.4
Belgium	–	66.8	66.9	71.3	61.1
Denmark	75.6	64.9	81.4	72.5	53.5
Finland	84.0	84.8	190.4	139.9	69.3
France	–	64.6	62.5	73.5	72.8
Germany	59.3	64.6	64.5	60.7	61.2
Italy	–	61.7	63.8	65.0	69.6
Netherlands	62.3	66.0	67.7	66.7	69.5
Norway	68.5	69.9	60.3	63.4	66.5
Portugal	67.0	46.8	53.0	58.2	56.5
Spain	64.0	60.9	60.3	59.7	63.8
Sweden	67.6	62.7	122.2	80.0	49.3
Switzerland	–	–	93.9	84.9	71.1
UK	66.9	64.8	65.9	64.1	60.3

Source: Institute of European Finance, Bangor.

been less successful. In other countries, tougher labour protection rules and union resistance have limited or delayed the opportunities for cost savings. Thus, in Spain, the merger between Banco Bilbao Vizcaya and Banco Central Hispano was a convoluted deal that took four years to generate cost savings and performance enhancement.

In general, M&A activity in Europe has accelerated (i.e. Scandinavian banks, Vereinsbank/Hypobank, Credit Suisse/Winterthur, Ambroveneto/ Cariplo, ING/ BBL, UBS/SBC) and is expected to increase significantly. This follows recent consolidation in US markets, including large universal banks, e.g. Citicorp/ Travellers, BankAmerica/NationsBank and the proposed deals in Canada between the Bank of Montreal/Royal Bank of Canada and CIBC/Toronto Dominion (Morgan Stanley Dean Witter, 1997). Overall, recent M&A activity (including deals that have taken place over the last decade – see Table 2.5) may be categorised into four main types:

1. Intra-country, overlapping-business, cost-based deal (Swedbank/ Foreningsbanken, Lloyds/TSB/Cheltenham & Gloucester Building Society, BankAmerica/NationsBank, Bank of Montreal/Royal Bank of Canada, CIBC/Toronto Dominion).
2. Intra-country, non-overlapping, critical mass-driven mergers and acquisitions (Ambroveneto/Cariplo, Credito Romagnolo/Credito Italiano).
3. Revenue/product-enhancement-based mergers in response to the disintermediation trend (bancassurance/asset management/investment banking) (Citicorp/Travelers, Credit Suisse/Winterthur).
4. Cross-border regional franchise building deals (Merita/Nordbanken, ING/ BBL, ING/Generale hostile bid).

Economic Integration and the EU Banking Industry

EU banking has been through significant changes in the last decade, many of them directly attributable to the pace and nature of European integration. With stage 3 of EMU having started on schedule and with a larger than expected number of countries in the first wave, there will be renewed impetus to change in the banking industry. This can be expected to pose new challenges to bank regulators and supervisors and, perhaps, to call into question some of the present arrangements.

Although progress has been slower than expected, the last few years have seen a gradual adaptation of EU banking to the single market. One of the principal aims of the EU in launching the single market in the 1980s was to open up services, and particular emphasis in this regard was given to financial services. The various directives affecting financial services had the common aim of reducing regulatory barriers to cross-border business, principally by allowing a

Table 2.5: Merger and acquisition activities in European banking, 1987–97

Date	Target	Acquirer	Country	Value ($ mn)
Oct. 87	Hill Samuel	TSB	UK	1 262
Oct. 88	Banco de Vizcaya	Banco de Bilbao	Spain	3 250
Nov. 89	Morgan Grenfell	Deutsche Bank	Germany/UK	1 483
Mar. 90	Algemene Bank Netherland	AMRO	Netherlands	2 414
Nov. 90	NMB Postbank	Nationale Nederland	Netherlands	7 458
Jan. 91	Oesterreische Landerbank	Zentralsparkasse und Kommercialbank Wien	Austria	1 201
Apr. 91	BCI & Banco Exterior	Caja Postal, Insituto Credito Local, Banco Hipotecario, Banco Credito Agricola	Spain	–
May. 91	Banco de Credito Industrial	Banco de Exterior de España	Spain	1 100
Mar. 92	Midland Bank	HSBC	UK	5 708
Jan. 93	Swiss Volksbank	CS Holding	Switzerland	1 101
May. 93	ASLK-CGER	Fortis	Belgium/ Netherlands	1 072
Jan. 94	Banesto	Banco Santander	Spain	2 287
Apr. 94	Cheltenham & Gloucester B. S.	Lloyds Bank	UK	2 872
Oct. 94	Credito Romagnolo	Credito Italiano	Italy	2 354
Mar. 95	Barings	ING	UK/ Netherlands	1 074
Apr. 95	National & Provincial B. S.	Abbey National	UK	2 151
May. 95	S.G. Warburg	SBC	UK/ Switzerland	3 159
Jun. 95	Kleinwort Benson	Dresdner Bank	UK/Germany	1 554
Jun. 95	Lloyds Bank	TSB	UK	15 316

Date	Target	Acquirer	Country	Value ($ mn)
Mar. 96	Credit Communal Belgique	Credit Local de France	Belgium/ France	3 070
Apr. 96	Banque Indosuez	Caisse Nationale de Credit Agricole	France	1 221
Oct. 96	MeesPierson	Fortis	Netherlands/ Belgium	1 436
Dec. 96	Stadshypotek	Svenska Handelsbanken	Sweden	3 344
Jan. 97	Creditanstalt	Bank Austria	Austria	1 537
Feb. 97	Forenings-banken	Sparbanken Sverige	Sweden	1 348
May. 97	Cariplo	Ambroveneto	Italy	3 920
Jul. 97	Bayerische Hypobank	Bayerische Vereinsbank	Germany	5 133
Sep. 97	First Austrian Savings Bank	GiroCredit	Austria	–
Oct. 97	Merita	Nordbanken	Finland/ Sweden	–
Nov. 97	BBL	ING	Belgium/ Netherlands	4 516
Dec. 97	UBS	SBC	Switzerland	19 838

Source: Institute of European Finance, Bangor.

bank to carry out business in any EU member state once it had been authorised by its home country (much the same philosophy was adopted for insurance undertakings and securities businesses). This so-called 'passport' meant that the costly and time-consuming burden of obtaining separate authorisation for each member state was avoided.

The effect of the single market was not dramatic and it is clear that its impact on EU banking has been much more muted than expected. Indeed, a study carried out for the European Commission as part of a major review of the single market found that substantial differences in the costs of banking persist across member states (Economic Research Europe, 1997). Banking today is still mainly an activity conducted at national level. Nevertheless, there have been moves towards pan-European banking, largely through cross-border mergers and alliances. In addition, most large banking groups have seen significant growth in non-domestic business. This is, however, more true of wholesale and investment banking than of the retail end of the business.

Industry Structure and its Likely Evolution

The banking industry in each EU member state is distinctive, reflecting the historical development of the financial sector and the impact of institutional factors such as accounting systems, tax rules and the character of corporate governance. In Germany, banks traditionally took substantial equity stakes in companies and this remains a cornerstone of corporate financing. The polar opposite is the UK, with its much more powerful stock market (Edwards and Fischer, 1994). This disjunction is apparent in the relative strengths of investment banking, with London dominant in this segment, although increasingly through US banks. An obvious corollary is that it is difficult to envisage a common regulatory framework that is suited to such diversity.

A second dimension of the present EU banking structure is the dichotomy between universal and specialist banks. Banks which offer a full gamut of financial services are exposed to different risks from those that specialise, so that once again, common rules are often inappropriate. Contagion within conglomerates is also an issue that is hard to resolve (Dale, 1992). There is also a division between wholesale and retail banking which particularly affects the extent of off-balance-sheet risks faced by different categories of banks. If an investment bank (i.e. one predominantly in the wholesale segment of the industry) trades substantially in derivatives (Barings being an extreme, recent example) its capital may be over stretched. Conversely, a wholesale bank which is only involved in asset management or major syndicated loans will tend to be less exposed than an ordinary retail bank.

EU banking has been affected by a diverse range of influences over the last two decades, including a progressive liberalisation of the market, the trends towards securitisation and disintermediation, advances in technology and the consequential changes in systems and their management, the internationalisation of financial markets, and now, the advent of monetary union. In response, banks have had to restructure internally and to adapt their competitive strategies. The banking industry has seen waves of mergers and acquisitions, all of which alter the demands on, and obligations of, regulators and supervisors.

Yet it is also clear that the banking industry has not become as 'Europeanised' as was presaged in the European Commission's 'Costs of non-Europe' studies (Price Waterhouse, 1988), nor has the single market yet had as great an impact on the sector as might have been expected (Economic Research Europe, 1997). The study found that there had been only limited convergence of bank prices and costs and that, although there was some increase in activity, there had been relatively little cross-border M&A activity involving larger banks. Instead, the main form of cross-border activity has been the acquisition by relatively large banks of smaller institutions, while most of the consolidation through mergers has been within member states, a strategy that is adjudged to be largely defensive. Competitive pressures have, however, obliged banks to focus on improving both their productive efficiency and their overall risk/return efficiency. Within countries, different institutional factors continue to characterise European banking systems (Altunbas and Chakravarty, 1998).

Much of the impetus for the restructuring of European financial services comes from the belief that bigger size is necessary for bank survival in the New Europe (see Pryce and Griffin, 1996; Morgan Stanley Dean Witter, 1997). Certainly, stock market expectations point in this direction and the recent spate of merger deals, notably amongst large US banks, could signal a renewed surge of bank merger activity in Europe. However, White (1998) is more circumspect, arguing that some of the leading European banks are already in the top league by international standards.

In an analysis of the manner in which banks have sought to internationalise their activity, Morgan Stanley Dean Witter (1997) identifies four broad global strategies:

- global/local (providers of financial services in local markets on a broad geographic basis, like Citicorp, HSBC, ABN Amro and ING);
- global operating services (specialist providers of specialised operating services like custody, treasury and cash management, such as Bank of New York, Citicorp, Chase Manhattan);
- global asset managers (third-party providers of asset management services to institutional and retail clients, for example UBS);
- global consumer services (firms that target broad or specialist product areas such as AMEX, top Swiss banks in private banking, Charles Schwab in discount brokerage).

These types of operations are increased mainly through acquisition but also through organic growth.

Other Key Factors

In considering the prospects for the European banking system, various characteristics of the system need to be recognised. Historically low returns have improved slightly since 1994, but as the ECB (1999) notes, they are still well below US levels. The ECB also observes that the low interest rates now prevailing in Euroland are 'beneficial to banks due to capital gains and increased income from maturity transformation, whereas in the long term, a low level of interest rates will reduce the margin earned by banks on their interest-free or low interest rate resources' (p. 2). Indeed, European margins are falling, reinforcing this point (Table 2.6). The generalised reduction in indebtedness of EU member states – motivated by their desire to be eligible for EMU and reinforced by the Stability and Growth Pact – has led to a shift in assets from public to private debt. The ECB comments that this could mean a more risky asset profile, and adds to the concern about bad loans to the Far East.

Table 2.6: Net interest margin in European banking, 1984–96

Country	1984	1989	1992	1994	1996
Austria	–	1.73	1.85	1.90	1.43
Belgium	–	1.57	1.51	1.33	1.32
Denmark	3.01	2.55	3.56	3.83	1.79
Finland	2.42	1.84	1.55	2.05	1.90
France	–	1.91	1.63	1.27	1.20
Germany	2.50	2.01	2.07	2.18	1.46
Italy	–	3.28	3.17	2.63	2.42
Netherlands	2.23	2.08	1.83	1.89	1.67
Norway	3.71	3.45	3.51	3.44	2.41
Portugal	1.86	4.12	4.11	2.78	1.95
Spain	4.15	4.05	3.59	3.00	2.54
Sweden	2.55	2.53	2.55	2.77	1.81
Switzerland	–	–	1.56	1.79	1.98
UK	3.00	3.10	2.60	2.40	2.10

Source: Institute of European Finance, Bangor.

The ECB believes that there are good reasons to assume that excess capacity exists in several member states and that EMU will accelerate industry consolidation and contribute to the reduction of excess capacity. Davis and Salo (1998) also analyse the excess capacity in the EU and discuss the causes (see Table 2.8). According to the ECB (1999, p. 4): 'in particular, the branch network and staffing levels, given the existing marked differences across countries, are expected to be affected, thus enabling banks to achieve efficiency gains'. Continuing disintermediation is expected to compound these difficulties by reducing further the share of banks in borrowing or savings markets.

A problem that may arise, however, is that because of social legislation in many Euroland countries, banks will find it hard to lay off staff. Indeed, White (1998, p. 15) points out that 'such laws have in some cases been reinforced by special legislation or regulations directed specifically to the banking industry'. Efficiency gains will, consequently, be slow to materialise and short-term profits may be further squeezed in a way that could worry supervisors concerned about already fragile balance sheets.

Banks and the state

The changing role of the state is a further important shift in the topography of banking. In several member states, public ownership or strong support of banks has been the norm (for example, mutual and co-operative banks, often having a regional nature), especially, as White (1998) notes, in France, Italy, Germany, Portugal and Spain among other countries. It is common for the state to offer specific forms of support, such as the credit guarantees offered by the Länder governments in Germany. White maintains that this philosophy has strongly influenced the approach to regulation and that 'public policy in this area has until recently tended to emphasise considerations relating to "stability" more than those of "efficiency"' (p. 12). The prospect of more bank privatisations can be expected to accelerate the trend towards a loosening of state links to banks.

Public attitudes can, moreover, affect the development of other forms of financial markets. White (1998) considers that 'the fact that state-supported social security funds are so well-developed in continental Europe, and that they have generally been of the unfunded variety … has in large part removed the need for private saving plans and the market infrastructure needed to support them' (p. 6). However, he detects a sea-change in this regard, mentioning in particular the case of Credit Lyonnais which he believes has prompted concern about 'the proper treatment of ailing banks within the context of the Maastricht Treaty'. The fact that Germany's Sparkassen and Landesbanken were not given special status in the Amsterdam Treaty is seen by White as another signal that the role of the state is fading. Whether or not these changes presage a general shift towards an 'Anglo-Saxon' model of banking across the EU remains to be seen.

Yet another issue is that of regulatory capture. If state and bank interests are too closely intertwined, political considerations may lead to outcomes that are either against the interests of consumers of banking services, or which weaken the application of regulation. As Honohan (1997, p. 5) puts it, 'all too often, the problem is not that the supervisors didn't know or suspect, but that the bank owners were too well-placed politically for their actions to be curtailed by supervisors without the most conclusive of evidence'.

Technology impacts

Banks are at the forefront of the information and communications technology (ICT) revolution and have been one of the sectors of activity most affected by their application, and the effects have been far-reaching. Advances in processing capability have transformed the organisation of banks, given rise to new techniques of risk assessment, altered the skill profiles demanded of bank employees (Rajan, 1996) and become an increasingly critical determinant of competitive success.

ICT has played a large part in new product development, both by facilitating new means of service delivery (for instance tele-banking) and by making possible the design of ever more elaborate or complex products. One facet of these developments that is of particular concern from a prudential perspective is the proliferation of trading in derivatives, together with the use of automated trading systems. The obvious danger of this is that off-balance-sheet risk may rapidly outgrow traditional on-balance-sheet liabilities, making an assessment of a bank's solvency more problematic.

2. THE LIKELY IMPACT OF EMU

A recent report by the European Central Bank concludes 'that EMU is likely to act in the medium and long term as a catalyst to reinforce already prevailing trends in the EU banking systems. In particular, EMU is expected to reinforce the pressure for the reduction of existing excess capacity, to put profitability under pressure and to lead to increased internationalisation and geographical diversification, also outside EMU, as well as to increased conglomeration and mergers and acquisitions' (ECB, 1999, p. 1). The analysis in the report also anticipates a significant increase in competition in banking within the euro area. Not surprisingly, the ECB believes that a stable monetary environment will favour the banking sector.

Although, at first sight, the banking systems of the EU (post-EMU) and the USA (after the 1994 Riegle–Neal Act) are subject to similar rules, Danthine et al. (1999) maintain that there is still much that separates them. In particular, liberalisation is still far from complete in the EU, because the single market in banking has yet to materialise and there are still major differences in corporate governance and accounting systems. Despite the various measures enacted under the single market programme and the pressures of 'globalisation', European financial markets today are still surprisingly fragmented, especially in retail financial services. Continuing national differences in tax regimes, corporate governance and accounting rules are identified in a study conducted by CEPS (Lannoo and Gros, 1998) as the main reasons for this fragmentation. The study predicts that change in these areas will occur only gradually, although EMU will provide a stimulus to more rapid integration. Integration is expected to advance more rapidly for fixed-income markets than for equities, while households will be the slowest to adjust. Monetary union will make a difference, but Danthine et al. believe that the persistence of non-regulatory obstacles such as taxation and corporate law will mean that the advent of 'the euro will not be enough to create a true single European financial market' (p. xvii).

As a result of continuing differences in the institutional setting, consolidation of the banking sector is likely to take place more rapidly within countries than across borders. Paradoxically, therefore, the early effects of the further European integration induced by EMU could be to increase the market power of the largest banks within each member country. This effect is likely to be more pronounced in retail banking than in investment banking and asset management. In the latter areas, Danthine et al. (1999) believe that potential economies of scope and key incentives to consolidation (technology and team-building) will favour cross-border mergers. Even though previous attempts at cross-border consolidation aimed at creating universal banks have had chequered results, they argue that 'the incentives of commercial banks will change' (p. xviii) to make such arrangements more attractive. But they also state that 'the outcome is uncertain' (p. xviii). Much will depend on the stance taken by regulators, especially in relation to off-balance-sheet risk.

If a single European market in banking and financial services is to be encouraged, the substantial continuing barriers to cross-border consolidation will have to be reduced. These touch on difficult areas of national sovereignty, such as corporate governance and corporate taxation. Danthine et al. (1999) also call for competition policy, both at EU level and by national authorities, to be applied rigorously to the banking sector. Plainly, if there were to be pan-European supervision, there would be a pressing need to design new procedures for pan-European business.

EMU is widely expected to accelerate the integration of the EU banking system and will also have a number of immediate effects on banks. Amongst the latter is the obvious need to adapt to the euro. Computer programs will have to be reconfigured, staff retrained and new settlement systems established. These changes, coinciding with the costs of dealing with the Y2K problem in computer systems, will impose a direct cost on banks which, while unlikely to be as steep as some of the more alarming forecasts suggest, will nevertheless depress short-term profitability.

A second direct effect of the euro will be to reduce income from certain forms of business. Foreign exchange trading in Euroland currencies has, self-evidently, stopped since the beginning of 1999. The generally lower interest rates expected in Euroland will see intermediation margins squeezed. In addition, as clients become accustomed to dealing in the euro, the need for fee-earning advice on intra-EU transactions will be expected to diminish. Thus, although demands for new financial services are bound to emerge in the integrated EU financial area, banks must expect to look beyond certain traditional services for revenue growth. Banking business will, in addition, be affected by the manner in which monetary policy impinges on the banking sector. Dermine (1998) sets out eight main effects that he anticipates EMU will have on the banking sector. These are shown in Table 2.7 below.

Table 2.7: Eight likely impacts of the euro on European banking

---

1. *The prospect of a European market for government bonds*, rather than national markets would be expected greatly to diminish the advantages enjoyed by national banks and lead to a cross-border consolidation by the major players seeking to exploit economies of scale and scope.
2. A similar consolidation of corporate bond and equity trading should occur.
3. As regards fund management, the importance of distribution channels controlled by national financial intermediaries will remain strong, but there should be some scope for *the development of pan-European funds*.
4. Little change will, however, take place in the deposit markets which are already efficient at European level.
5. *Much foreign exchange business will disappear* and the competitive advantage of national banks in trading in their own currencies will cease to be significant when the trading is in the single currency.
6. Some gains may emerge for European banks as the international role of the euro expands, but given the pre-eminence of the dollar, the effect will be limited.
7. The 'one size fits all' monetary policy in *Euroland* will mean *some increase in credit risk* where a national economy diverges from the mean, as monetary policy will be less likely to provide a means of adjustment.
8. A lower inflation environment could mean *lower intermediation margins*, but will be affected by how personal loans are priced and by how the 'inflation tax' shifts.

Source: Dermine (1998).

Further pressures on the supply-side of the banking sector will come from the dynamic effects of monetary union. It is widely forecast that bond trading will concentrate in a few core centres, such as Paris, Frankfurt and, especially, London. More generally, EMU will intensify competition and can be expected to expose excess capacity in the banking industry. The notion of excess capacity in banking is, as Davis and Salo (1998) show, not an easy one to define in banking (see Table 2.8). Assuming that the forecasts are correct, excess capacity in European banking will manifest itself in two ways. First, profitability in the sector will fall; and, second, there will be strong incentives to rationalise.

Table 2.8: Reasons for excess capacity in the EU context

---

1. *Cyclical or structural decline in demand* for the industry's product. With the advance of securitisation (Revell, 1997) in the EU, it can be argued that such a structural change is occurring, and it may have been exacerbated by the slow growth in stages 1 and 2 of EMU.
2. *Technological shocks* which make existing capacity redundant. New methods of distribution in financial services including telephone and internet banking are growing in the EU and facilitating the entry of new providers of banking services.
3. *Redistribution of demand* between banks means that the more attractive intermediaries gain market share at the expense of others, who are pushed into a situation of excess capacity, even if demand at the industry level is unchanged.
4. *New competitors* have been entering the industry in the EU either from other countries or from other sectors such as retailing. Unless the banks which are directly challenged 'downsize' they will find themselves subject to excess capacity or if entry is sufficiently large scale, such problems may arise for the entire industry.
5. *Changes in regulation* constitute a specific potential cause of excess capacity in the EU. In particular, it may arise as a consequence, on the other hand, of the single market measures, which affects costs of or even feasibility of entry and exit; and, on the other hand, of putative changes in supervisory arrangements linked to EMU which oblige some banks to curb their activities.
6. *Strategic competitive imperatives* may surface where there are sunk costs which banks try to offset by seeking to reap economies of scope. These may induce banks to expand their activity in new markets in other EU member states, leading to excess capacity amongst indigenous banks. One form that this appears to have taken in the EU is rationalisation following merger or acquisition, especially where the dominant partner brings more advanced management practices and/or new technology to bear.

Source: Adapted from Davis and Salo (1998).

An interesting essay by Rybczynski (1997) distinguishes three stages of development of the banking system: a bank-oriented phase; a market-oriented phase; and a securitised phase. He relates these to the evolution of capitalism from a system dominated by owner–managers through one in which 'managerial capitalism' is dominant through to a phase (characteristic of the most mature EU economies) in which the securities markets via institutionalised savings are the norm. It can be argued that this model not only has implications for the EU banking system under EMU, but is also especially relevant in considering how supervision should be designed and implemented in the transition economies.

The ECB (1999, p. 5) research suggests that banks have a number of aims in responding to EMU, including 'cost and efficiency improvements (economies of scale and scope), product diversification, new distribution channels (electronic banking) and geographical expansion'. To achieve these aims, the ECB identifies three main strategies:

- improvements in services and procedures (concerning the quality of services, staff and IT; risk management and internal control systems, cost-cutting and efficiency improvements);
- changes in product ranges (shift from operating services to consulting; reconsideration of product ranges, development of alternative sources of income, e.g. through geographical expansion);
- mergers, strategic alliances and co-operation agreements, with signs that the start of EMU has revitalised the trend towards cross-border mergers and alliances of different kinds. There was a big surge in mergers in 1997 (Goldman Sachs, 1998) and further deals are in progress.

The likely impact of EMU on risks is hard to judge. Increased competition, by driving down margins, could well increase prudential risk both by tempting banks to take loans with higher credit risk and by offering finer terms with less margin for bad debt provisions. Thus, although EMU will reduce exchange rate risk, it could see increased credit risk. The ECB (1999, p. 6) is, however, confident that the 'positive macroeconomic effects of EMU ... [will] ... mitigate credit risk in the euro area', but is concerned that there may be 'a concentration of likely "EMU losers" among individual bank's debtors that could increase credit risk'. The ECB worries about small businesses and fears that 'under competitive pressure banks might shift their business towards more profitable but also more risky business'. On the other hand, 'market risk under EMU is expected to decrease, especially with regard to foreign exchange and interest rate risk', although if banks react by trying to win forex business in non-EMU markets, country risk may increase. Because EMU will result in deeper financial markets, the ECB expects liquidity risk to decrease.

For supervisors, this re-balancing of risk is bound to be problematic and will call for both imagination and care in assessing not only how solvency will be affected, but also how well the internal procedures of banks adapt to take account of the new risk profiles.

3.   REGULATORY POLICY TENSIONS

Regulation of banking has disparate aims, some of which may be in conflict with one another. The rationale for the single market programme and the principle of home country control is that by making it easier for firms to compete in other EU countries, competition will flourish and the costs of banking services to consumers and businesses will fall. As a result, the cosy world of banking will be irreversibly changed by the need to be competitive, prompting Danthine et al. (1999) to observe that 'the days in which banking was off-limits for competition policy have passed and should not return' (p. 109). More generally, lighter regulation allows banks more freedom in their conduct of business and thus facilitates efficiency gains. In both respects, the role of banks as core economic services should be enhanced.

Prudential concerns include the avoidance of systemic collapse and the protection of depositors. While both aims are served by assuring the solvency of banks, there may be differences in philosophy about the degree of oversight that should be exercised by supervisors. Though strictly separate, supervision can play a role in facilitating the conduct of monetary policy in so far as the techniques of supervision and the instruments of monetary control operate on the same monetary aggregates. But there are institutional issues to consider, notably the fact that the ECB has a fully articulated Treaty mandate and unambiguous responsibility for monetary policy, whereas the Treaty is vague on how prudential supervision should evolve. Article 105 (5) of the Treaty states that the ESCB 'shall contribute to ... prudential supervision of credit institutions and the stability of the financial system' and in 105 (6) there is reference to the possibility that the ECB may be asked to undertake specific tasks in relation to 'prudential supervision of credit institutions and other financial institutions with the exception of insurance undertakings'. However, no other Community or national bodies are mentioned in this regard, and the possibility of a separate supervisory authority of the kind found in a majority of member states is not mentioned.

There is, therefore, a significant regulatory challenge in adapting to the single currency environment. With the ECB now at the pinnacle of the European System of Central Banks, the various national regulators and supervisors will have to rethink their relationships with national central banks and learn how to work with the new monetary authorities. In parallel, actors in financial markets have to learn how to interpret signals emanating from authorities. Any regime change is prone to being a flash-point for change and can affect established norms and procedures. Honohan (1997) identifies sources of disruption in banking that can give rise to solvency or other regulatory problems (Table 2.9) and thus be of concern to supervisors. All have the potential to cause a shake-up in the banking industry.

Table 2.9: Sources of disruption of banking industries

---

1. Financial repression occurs where regulatory controls inhibit innovation in product development and thus make the regulated banks vulnerable to other providers of intermediation services.
2. Financial liberalisation has occurred, to differing degrees, in most EU countries in recent years. By stimulating market entry, competition is intensified, obliging supervisors to accommodate new financial intermediaries. Liberalisation also tends to blur boundaries between market segments, with the risk of contagion between different types of financial services and increased complexity in assessing exposures.
3. Macroeconomic instability affects the lending and borrowing activity of the corporate and personal sectors, and leads to gyrations in interest rates which inevitably disrupt financial intermediation. The processes can become self-reinforcing, for example if bad debts trigger a credit crunch by banks as they seek to shore-up their balance sheets.
4. Structural economic transformation often results in turbulence in the supply-side of the economy with companies being taken over, rationalised or even going out of business.
5. Political developments may affect credit risk and have a variety of other impacts on the stability of banking.
6. Privatisation lessens the direct operational control of the state over the banking sector, but also calls for a recasting of regulation.
7. Innovation and globalisation in finance again stimulates market entry. In addition, by offering new forms of financing to borrowers, it calls into question accepted bank procedures.

Source: Based on Honohan (1997).

One of the most immediate challenges for supervisors will be to ensure that the anticipated shake-out in EU banking triggered by the single market and likely to be given renewed impetus by the start of monetary union takes place without undue trouble. The authorities will have to come up with procedures for managing a shake-out in bank numbers which could, moreover, be uneven between countries. White (1998) also makes the telling point that, in addition to the well-known problem of banks considered 'too big to fail', there may also be an issue about 'financial firms that had grown "too big to save"'. The moral hazard problems associated with the former case are familiar in the literature – indeed, the whole story of Crédit Lyonnais illustrates them. But as banks become increasingly Europeanised, the cost of a rescue not only grows, but becomes much more difficult to apportion between member states. Hence the latter case,where, if the cost of rescue is very high because of multi-country exposures, it may be beyond the means of a small country, even though home-country control might make the national supervisor responsible, and the same nation's fiscal authority liable for any rescue. Could Ireland or Portugal, let alone Luxembourg, have afforded the Crédit Lyonnais rescue if, for whatever reason, the bank had chosen to be authorised in any of those countries?

Because of its mandate, the ECB is less likely to be able or willing to provide liquidity to banks. For Danthine et al. (1999, p. xxi), 'the implication is that ex ante regulation and supervision are correspondingly more important in EMU than they are in the United States'. A related issue is how (or, indeed, whether) the Eurosystem offers a 'lender of last resort' facility to banks and other financial intermediaries. In the European System of Central Banks, this could be a function performed by the ECB or national central banks. But the Treaty is vague on this matter. Lending in the last resort is justified in theory where an otherwise solvent bank faces a liquidity crisis which can be overcome by a temporary loan from the central bank, although the notion is sometimes criticised as academic rather than practical. Nevertheless, Buiter (1999) is especially critical of the lack of clarity, noting that 'the view that the Maastricht and Amsterdam Treaties were severely deficient in not dealing explicitly with the lender of last resort responsibilities of the ECB and the ESCB is widely shared in the international financial community' (p. 201).

4. NEW CHALLENGES FOR SUPERVISION

In many ways, the curious feature of the development of EU banking in the 1990s is that it has not, despite the single market and the prospect of the euro, become more integrated. Now that the euro is a reality, change may well accelerate, so that supervision will have to respond. There are general issues for supervisors to confront that derive from trends in banking, notably the intensification of competitive pressures.

The single market rules made home-country control of banking entities the principal underpinning supervision in the EU. Once a bank is authorised in its home country, it is entitled to operate in others. This entitlement applies even where the proportion of business in the home country is very small, an extreme example of which was BCCI, supervised from Luxembourg, but conducting the bulk of its business in the UK. The home-country control principle was motivated primarily by competitive considerations, since it was implemented as a means of reducing the regulatory burden and avoiding regulatory barriers to market access.

As more pan-European financial groups are created, the home-country control principle may need to be re-examined, as it is likely that a growing proportion of the activity of financial intermediaries will take place outside the home country, especially for the smaller member states. Difficult questions would then arise about, on the one hand, the incentives facing supervisors and their accountability to customers elsewhere, and on the other hand, the issue of redress and the obligations on national authorities to fund any rescue packages for failing banks. Such rescues have, traditionally, been extremely costly for taxpayers and even if the prevailing philosophy is to allow the market to exercise its own discipline to a much greater extent than in the past, it is unrealistic to expect that no burden will fall on tax payers. Acute controversy would arise if inadequate supervision – on the home-country control principle – in country 'x' led to demands on tax payers in country 'y'.

In parallel, supervision will have to evolve to reflect the changing institutional and political context of the EU. Specifically, the key question is whether home-country control – the guiding principle of the single market – can (or should) survive, or ought to be replaced (or complemented by) supranational supervision.

Many of the arguments are well known. Thus, it is accepted that supervisors close to the financial intermediaries under their jurisdiction will be more adept at understanding them, will be immersed in the same financial culture and thus be better at interpreting the data emerging from the supervisees. Equally, as the proportion of non-domestic business of banks grows, the force of these arguments diminishes.

Systemic risk provides one of the more persuasive arguments for Europeanisation of supervision. The advent of cross-border banking means that the risks of contagion spreading from one member state to another must be expected to increase. Especially in a period of intensifying competition with the prospect of large-scale rationalisation across the EU, there could be a jump in the probability of default. Danthine et al. (1999) suggest that the likely emergence of pan-European universal banks could mean that these intermediaries will engage in what the IMF has dubbed 'regulatory arbitrage' or others have called 'supervisor shopping' (Smits, 1997), leading to a general decline in the standard of oversight. Recognising the force of these arguments, Goodhart et al. (1998), though hesitant about European supervision, consider that systemic stability arguments may justify supranational involvement.

Incentives for national supervisors and, perhaps more important, budgetary authorities also have to be considered. If the costs of allowing a bank to fail for a single country are small, the authorities may be reluctant to intervene, even if the damage done to the financial system in other countries is greater. Similarly, if the budgetary cost of dealing with a default falls outside the country which has formal responsibility for supervision, there are obvious moral hazard problems. The immediate answer to these concerns is that supervisors are a close-knit club and have a vested interest in making things work. Moreover, through the BIS and the various EC sponsored fora, they have sufficiently well-developed co-ordination mechanisms to make such fears unfounded.

In dealing with systemic threats, speed of action is universally agreed to be vital. It is argued by Danthine et al. (1999) that centralisation helps to bring all parties together and thus to avoid regulatory buck-passing, justifying a European-level supervisor: 'As universal banking makes it increasingly difficult to distinguish between market risk and the risk of individual banks, the argument for combining the two functions of bank and market supervision in a supra-national EU independent agency seems overwhelming' (p. xxii).

To centralise or not is, thus, a key question about supervision, although there are, in practice, two distinct questions here. The first is whether there should be a single supervisory system covering all the EU countries, thereby creating a counterpart to the integration of monetary policy. The second is whether the ECB should be the agency charged with the task. The arguments for and against giving any central bank the primary responsibility have been well-rehearsed (see, for example, Goodhart et al. 1998). Separation has the merit that the supervisor then has an unambiguous mandate to assure solvency, whereas a central bank may be tempted to confuse monetary policy and systemic stability aims. One argument cited by McCauley and White (1997) is that the result could lead the central bank to be overly expansionary in monetary policy so as to lessen systemic risk. Consolidation, on the other hand, would mean that the central bank could react quickly to forestall any market disruption.

However, a national supervisor may be closer to the action, culture and mentality of the banks in its jurisdiction and may therefore be quicker to spot problems and, equally important, to devise ways of mitigating them. McCauley and White (1997) argue that if national supervision continues, it will 'make it harder to monitor exposure to single creditors borrowing in different parts of the integrated market, and will put a big premium on the efficient exchange of information. It also seems likely to encourage the maintenance of existing differences in both supervisory practices and capital standards among member nations, which, as noted above, continue to impede formation of the single market' (p. 29).

The obvious solution, suggested by, for example, Levitt (1995) is to activate the limited provisions in Article 105 that open to the door to ECB involvement in the supervisory area. Typically, a change of this magnitude only occurs if it is precipitated by a crisis, although this would clearly not be the best way for such a change to be instigated. An alternative justification for assigning competence in supervisory matters to the EU level, identified by a number of commentators (Begg and Green, 1996; McCauley and White, 1997), would be if there were a surge in the number of pan-European banks which outgrew their respective national supervisors. Schoenmaker (1995) suggests a more limited approach in which only those banks whose failure would have systemic implications be supervised at European level.

Striking the right balance is, thus, a practical question rather than an issue of principle, suggesting that the emphasis should be on establishing procedures that work well. These may involve a functional splitting of supervision (Begg and Green, 1996) in which matters of supervisory policy or interaction with monetary policy are assigned to an EU-level body, while the detailed implementation is delegated to national authorities. There is also a political and constitutional question about which body should take on EU-wide supervision. The ECB is the only EU institution theoretically mandated to carry out prudential supervision, although as noted in Begg and Green (1996, p. 378), 'the choice between the Bank and a putative European Banking Commission is a matter of detail rather than principle'.

The division of labour should also take account of the nature of the intermediaries being supervised. Small, local banks with their activity confined to a single member state (and often only to a region within it) will typically have little bearing on the overall stability of the financial system and can, consequently, be well supervised by a decentralised agency. The Sparkassen in Germany, the Spanish cajas or the British building societies are all examples of such intermediaries: their borrowing and lending is geared to local conditions and institutions – housing markets for example – and they generally have simple products.[1]

More important is how supervision should be conducted and how rules are to be set. It was argued in Begg and Green (1996, p. 379) that 'the accumulated knowledge and experience of national supervisors leads us to argue that a collegiate or federal supervisory system would be most effective'. Honohan (1997, p. 26) emphasises the role of incentives, not just for those subject to regulation but also for the regulators and supervisors: 'from the economist's perspective, the most interesting way of curbing abuse is by altering the incentive structure faced by the various participants: bankers, depositors, regulators and the government itself. When it comes to the incentive structure for government, we move into the grey area between fiscal policy on the one hand and issues of governance and even of political corruption on the other.' Plainly, if the emergent Eurosystem is to prosper, it will have to face up to these issues and devise forms of supervision that minimise the dangers of financial fragility while ensuring that the banking system of the EU plays its part in advancing the prosperity of the Union.

NOTE

1. The US Savings and Loans crisis might be put forward as a counter-example. However, the issue there was that the deposit insurance in the system as a whole provided a one-way bet for

risk-takers (and fraudulent operators). Hence it was the nature of the supervisory system rather than its geographical level that was to blame.

REFERENCES

Altunbas, Y. and S.P. Chakravarty (1998), 'Efficiency measures and the banking structure in Europe', *Economic Letters* 60, 205–208.

Arthur Andersen (1993), *European Banking and Capital Markets: A Strategic Forecast*, London: The Economist Intelligence Unit.

BankScope (1998), Database (various), Brussels: Burreau van Dijk.

Begg I. and D. Green (1996), 'Banking supervision in Europe and economic and monetary union', *Journal of European Public Policy* 3, 381–401.

Buiter, W. (1999), 'Alice in Euroland', *Journal of Common Market Studies* 37(2), 181–209.

Council of the European Communities and Commission of the European Communities (1992), *Treaty on European Union*, Luxembourg: OOPEC.

Dale, R. (1992), *International Banking Deregulation: The Great Banking Experiment*, Oxford: Blackwell.

Danthine, J.-P., F. Giavazzi, X. Vives and E.-L. von Thadden (1999), *The Future of European Banking*, London: CEPR.

Davis, E.P. and S. Salo (1998), 'Excess capacity in EU and US banking sectors: conceptual, measurement and policy issues', *LSE Financial Markets Group* Special Paper No. 105.

Dermine, J. (1998), 'Eurobanking, the strategic issues', INSEAD Working Paper No. 98/74/FIN.

Dewatripont, M. and J. Tirole (1994), *The Prudential Regulation of Banks*, Cambridge, MA: MIT Press.

Economic Research Europe (1997), *A Study of the Effectiveness and Impact of Internal Market Integration on the Banking and Credit Sector*, London: Kogan Page.

Edwards J. and K. Fischer (1994), *Banks, Finance and Investment in Germany*, Cambridge: Cambridge University Press.

European Central Bank (1999), *Possible Effects of EMU on the EU Banking Systems in the Medium to Long Term*, Frankfurt am Main: European Central Bank.

Goldman Sachs (1998), 'Restructuring? Its all happening!', *European Banks Fact Sheet*, May 1998, London: Goldman Sachs.

Goodhart, C., P. Hartman, D. Llewellyn, L. Rojas Suarez and S. Weisbrad (1998), *Financial Regulation: Why, How and Where Now?* London: Bank of England.

Honohan, P. (1997), 'Banking system failures in developing and transition countries: diagnosis and prediction', BIS Working papers No. 39.

Lannoo, K. and D. Gros (1998), *Capital Markets and EMU: Report of a CEPS Working Party*, Brussels: CEPS.

Levitt, Malcolm (1995), *Economic and Monetary Union Stage III: The Issues for Banks*, London: Centre for the Study of Financial Innovation.

Louis, J.-V., I.G. Begg, E. de Lhoneux, E. Garcia de Enterria, N. Horn, L. Radicati di Brozolo, R. Smits and J. Stoufflet (1995), *Institutional Aspects of Banking Supervision in the European Community*, Brussels: Editions Universitaire de Bruxelles.

McCauley, R.N. and W.R. White (1997), 'The euro and European financial markets', BIS, Working papers No. 41.

Morgan Stanley Dean Witter (1997), *European Banking: The Pace of Consolidation Accelerates*, UK and Europe Investment Research, 16 December.

Morgan Stanley Dean Witter (1998), *European Banks and Restructuring Potential: Know Why You Own What You Own*, UK and Europe Investment Research, 20 March.

Price Waterhouse (1988), *The Costs of Non-Europe in Financial Services*, Luxembourg: OOPEC.

Pryce, V. and N.B. Griffin (1996), 'They have a dream', *The Banker*, April.

Rajan, A. ed. (1996), *Shaping Up for Change Through Investors in People*, London: Investors in People.

Revell, J. ed. (1997), *The Recent Evolution of Financial Systems*, Basingstoke: Macmillan.

Rybczynski, T.M. (1997), 'A new look at the evolution of financial systems', in J. Revell (ed.), *The Recent Evolution of Financial Systems*, Basingstoke: Macmillan.

Schoenmaker, D. (1995), 'Banking Supervision in Stage Three of EMU', Financial Markets Group Special Paper No. 72, London: London School of Economics.

Siems, T.F. and J.A. Clark (1997), 'Rethinking in bank efficiency and regulation: how off-balance-sheet activities make a difference', *Federal Reserve Bank of Dallas Financial Industry Study*, December, 1–12.

Smits, R. (1997) *The European Central Bank: Institutional Aspects*, The Hague: Kluwer Law International.

White, W.R. (1998), 'The coming transformation of continental European Banking?', *Bank For International Settlements Monetary and Economic Department*, Working Papers No. 54, June.

3. Harmonisation and Legal Transplantation of EU Banking Supervisory Rules to Transitional Economies: A Legal Approach

Michel Tison

INTRODUCTION

The Agenda 2000 programme of the European Commission[1] outlines the main principles along which negotiations between the European Union (EU) and Central and Eastern European Countries (CEECs) should be pursued with a view to possible EU accession. As an initial stage, it recommends the opening of negotiations with a selected group of CEECs: Hungary, Poland, Estonia, the Czech Republic and Slovenia.[2] Notwithstanding this two-step approach, the signal has nevertheless been clearly given by the European Commission: in the long run, all CEECs should be entitled to join the European Union, and the conclusion of Association Agreements ('Europe Agreements') is to be considered a first step towards a more comprehensive policy of convergence with EU regulations. Countries which were not part of the first group of potential EU member states (Slovakia, Lithuania, Latvia, Romania and Bulgaria) have nonetheless stepped up their efforts to incorporate EU regulatory standards into their national laws as part of a comprehensive pre-accession strategy. This movement is particularly strong in the field of banking, as a strong and reliable financial industry constitutes an important foundation of a sound economy.

This chapter examines how different CEECs belonging to the group of privileged accession candidates (Slovenia, Hungary, Czech Republic) are adapting their banking systems to the *acquis communautaire*, and the effects and possible limits of the transplantation of EU rules to economies in transition. The first section will outline the general principles of the relations between the EU and individual transitional countries, in order to find out to what extent the latter are bound to incorporate the *acquis communautaire* into their national legal systems. The second section examines the changing legal environment of

banking in the selected CEECs and compares some of its features with the
existing European and international supervisory standards. Section 3 will analyse
the scope, effects and possible limits of transplantation of EU supervisory
standards to the CEECs. In particular, attention will be paid to the specific
functions of EU harmonisation in a perspective of market integration, and the
question whether these rules should be adapted to the specificities of the market
environment in which these rules will have to operate.

1.   TRADE RELATIONS BETWEEN THE EU AND SELECTED CEECS: EUROPE AGREEMENTS AND THE *ACQUIS COMMUNAUTAIRE*

1.1   From Bilateral Co-operation to Association

Although the process has not been carried out simultaneously in each country,
the CEECs examined in this study have at present all entered into 'Europe
Agreements' with the European Union.[3] A first wave of Europe Agreements
was concluded in December 1991 with Poland, Hungary and Czechoslovakia.
Following the splitting up of the last country into the Czech and Slovak Republics
respectively, the Europe Agreements were renegotiated, which led to the
conclusion of almost identical agreements with both countries in 1993.[4] The
Europe Agreement concluded with Slovenia in June 1996[5] constitutes the last
in a 'third wave' of agreements, initiated by agreements signed with the Baltic
states in 1995. Before the completion of the ratification process for the Agreement
with Slovenia, an Interim Agreement containing most of the trade-related
provisions of the Europe Agreement was in force.[6] The Europe Agreement with
Slovenia effectively came into force on 1 February 1999.

The structure and contents of the Europe Agreements concluded with the
different CEECs are very similar. This leads to the conclusion that, in legal
terms, the CEECs are broadly speaking in a similar position as to their
relations with the EU. This is the consequence of a deliberate policy of taking a
'global approach' to these agreements adopted by the European Commission.
This has, however, not always been fully welcomed by the economically
more advanced CEECs, such as Hungary or the Czech Republic.[7] The latter
countries expressed the fear that the globalising approach would slow down
the integration process, as 'the slowest ship determines the speed of the
convoy'.[8] The Agenda 2000 programme of the European Commission seems
to have at least partially met these objections by dividing the applicant
CEECs into two categories according to the possible timing of EU accession
(see below).

1.2 The Europe Agreements and the *Acquis Communautaire*

Perhaps surprisingly, the Europe Agreements do not contain explicit provisions on the implementation of the *acquis communautaire* by the associated countries. This is due to the fact that the conclusion of these agreements was not initially considered by the European Commission as forming part of a pre-accession strategy. On the contrary, the Europe Agreements, putting into place an association with the European Union, were originally devised as an alternative to accession.[9] The inclusion of the Europe Agreements in a pre-accession process only came later, and was mainly inspired by successive political declarations and decisions taken by the European Council from 1994 on.[10]

In fact, the economic part of the Europe Agreements focuses mainly on the liberalisation of trade relations between the EU and the partner country, continuing the objectives already contained in the bilateral co-operation agreements which preceded the Europe Agreements.[11] The Association will gradually create a free trade area between the European Union and the partner country, leading to the abolition of all customs duties in the movement of goods, and to the elimination of all discriminatory treatments in the cross-border movement of workers, services and establishment.

1.3 The Europe Agreements and Financial Services

1.3.1 Liberalisation and its limits
In the field of financial services, all Europe Agreements contain specific transitional rules and derogations from the general principles of (gradual) liberalisation. The exceptions should enable the CEECs to spread the adjustment costs relating to the liberalisation of their financial markets over a longer period of time. The activities covered under the heading of 'financial services' include both direct and life insurance business and more traditional banking activities.[12] As for the latter, the Europe Agreements have copied the extensive list of 'banking activities' contained in the Second Banking Directive, which is largely consistent with a universal banking model. The derogations, which are largely similar in all Europe Agreements, apply to all freedoms at stake (establishment, services and capital movements). A comparative overview of the applicable rules is provided in Table 3.1.

A first exception relates to the cross-border *establishment* of companies, i.e. the setting-up[13] and management of subsidiaries or branches. The general obligation for the CEECs gradually to grant national treatment[14] to the establishment of EU companies and nationals either at the entry into force of the Agreement (Czech Republic, Slovenia), or at the end of the first stage of the transitional period (Hungary), does not apply to financial services, where national treatment should in all cases be granted only at the end of (i.e. the second stage

Table 3.1: Liberalisation of establishment, services and capital movements in the area of financial services: a comparative overview

		Hungary	Czech Republic	Slovenia
Establishment	Establishment of companies	National treatment by end of first stage (1 Feb 1999)	National treatment by end of transitional period	National treatment by end of transitional period
	Operation of established companies	National treatment by 1 Feb. 1999	National treatment	National treatment
	Standstill obligation	Yes, with exception (art. 50)	Yes, with exception (art. 51)	Yes, with exception (art. 52)
	Acceleration of liberalisation	Possible (decision by Association Council)	Possible (decision by Association Council)	Possible (decision by Association Council)
	Prolongation of derogation regime	Exceptionally and for limited period of time (decision by Association Council)	Exceptionally and for limited period of time (decision by Association Council)	Exceptionally and for limited period of time (decision by Association Council)
Services	Timetable for liberalisation	Progressive liberalisation through decisions of Association Council	Progressive liberalisation through decisions of Association Council	Progressive liberalisation by Association Council within 8 years
	Standstill obligation	No	No	Yes (no measures which are 'significantly more restrictive')

	Direct Investments	Freedom for liberalised establishments	Freedom for liberalised establishments	Freedom for liberalised establishments (Exception: privatised companies)
				• Full freedom of commercial credits and financial loans
				• From fourth year: full freedom for portfolio investment
Capital movements	Financial Services	• First stage: 'creation of necessary conditions for gradual liberalisation'	• First stage: 'creation of necessary conditions for gradual liberalisation'	• First stage: 'creation of necessary conditions for gradual liberalisation'
		• Second stage: possible full liberalisation through decision of Association Council	• Second stage: possible full liberalisation through decision of Association Council	• Second stage: possible full liberalisation through decision of Association Council
	Standstill obligation	Yes (only after end of first stage)	Yes (only after end of first stage)	Yes

of) the transitional period.[15] The Agreement nevertheless provides for the possibility of either an accelerated or (in exceptional circumstances) a delayed transition to national treatment in the area of financial services, subject to the decision of the Association Council.[16] In contrast, the *operation* of companies and nationals duly established in the associated country should be granted non-discriminatory treatment from the initiation of the agreements.[17] No derogation applies with respect to financial services.

With respect to *cross-border services*, no specific regime is envisaged for the area of financial services. The Europe Agreements only prescribe the gradual liberalisation of cross-border services by way of decisions adopted by the respective Association Councils.[18] These decisions should take into account the development of the services sector in the associated countries.

Despite its apparent similarity with the other Europe Agreements, the Agreement with Slovenia seems much more compulsive in formulating the liberalisation principle in the area of services: for example, it states that the Association Council shall take the measures to progressively implement the liberalisation process within eight years from the enactment of the Agreement. In this case, the Agreement formulates a clear obligation to achieve a specific result, which can be seen as having a direct effect in member states at the end of the term.[19] This more stringent approach in the agreement with Slovenia with respect to liberalising cross-border services may be due to the more recent date of conclusion of the Agreement, which allowed the inclusion in the Agreement itself of achievements which were already made in the implementation of the Agreements with other CEECs by way of the later decisions of the respective Association Councils.

Finally, with respect to *capital movements*, the Agreements make a distinction between capital flows related to direct investments and other capital movements not related to current account payments. With respect to direct investments, the Agreements allow the free movement of both the investments and the liquidation or repatriation of these investments, as far as the underlying investment (establishment) is liberalised. As a consequence, the derogation for financial services on national treatment for cross-border establishment equally extends to the capital movements connected with it.

For other cross-border capital movements, a two-stage liberalisation of capital flows is envisaged in the Europe Agreements: during the first stage, the contracting parties should take the necessary measures to 'create the conditions for the further gradual application of Community rules on the free movement of capital'. In the second stage, the Association Council will be competent to examine ways of fully liberalising cross-border capital movements at the end of the transitional period.[20] This general regime, which does not create any obligation for the Association Council to remove obstacles to free movement of capital, fully applies to capital movements associated with financial services.

Again, the Europe Agreement with Slovenia shows a more prescribed approach: although the Agreement endorses the two-stage approach with respect to capital movement liberalisation, it also stipulates the immediate liberalisation of credits related to commercial transactions and financial loans. Moreover, capital movements relating to portfolio investment should be free from the fifth year after entry into the Agreement.[21]

1.3.2   Banking and financial sector development

Beside some specificities in the different Europe Agreements with respect to the *liberalisation* of financial services, all Europe Agreements also stress the importance of *technical co-operation* in the field of banking and financial sector development.[22] In general, bilateral co-operation should ensure the creation or further development of a suitable framework for the conduct of banking, insurance and other financial activities in the associated country. These co-operation efforts should, according to the text of the Agreements, focus on both operational aspects of financial sector development and the improvement of the supervisory framework. The co-operation is intended to include the provision of technical assistance and training.

Although drafted in largely similar terms, the provisions of the Europe Agreements which deal with these aspects of co-operation show some noticeable differences, which reflect the different stage of financial sector development and the ensuing priorities in terms of technical assistance to each of the associated countries. In Hungary, for instance, where the development of the financial sector and the supervisory framework was perceived as being relatively satisfactory, the Agreement mainly focused on co-operation on the harmonisation of the regulatory and supervisory framework with the European practices. In contrast, the Agreement with Slovenia indicates the need for co-operation in order to strengthen and restructure the financial sector, which reflects the less advanced stage of transition in Slovenia at the time of conclusion of the Agreement compared to the Hungarian situation. Moreover, the Agreement with Slovenia points to the need to improve the supervision and regulation of the financial sector, not simply to 'harmonise' the existing rules and practices. A similar picture also emerges in the Agreement with the Czech Republic. In the case of Slovenia, co-operation aims at *establishing* and developing a suitable framework for the encouragement of the financial sector.

Finally, all Europe Agreements provide for technical co-operation with respect to the translation of legislation of both the EU and the partner country. Indeed, the main sources of banking legislation in the countries examined are available in English, which substantially enhances the transparency of the regulatory system and is likely to stimulate market access by EU companies.

1.4   The 1995 White Paper

An important step towards regulatory convergence between the EU and the CEECs was made by the adoption in 1995 of a Commission White Paper on the 'Preparation of the Associated Countries of Central and Eastern Europe into the Internal Market of the European Union',[23] which was subsequently backed by the European Council at its 1995 Cannes Summit. The White Paper, though a unilateral, and therefore not legally binding, instrument for the European Community,[24] clearly expressed the view that the incorporation of the *acquis communautaire* by CEECs would substantially facilitate accession negotiations, even though this has never been formulated as a formal condition for accession.[25]

Specifically in the field of financial services, the White Paper proposed a gradual approach to regulatory convergence: the CEECs should as a first stage take the necessary measures required to enhance the confidence of domestic and foreign investors in the financial system: the training of personnel, the enactment of appropriate legislation and the creation of qualified supervisory bodies. It is only in a second stage that co-ordination measures could be adopted to realise the freedom of establishment and free provision of services in the legislation of the CEECs.[26]

1.5   Agenda 2000

The Agenda 2000 programme relies heavily on the principles set out in the 1995 White Paper. It stresses the importance of applying *in advance of accession* all the elements of the 1985 White Paper on the Single Market,[27] leading to the abolition of border controls, through a specific set of procedures.[28] This is reflected in the strategy for enlargement which the Agenda 2000 programme puts forward, which is based on two principles:[29]

- the conduct of negotiations between the EU and applicants, based on the principle that the *acquis communautaire* will be fully applied upon accession;
- a reinforced pre-accession strategy for all applicants, designed to ensure that they take on as much as possible of the *acquis communautaire* in advance of membership.

The above principles also apply in the field of financial services. In the opinion of the European Commission, 'strengthening the solidity and efficiency of the financial system in all candidate countries seems indispensable. Financial supervising authorities must acquire the qualifications and capacity to implement fully relevant Community legislation'.[30]

Finally, it should be noted that all CEECs have elaborated pre-accession plans and set up a pre-accession institutional framework in the period 1995–97, in order to implement the *acquis communautaire* into their national laws.[31]

By way of conclusion, the analysis of the different legal instruments and political decisions with respect to both the liberalisation of trade relations between the EU and the CEECs, and the preparation for accession by the latter, illustrate that there is no formal legal obligation for the CEECs to incorporate the *acquis communautaire* into their national legal systems. However, adopting the *acquis communautaire* is clearly considered to be an important political commitment and *de facto* precondition for serious negotiations on possible accession to the EU.

2. THE LEGAL FRAMEWORK OF BANKING SUPERVISION IN SELECTED CEECS COMPARED TO EUROPEAN AND INTERNATIONAL STANDARDS

Banking regulation has witnessed dramatic changes since the CEECs have oriented their regulatory strategies towards incorporating the *acquis communautaire*. In Slovenia, a new banking law was approved by Parliament in February 1999, which adapts the Law on Banks and Saving Banks of 1983 to most of the EU banking directives, even including the principles of single licence and home-country control contained in the Second Banking Directive.[32] In the Czech Republic the Act No. 21/1992, which was substantially modified in 1997,[33] is in line with most of the EU banking supervisory standards, as are the regulations adopted by the Czech National Bank.[34] In Hungary, an important move towards European convergence has been made by the adoption of Act No. CXII of 1996 on the Credit Institutions and the Financial Undertakings.

The effort to incorporate the *acquis communautaire* into the laws of CEECs should not be seen as a goal on its own. In fact, European prudential standards in turn reflect commonly accepted prudential principles, as they develop within the Basle Committee for Banking Supervision. By incorporating the European *acquis,* the CEECs not only facilitate their possible accession to the European Union, but at the same time adapt their banking laws to international prudential standards, promoting their integration in the international banking community.

Though not legally binding, the *Core Principles for Effective Banking Supervision*, launched by the Basle Committee in September 1997, constitute a landmark document in the codification of international prudential standards. As the introduction to the document states, '[t]he Basle Core Principles are intended to serve as a basic reference for supervisory and other public authorities in all countries and internationally'.[35] This equally applies to the CEECs in the transformation of the legal framework for banking. In fact, some CEECs have been actively involved or associated in the elaboration of the 25 Core Principles (e.g. Czech Republic, Hungary), and accept them as current international prudential standards.[36]

A general comparison between the Core Principles, the current European prudential standards and the legislation currently in force in the selected CEECs, as shown in Table 3.2, leads to the following considerations.

Table 3.2: Overview of the implementation of the core principles for effective banking supervision in EU directives and in selected Central and Eastern European countries

Core Principles	EU	Czech Republic	Hungary	Slovenia
Preconditions				
1. Suitable legal framework for banking supervision	Yes	Yes	Yes	Yes
Licensing and structure				
2. Protection word 'bank'	Yes	Yes	Yes	Yes
3. Licensing criteria:				
- Ownership structure	Review of 10% shareholders	Review of 10% shareholders	Review of 10% shareholders	Review of 10% shareholders
- Fit & proper directors	Yes	Yes	Yes	Yes
- Operating plan	Yes	Yes	Yes	Yes
- Internal controls	Yes	Yes	Yes	Yes
- Capital base (mn euro)	5	14.26	7.96	5.2[a]
4. Review of transfer of significant ownership in bank	Thresholds: 10, 25, 33, 50%	Thresholds: 10, 25, 33, 50%	Thresholds: 10, 15, 33, 50, 75%	Thresholds: 10, 20, 33, 50%
5. Review of major acquisitions or investments by bank	Max. 15% own funds	Max. 15% own funds[b]	Max. 15% own funds	Max. 15% own funds
6. Minimum capital adequacy requirements	Solvency ratio: 8%	Solvency ratio: 8%	Solvency ratio: 8%	Solvency ratio: 8%
7. Evaluation of bank's policies with respect to granting of loans	+/−	Yes	+/−	Yes
8. Internal procedures for evaluation of bank assets	+/− Adequate accounting procedures	-	Yes	Yes
9. Restrictions on exposure to single borrowers	25% own funds	25% own funds	25% own funds	25% own funds
10. Lending to related companies at arm's length	+/− (20% own funds)	Yes	+/− (Max. 15% own funds)	+/− (20% own funds)

11. Monitoring/control of country risk	+/− (Cooke ratio)		+	+/− (Cooke ratio)
12. Monitoring/control of market risk	Yes (CAD)	Limited (Yes, as of 1 Jan 2000)	Yes	Yes
13. Adequate risk management process for other material risks	-	No	Yes	Yes
14. Adequate internal controls	+		Yes	Yes
15. Promotion of high ethical/professional standards	+/− Money laundering	+/− Money laundering	-	-
Ongoing banking supervision				
16. On-site and off-site inspection	+/− (Cross-border inspection)	Yes	Yes	Yes
17. Regular contacts with bank management	-	-	Yes	-
18. Collection of prudential reports	+/−	Yes	Yes	Yes
19. Independent validation of supervisory information	Yes	Yes	Yes	Yes (annual account)
20. Ability to exercise consolidated supervison	Yes	+/−	Yes	Yes
Information requirements				
21. Adequate accounting and record keeping	Yes	Yes	Yes	Yes
Formal powers of supervisors	Yes	Yes	Yes	Yes
22. Adequate supervisory measures in case of emergency	+/−	Yes	Yes	Yes
Cross-border banking				
23. Consolidated supervision	Yes	No	Yes	Yes
24. International exchange of information between supervisors	Yes	Yes	Yes	-
25. Adequate supervision of local operations of foreign banks	Yes	Yes (local branches)	Yes	Yes (local branches)

Notes:
[a] 0.94 mn euro for savings banks.
[b] The law furthermore prohibits banks from acquiring control of a non-financial company.

First, most of the Core Principles have been incorporated into the European directives, either in a general manner or through more detailed rules, often quantifying the general principles. However, some Core Principles do not have a clear transcription in the European directives. To explain this, one must take into account the specific nature and function of EU harmonisation: the directives do not aim at creating a European 'banking law' which gives an exhaustive account of prudential standards to be applied by the member states. EU harmonisation is merely confined to setting the *minimum* standards to be observed by all credit institutions active in a EU member state, with a view to granting them the right to expand their activities in other member states. Indeed, the banking directives are based on Article 57, paragraph 2 of the EC Treaty, which empowers the Council and the European Parliament only to adopt the directives which are *necessary* to realise the free movement of services and the freedom of establishment for economic actors.

Second, from a formal point of view, it appears from Table 3.2 that the present legal framework for banking in the CEECs under examination already complies to a great extent with both the Basle Core Principles and EU standards. Nevertheless, differences still exist between different countries. In general, Hungary appears to have introduced most of the EU and BIS standards in its banking law.

With some notable exceptions (principle of consolidated supervision; management of market risk and general risk management models), the same can be concluded for the Czech Republic. In Slovenia, the present regulatory framework appeared to lag somewhat behind, but the new banking law approved in February 1999 has incorporated most of the European directives into the national legal order. As a matter of fact, the Slovenian legislature had the relative advantage of being able to rely on the Basle Committee Core Principles. Compared with the present legal framework in the Czech Republic and in Hungary, Slovenian banking law can at present be considered most clearly to reflect current international prudential standards.

One should not, however, rely solely on a formal legal framework. It is not sufficient for a regulator to enact formal prudential standards. It is much more important to examine whether and how the formal rules are effectively applied, and how this is reflected in the day-to-day supervisory practice. On the other hand, it may be the case that the actual supervisory practice in a given country is more in line with the Core Principles than is sometimes suggested by the results of Table 3.2, which has been made on the sole basis of the formally enacted laws and regulations. For instance, it is possible that the supervisor actually imposes stringent risk management procedures, although banking law does not explicitly contain a rule in this sense. Setting the prudential standards by way of formal (legal) rules nevertheless has the advantage of transparency as to the applicable rules and expectations from the supervisory authority.

3. PROSPECTS AND PITFALLS OF LEGAL TRANSPLANTATION OF EU SUPERVISORY RULES: GENERAL CONSIDERATIONS

3.1 General Remarks

The incorporation of the *acquis communautaire* with respect to EU banking regulation in CEECs is not solely a matter of 'legal transplantation'. It is widely accepted in the legal theory of comparative law that legal rules are not purely abstract normative instruments, but should always be seen as they operate within their specific legal, economic and sociological environment. Against this background, it can be asserted that the successful reception of foreign legal rules in a legal system will generally be limited. However, the degree of the international permeability of legal rules across different countries varies considerably, according to the nature and objectives of these rules. The move towards the internationalisation and globalisation of the economy in the past decades has shown that in the field of economic regulation it is relatively easy to elaborate common rules and standards, and to produce co-ordinated, or even unified, rules. This is not to say, however, that identical rules and standards will produce the same effects and operate as efficiently in all countries. In particular for new 'entrants' in the international economic community, such as CEECs, it will be important to examine to what extent the level of standards and rules is adapted to the local market structure and environment. As in medical practice, mere 'transplantation' to a foreign body could produce powerful rejection effects which annihilate the expected benefits of the transplantation.

The same danger exists with respect to the 'transplantation' of the *acquis communautaire* to transitional economies: legal transplantation should not be an aim in itself, but rather must be examined against the background of finding operative ways to promote economic development and the transition to a market economy in the CEECs. Legal transplantation will only be successful when the rules are effectively applied and accepted by the recipients. Imposing the incorporation of the *acquis communautaire* as a pre-condition for accession will in this approach come down to requiring a sufficient level of economic development and stability in the applicant countries, such as to enable the effective operation of EU rules and standards.

3.2 Transplantation of EU Banking Supervisory Rules

3.2.1 Prospects for transplantation
Looking specifically at the area of banking supervision, different elements appear to facilitate a successful transplantation of the *acquis communautaire* to CEECs. These are examined below.

3.2.1.1 Convergence of EU and international prudential standards First, the high degree of convergence between the EU standards and the Basle Committee Core Principles enhances the permeability of EU rules to CEECs. The involvement of some CEECs in the elaboration of the Core Principles cannot be underestimated in this respect. As can be seen in Table 3.2 above, the banking law reforms in the CEECs under examination have been influenced to a large degree by both EU rules and the different recommendations outlined by the Basle Committee. As the case of Slovenia further demonstrates, this influence is even stronger for more recently enacted reforms which are posterior to the publication of the Core Principles. Indeed, the structure of these new banking laws follows the format of the Core Principles to a great extent.

3.2.1.2 EU supervisory standards are 'minimum' standards Second, the very nature of EU supervisory rules could possibly facilitate their transplantation to the CEECs: the prudential rules and standards only constitute a *minimum* harmonisation. In line with the 'new approach' to harmonisation adopted in the 1985 Single Market White Book, harmonisation will be effected to a level deemed sufficient to create the necessary climate of mutual confidence between member states when credit institutions and investment firms wish to expand their activities, either through cross-border establishments or the direct provision of services. The principle of 'minimum' harmonisation has a double advantage for member states: on the one hand, member states are in line with their European obligations as soon as they incorporate these 'minimum' standards. On the other hand, member states remain free to regulate above the minimum set by the European directives.

However, the principle of mutual recognition which is part of the single European licence prohibits a member state from imposing these stricter rules on a credit institution or investment firm licensed in another EU member state. This paradigm of minimum harmonisation–mutual recognition theoretically induces a form of competition between regulators, with the EU minimum level as the bottom line: member states will have to balance the benefit of having stricter supervisory standards imposed upon their domestic financial institutions with the competitive disadvantage these domestic institutions will suffer compared to foreign entrants which are subject to less strict rules in their home country. Theoretically at least, this competition between regulators should in fact lead to the overall convergence of national supervisory standards to the EU 'minimum' level. The same theoretical conclusion is valid for CEECs.

In line with the principle of subsidiary, member states retain the possibility to subject their domestic financial institutions to stricter rules than the European minimum standard. Being limited to 'minimum' standards, the burden for CEECs to incorporate these standards should be relatively low. Furthermore,

CEECs could equally introduce or maintain stricter standards, reflecting specific regulatory choices. This may be further illustrated with reference to the minimum capital for credit institutions: the legislation of most EU member states imposed relatively low initial capital requirements. When it came to implementing the Second Banking Directive, which imposed a minimum capital of EUR 5 mn, most member states adopted the EU minimum.[37] In contrast, the CEECs under examination provide a less uniform picture: only Slovenia approximately sticks to the EU minimum (EUR 5.2 mn). Hungary and the Czech Republic clearly impose higher minimum capital rules (EUR 7.96 and 14.26 mn respectively). These higher standards reflect a deliberate policy objective: by imposing a higher initial capital standard, the regulator indirectly influences the market structure by allowing only highly capitalised actors in the market. As a consequence, the concentration of the market will be relatively high, with fewer banks, but those that exist will be highly capitalised, and will most likely be operating as universal banks. These policy moves may also in part be ascribed to the consequences of the banking crises that these countries experienced in the early transition, which drove out of the market many of the newly established small and medium-sized banks.[38]

However, the reality behind the qualification of EU supervisory standards as a regulatory 'minimum' might be somewhat different. Though qualified as a 'minimum', a comparison between the EU supervisory standards contained in the banking directives and the pre-existent standards in most member states indicates that the 'minimum' standards in fact very often were higher than the pre-existent standards in the member states. In these cases the implementation of banking directives into national law often merely meant increasing existing standards up to the European 'minimum'. The situation is similar in most CEECs, which before the transition did not have a comprehensive banking law. Introducing the 'minimum' EU standards thus necessitates a substantial 'upgrade' of the existent regulatory framework. As a result, as a rule the CEECs under examination have not surpassed the EU minimum level.

3.2 Pitfalls of Transplantation

The specificities of EU harmonisation in the banking supervisory field must not be lost sight of when it comes to building up a comprehensive system of banking regulation and supervision in CEECs. Mere incorporation of EU directives might prove insufficient in this respect, as the directives only constitute a minimum, and moreover mainly serve the specific aim of promoting market integration. More important, however, than the formal regulatory framework is the quality and effectiveness of supervision, which is an essential element in successful transplantation of rules. The issue of the quality of supervision becomes even more important within the perspective of stronger integration, with the possible application of the principles of single licence and home-country control as a future prospect.

3.2.1 Non-exhaustive harmonisation

First, the European directives do not provide for an exhaustive account of banking supervisory rules. When comparing EU harmonisation with the Core Principles, it appears that a number of issues listed in the Core Principles have not (yet) been made the subject of EU harmonisation. For instance, EU prudential standards with respect to capital adequacy impose specific capital ratios to cover solvency, concentration and market risks, but do not contain specific rules on liquidity risks for credit institutions. The lack of EU rules is often due to the impossibility to reach the qualified majority among member states necessary to adopt such measures. However, this does not mean that there is no objective need for supervising liquidity risk generally, and also possibly a need for the elaboration of specific prudential ratios in this respect for individual countries. In fact, a number of EU countries do impose a general *gearing ratio*, imposing a minimum ratio of own funds in relation to liabilities. This ratio is often devised as an additional instrument aimed at covering general risks (liability, fraud, etc.). Here again, the possible introduction of additional capital ratios should be considered in CEECs in order to cover such risks.

In some fields of banking regulation, such as emergency and 'winding up' measures, no consensus has yet been reached at EU level to adopt a directive. It is clear that the inclusion of these kinds of measures in banking regulation is essential for effective banking supervision, as also appears in the Core Principles. The EU can therefore not be satisfied with the mere adoption of the *acquis communautaire* by CEECs, but should also be assessing the adequacy of the legal framework and how fully it takes into account the Core Principles as an additional source of regulation.

3.2.2 Quality of supervision

Most CEECs have now more or less incorporated the EU and Basle Committee regulatory standards into their national legal systems. The effectiveness of the transplantation of rules will however be illusory unless the regulations are supplemented by an effective and efficient system of monitoring and supervision. In other words, the quality of prudential supervision is an essential element in building up a sound financial system. The importance of this issue has also been reflected in the Europe Agreements and the Agenda 2000 programme, which also call for specific assistance to the CEECs by the European Union in training of personnel.

The main difficulty in implementing this issue is to find objective criteria or references to assess the quality of supervision. The EU directives themselves do not contain any reference to this, but are apparently built upon the assumption that all member states will take up the moral obligation to ensure high-quality supervision, and to adapt the number and qualifications of supervisory staff to the tasks and functions of the supervisory authority. A recently conducted external audit of the Belgian supervisory authority has highlighted the problems in finding adequate assessment criteria. In this case, the quality of the internal organisation and exercise of prudential supervision has been assessed by using a benchmark approach based upon existing structures and organisation methods in neighbouring countries.

Specifically for the supervisory authorities in the CEECs, continuous technical assistance will be essential in consolidating high-quality supervision. The assistance should extend to, *inter alia*, the methods of supervising on the basis of bank records, the ways to conduct on-site investigations, to continuously monitor banks facing financial difficulties etc. In assessing the quality of supervision, the specificity of the banking industry in these countries and its higher vulnerability to crises in the period of transition should also been taken into account. The authorities should, probably more so than is the case in EU countries, be trained in dealing with emergency situations, bank runs and the possible domino effects of a bank collapse.

In legal terms, the issue of deficient quality in supervision raises questions as to the remedies and sanctions for such deficiencies. This problem has gained importance as recently bank failures (such as the BCCI scandal, which has a strong international dimension) in different countries have given rise to liability claims formulated by the depositors of failed banks against the state or the supervisory authorities for alleged negligent supervision. In different EU countries, when the liability of the supervisor or the state was accepted, the legislature has reacted by modifying banking law to the effect of excluding, or at least substantially limiting, the liability of supervisory authorities to cases of gross negligence.[39] In other countries, in the absence of specific legislation, this limit has been set by jurisprudence, taking into account the specific functions and objectives of prudential supervision.[40] A third group of jurisdictions does not have any specific rules, so that general liability principles apply.[41]

To the extent that prudential standards are derived from obligations imposed by EU directives, the question then arises as to whether deficient supervision by the prudential authorities of a member state could find a legal basis directly in the EU legal order. Recent case law of the Court of Justice of the European Communities, in particular the *Brasserie du Pêcheur/Factortame* cases, suggests that liability could indeed be based directly on European law, to the extent that negligent supervision is considered the non-fulfilment by a member state of its obligations under European law to fully implement EU directives. This conclusion is of particular importance, as claimants could find in European law a method of circumventing possible limitations on the liability of a supervisor which exists in national law. As a matter of fact, a UK Court of Appeal judgment delivered in the aftermath of the BCCI failure has accepted liability of the Bank of England and the United Kingdom on the basis of the *Brasserie du Pêcheur* jurisprudence, for not having supervised BCCI's operations in accordance with the requirements set by the First Banking Directive. However, in view of the conditions set on liability in the *Brasserie du Pêcheur* case, liability under European law will also be limited to cases of gross negligence of the supervisory authority in the exercise of its functions.

The issue of the possible liability of the prudential supervisor in CEECs should be carefully considered when building up the regulatory framework for banking activities. Liability actions will indeed be the ultimate test for assessing the quality of supervision, though this would then be left in the hands of the courts. On the one hand, the law could restrict or even exclude the liability of supervisors, with a view to preserving the financial resources of both the supervisory authority and the state. On the other hand, such a restriction could in itself partially undermine the credibility of the supervisors in the market, as they wish to protect themselves from any consequences of misconduct or negligence in exercising their functions. Maintaining a possible liability could then be seen as a way to stimulate good-quality supervision. In the prospect of future accession and of the incorporation of the *acquis communautaire*, the applicant CEECs should furthermore take into account the basis for liability arising from European law, which cannot be completely ruled out.

In conclusion, it is clear that the issue of enhancing and maintaining high quality standards in prudential supervision is an essential element in preserving the credibility of the prudential standards contained in the banking laws and regulations. In the absence of clear criteria for assessing the quality of supervision, it could be useful regularly to conduct external audits of the supervisory authority, based on a benchmark approach, and taking account of the specificities of the local banking market. Eventually, the main legal remedy for insufficient quality in supervision lies in the possible liability of the supervisory authority towards aggrieved depositors. A legal basis for this liability might be found in national (liability) law, but possibly also in European law. In the prospect of accession, applicant CEECs should be aware of this liability risk.

3.2.3   Prospective evolution: single licence and home-country control
The move towards the liberalisation of trade relations between the EU and CEECs following from the Europe Agreements is not currently as far-reaching as intra-EU liberalisation. While the Agreements provide for the gradual realisation of the freedom of establishment under conditions of non-discrimination, the freedom to provide services is in general much more dependent upon additional decisions to be taken by the respective Association Councils.

It is clear that this situation is far removed from the level of market integration reached within the European Union: since the entry into force of the Second Banking Directive and the Investment Services Directive, the cross-border establishment and direct provision of services by credit institutions and investment firms operates within the system of 'single-licence' and 'home-country control'. As such, a financial institution licensed in one member state is allowed to open branches and provide services directly in other member states without additional authorisation in the host countries. With a few exceptions, supervision on activities undertaken with the use of this single licence is allotted exclusively to the prudential authorities of the financial institution's home country.

In contrast, the level of liberalisation between the EU and individual partner countries in the Europe Agreements can be compared to the system which existed after the adoption of the First Banking Directive: the creation of an establishment abroad is subject to non-discriminatory treatment, allowing the host state to impose an authorisation regime similar to the regime applicable to domestic institutions. Furthermore, the host country may exercise its supervisory powers on the activities of foreign bank branches, as it is competent to supervise the activities of a foreign financial institution providing services within its territory without establishment.

It should also be noted that the liberalisation principles contained in the Europe Agreements only apply to the *individual* relations between the EU and each associated country. The agreements do not institute a multilateral framework for the liberalising of trade relations between the European Union and CEECs as a whole. Hence, mutual market access and integration *between* CEECs is still limited, and is in any case not subject to the same principles as those that apply in their relations with the EU.

The limited liberalisation imposed by the Europe Agreements does not preclude an associated country from unilaterally granting the benefits of a single licence and home-country control to EU financial institutions wishing to set up a branch or provide services in its territory. While Hungary and the Czech Republic presently still apply the non-discrimination principles outlined above, Slovenian law already endorses the principles of the Second Banking Directive: a credit institution with its head office in an EU member state is allowed to use its single licence in Slovenia under the same conditions as in another EU member states, i.e. without additional authorisation requirements and with the application of the home-country control principle. Slovenian law further allows the supervisory authority of the home member state to conduct on-site investigations.

However, these provisions will only enter into force upon Slovenia's entry as a member of the EU.[42] The incorporation of the single-licence and home-country control principles should therefore be regarded as merely symbolic, as it is clear that upon effective accession these provisions will anyway belong to the *acquis communautaire*. Pending the accession negotiations, EU credit institutions will be treated in Slovenia like other foreign credit institutions: banking operations in Slovenia should be conducted through a local branch which is subjected to the authorisation and supervision by the Bank of Slovenia.[43]

It should nevertheless be pointed out that, as a rule, there is no obstacle that prevents a non-EU country such as Slovenia from applying the principles of single-licence and home-country control in the case of EU credit institutions. Its effects will however only work in a single direction: it only applies to EU credit institutions entering the non-EU market. In contrast, entry into an EU member state by a non-EU-based credit institution is subject to the general regime that regulates such matters.[44] Therefore, the creation of an EU branch by a Slovenian bank would require a separate authorisation according to the national law of the host state, while the direct provision of services without establishment is generally not allowed. The main consequence of the Europe Agreements in this respect is to guarantee non-discriminatory treatment for branches, and possibly the right to provide services without establishment by virtue of a decision of the Association Council. The host EU state is not empowered to grant 'Second Banking Directive' status to a non-EU bank, to the extent that this relation falls under the exclusive competence of the EU institutions for the (external) commercial policy (Art. 133 EU Treaty).

While an EU member state lacks the power unilaterally to grant 'Second Banking Directive' status to a credit institution from an associated country, the Association Council created under all Agreements could decide to grant such status as part of the realisation of the freedoms of establishment and the provision of services in each Agreement. This would in any case require prior implementation of EU directives regarding banking supervision in the associated country, as harmonisation is devised as a necessary precondition for application of the principles of mutual recognition of banking licences and supervisory regimes. The need for high-quality standards in the exercise of prudential supervision becomes even more important in this perspective: the principle of home-country control requires the full confidence of the host country in the adequacy of supervision exercised by the home-country authority on the activities of a credit institution or its branch in the host country.[45] As recent case law of the European Court of Justice and of national courts suggests, a host country is not allowed unilaterally to restrict or revoke the benefit of the single licence if the supervision exercised by the home country is allegedly insufficient, or if the licence granted to the credit institution in its home country is not in conformity with the prudential standards imposed by the EU directives.

Illustrative in this context is a judgment of the Belgian *Conseil d'Etat* with respect to the cross-border distribution of units in a collective investment undertaking. The plaintiff, *Fleming Flagship Fund*, was a Luxembourg-based collective investment undertaking (UCITS), authorised under Luxembourg law and benefiting from a European passport under the 1985 UCITS Directive. When applying for distribution of units relating to a specific compartment in Belgium with use of its European passport, the Belgian Banking and Finance Commission refused to grant authorisation, under the rationale that *Fleming Flagship Fund* did not abide by all provisions of the UCITS directive, despite the authorisation granted by the Luxembourg competent authority. Upon appeal, the Belgian Ministry of Finance confirmed the refusal: host-state authorities are entitled to refuse the benefit of the European passport to a financial institution authorised in another EU member state which does not conform to the substantive rules of the applicable directives which constitute the preconditions of the right to rely on mutual recognition of home-state authorisation and supervision.

However, the action of annulment against these decisions brought by *Fleming Flagship Fund* before the *Conseil d'Etat* succeeded. Relying mainly on the text of the UCITS directive and the Belgian implementing legislation, the *Conseil d'Etat* held that the host state should exclusively make use of the mechanisms provided for in the EU Treaty and its relevant directives when the home country allegedly does not properly authorise or supervise the financial institutions falling under its jurisdiction. Surprisingly, the *Conseil d'Etat* did not deem it necessary to refer a preliminary question on the interpretation of the EU Treaty or the UCITS Directive to the Court of Justice. However, it can be argued that the solution adopted by the *Conseil d'Etat* is in line with the case law of the Court of Justice, and that the same principles should apply with respect to the use system of mutual recognition under the Second Banking Directive.

In the event of alleged insufficient home-country supervision over the banking activities conducted in the host country, the latter would only be entitled either to file a complaint with the European Commission or bring an action against the home state before the Court of Justice (Arts. 226 and 227 EU Treaty). In a case of emergency, the host state could ask the Court to revoke the single licence by way of an interim measure (Art. 241 EU Treaty). This case law strongly relies on the assumption that in a system of economic integration the member states should as a rule have full mutual confidence in the quality of each other's supervision. Supervisory practice within the EU seems to show that difficulties sometimes arise, although the strongly institutionalised co-operation mechanisms between supervisory authorities are likely gradually to reduce possible tensions and conflicts. When it comes to extending the principles of the Second Banking Directive to the economies in transition with a limited experience in banking supervision, this issue will become even more important, in light of the far-reaching legal consequences of the supervisory system introduced by the Second Banking Directive.

4. PROSPECTS AND PITFALLS OF LEGAL TRANSPLANTATION: THE CASE OF DEPOSIT GUARANTEE

The principles set out in Section 3 with respect to the possibilities and limits of legal transplantation of EU banking directives can be further illustrated with reference to the issue of deposit guarantees. At EU level, deposit guarantees were first regulated by a recommendation which was more recently replaced by the Deposit Guarantee Directive. The directive is a key legal instrument in maintaining public confidence in the banking industry, as it provides for compensation to (mainly small) depositors in case of bank failure, and therefore could avoid confidence-based runs on solid banks. Its implementation and possible transplantation to CEECs can therefore be considered an important element in the building of a sound banking system.

4.1   The Deposit Guarantee Directive: Scope for Minimum Harmonisation

The Deposit Guarantee Directive introduced the obligation to join a deposit guarantee scheme as a formal authorisation requirement for all credit institutions. The maximum coverage granted to a single depositor in case of bank failure should amount to at least EUR 20,000 (EUR 15,000 until 31 December 1999), with the possibility to limit the coverage to 90 per cent of deposited funds. Further, the directive allows member states to exclude some deposits or depositors from coverage in order to avoid moral hazard problems and to focus the protection on small depositors. The regulatory approach is, as in the Second Banking Directive, based on the paradigm of minimum harmonisation and mutual recognition: the coverage level imposed by the directive only constitutes a minimum, and does not preclude a member state from introducing or maintaining a higher coverage in its guarantee system.

   In line with the principle of mutual recognition, a credit institution will fall under its home-country deposit guarantee system for its deposit-taking activities undertaken in other EU member states by use of its single licence, i.e. under the regime of the free provision of services or through branches. The mutual recognition principle conversely implies that a member state must accept that credit institutions licensed in another member state with a lower level of deposit guarantees are nevertheless allowed to offer banking services in its territory, either by the direct provision of services or through a branch, without having to join the host-country deposit guarantee system.[46] The application of the paradigm of minimum harmonisation/mutual recognition implies that, in the opinion of the European Parliament, the directive has laid down a sufficient level of harmonised protection so as to create the necessary climate of mutual confidence between member states under a system of mutual recognition of deposit protection schemes.

However, the scope of harmonisation realised by the Deposit Guarantee Directive is limited. The directive does not contain detailed provisions with respect to the organisation of the guarantee systems or the legal technique to achieve coverage of deposits (guarantee, insurance scheme, etc.): both a self-regulatory scheme resulting from an agreement between credit institutions, and government-organised or -supervised systems are conceivable, as long as membership of one or the other system is compulsory and the systems provide for a legally enforceable right to compensation in case of bank failure.[47]

Neither does the directive lay down specific provisions for the funding of deposit guarantee schemes in the member states. The only principles relating to funding are to be found back in the preamble to the directive: as a rule, it is up to the credit institutions, and not to the member states, to take the responsibility for funding deposit guarantee schemes. Shifting the cost of deposit guarantees to public authorities could qualify as a state aid, prohibited by Art. 87 EU Treaty. Furthermore, the preamble to the directive states that the funding capacity of the guarantee schemes should be proportionate to their potential obligations.[48] Although the European Parliament did not deem it 'absolutely necessary' to lay down more detailed rules in this respect, it is clear that the absence of any harmonisation of rules on funding substantially reduces the harmonisation effect of the guarantee systems. Given the wide diversity of systems in EU countries, achieving a consensus on common funding rules would in any case have been very difficult.

4.2 Implementation of the Deposit Guarantee Directive in EU Member States

With respect to the level of deposit coverage, the implementation of the Deposit Guarantee Directive in the EU member states exemplifies the patterns of implementation described above: member states which did not have deposit guarantee coverage reaching the minimum imposed by the directive have in general adapted their internal systems to the European minimum. This is the case in the Netherlands, the United Kingdom, Luxembourg and Belgium. On the other hand, member states with higher deposit guarantee coverage than the European minimum have maintained this higher level, which seems to confirm the paradigm of competition for excellence in banking regulation. One country which has done this is France, where the limit of approximately EUR 60,000 has been maintained. The German reaction to the directive is also significant: Germany unsuccessfully challenged the directive before the Court of Justice, on grounds of the incompatibility of the limits on mutual recognition of deposit guarantee regimes with the principles of free movement.[49] Germany wished to preserve its system of almost unlimited deposit coverage under a system of mutual recognition. The non-implementation by Germany of the Deposit Guarantee Directive has recently led the European Commission to bring an infringement action against Germany before the Court of Justice.

As the organisation and funding of deposit guarantee schemes fell outside the scope of the EU directive, only limited data are available as to the present situation in the EU member states. As can be seen in Table 3.3, the directive did not provoke a strong convergence between the member states. With respect to the organisation of protection schemes, most member states which implemented the directive have opted for protection through the creation of either one or several funds. However, the financial arrangements within the protection systems still differ strongly between member states. While some states impose actual contributions to be made to the fund(s), other systems are based exclusively on

Table 3.3: Deposit guarantee systems in different EU member states after the implementation of the Deposit Guarantee Directive

	Deposit coverage ceiling, domestic currency	Deposit coverage ceiling, EUR	Annual contribution or commitments to guarantee fund (in % of total deposits)
Belgium	BEF 807,000	20,000	0.02
			0.06
Denmark	DKK 300,000	40,350	0.2
Germany	30% of bank's own		0.03
	funds per depositor		0.06
Greece	GRD 6,000,000	20,000	1.25–0.025
Spain	ESP 2,325,000	20,000	0.1
France	FRF 400,000	60,980	0.03
Italy	ITL 200,000,000	100,000	0.4–0.8%
Netherlands	NLG 44,075	20,000	Max. 10% own funds of member bank
Austria	ATS 260,000	20,000	Max. 0.83% risk-adjusted assets
Portugal	PTE 6,750,000	33,750	0.8–1.1
Finland	FIM 150,000	25,000	0.05–1% of assets
Sweden	SEK 250,000	27,870	0.4–0.6
UK	GBP 20,000	20,000	Max. 0.3%

Source: European Banking Federation (1997), Tables I & III.

commitments to pay from the part of the member credit institutions when the fund has to intervene. Some systems use a mixed funding system, based partly on (annual) contributions, supplemented by commitments which can be called upon by the fund in case of emergency.

Moreover, different methods are applied to the calculation of contributions or commitments to pay: in most cases, the contribution/commitment of a single credit institution is expressed in relation to the amounts of deposits held with it. The figures show, however, substantial differences between the protection schemes, where actual contributions can vary from 0.01 to 1.25 per cent of the deposit volume. In commitment based protection schemes, the amounts are generally slightly higher (on average 0.6 per cent of deposits). Some member states use other criteria to calculate the contributions or commitments to be made by credit institutions, such as the amount of own funds (Netherlands) or the total assets (Austria). In Portugal, the amount of the contribution is inversely related to the solvency ratio of the banks. This should reduce moral hazard on the part of participating credit institutions, as better-capitalised banks benefit from a lower financial burden in regard to contributions to the deposit protection scheme.

When focusing on the capacity of protection funds to cover deposits in case of bank failure, the figures again show strong differences as to the actual or potential size of the protection funds in absolute figures. More important, however, is the relative size of the protection fund in relation to its potential liabilities, i.e. the total amount of covered deposits. In absence of precise data on the latter, the coverage capacity is extremely difficult to assess. Relating the size of the protection funds in a country to the total amount of non-bank deposits, as shown in Table 3.4, only provides a partial picture on the coverage capacity of protection funds, as no account is taken of the coverage ceilings in the protection schemes and the exclusion of some deposits from protection. In fact, one should also include in the figures the relative importance of retail deposits in the aggregate of non-bank deposits and the average size of such retail deposits. Nevertheless, the figures give some rough indications as to the possible coverage capacity of the protection schemes. Here again, we can see strong disparities between the countries under examination, varying from less than 0.01 per cent to 0.7 per cent. In Sweden the objective of the protection fund is to attain a coverage ratio of 2.5 per cent of client deposits. This relatively high proportion can probably be ascribed to the experiences of the 1994 banking crisis in this country.

Once more, the conclusion seems to be that EU-level harmonisation of the minimum protection to be granted to depositors in case of bank failures is not reflected in the actual financial situation and coverage capacity of the protection funds. In most member states, the elaboration of the funding arrangements and the financial objectives of the protection funds do not seem to be based on the

Table 3.4: Coverage capacity of deposit protection schemes in EU countries (as of 31 December 1996)

EU Member	Amount available in the deposit protection fund, actual contributions + commitments (in EUR mn)	Amount of non-bank deposits (in EUR mn)	Coverage capacity of deposit protection fund (%)
Belgium	334.6	227,618	0.147
Denmark	100.9	83,452	0.121
Germany		1,680,093	
Greece	9.2	15,223	0.06
Spain	n.a.	n.a.	
France	381.1	813,088	0.047
Italy	1600–3200	490,471	0.326
Netherlands	n.a.	333,930	
Austria	1529	n.a.	
Portugal	259.4	37,061	0.7
Finland	n.a.	61,226	
Sweden	2.7 (objective: 2.5% deposits covered)	87,902	0.003
UK	4.55–9.11	843,283	0.001

Sources: Banking Federation of the European Union (1997), Tables IV–V: amount of protection funds; OECD, *Bank Profitability* (1998): amount of non-bank deposits.

assessed needs of the protection schemes themselves, as in most cases precise data on the amount of potential liabilities (covered non bank deposits) does not even exist.

The above figures demonstrate that substantial differences still exist between member states with respect to the aspects of deposit protection which were not harmonised at EU level, in particular the rules regarding the financial contributions made by credit institutions to protection funds, and the actual size (in absolute and relative terms) of the protection funds. In those member states which have been confronted with important banking failures in recent years, such as Sweden, more attention seems to be paid to the funding capacity of the protection schemes. It is clear that the financial resources of the protection funds in some member states would be insufficient to absorb the failure of even a middle-range bank. In this respect, it is essential for the protection schemes to allow for additional contributions/commitments to be made by the banks, in order not to shift the cost of most banking failures to the state.

The main conclusions that may be drawn are that incorporating the Deposit Protection Directive into national law is clearly not sufficient to create a sound and credible deposit protection system. Member states should assess on economic criteria whether the funding arrangements and the actual size of the protection funds are adequate. In this analysis, an overall sectoral approach of the financial soundness of the banking industry should also be effected, as it could influence the probability of individual banking failures.

4.3 Legal Transplantation to the CEECs

The issue of the legal transplantation of the Deposit Guarantee Directive to transitional economies illustrates the apparent simplicity and underlying risks of the mechanical transplantation of the formal rules of a directive. The Deposit Guarantee Directive has been elaborated in an economic environment where banking failures generally do not occur, and where most guarantee systems were at all times sufficiently funded in order to cover individual failures of mostly smaller banks.

The situation is very different in CEECs. The banking systems of these countries have, at least in this stage of privatisation and transition, not been immune from important banking failures and even widespread banking crises. As the privatisation of state-owned banks mostly implied the abolition of the previously existing explicit state guarantee, deposit protection schemes became the only safety net for ensuring depositor confidence beside an implicit state guarantee. Most CEECs have indeed made substantial efforts to establish a separate deposit insurance system (Hungary since 1993; Czech Republic since 1995) or are in the process of setting up such a system (Slovenia, effective from 1 January 2001).[50]

The early years of operation of these systems have proved to be difficult. The frequent occurrence of banking failures led to a situation where guarantee funds were virtually exhausted, as happened in the Czech Republic in 1995 after two major bank failures.[51] This means that at present the protection schemes operate under financially precarious conditions. As a result, the state guarantee for bank failures could well turn out to be less implicit than it ought to be.

Discussing the different pros and cons of deposit guarantee systems and the existence of explicit or implicit state guarantee falls outside the scope of this study. The case for deposit guarantee in the economies in transition (and more generally in developing countries) has, however, gained attention in economic literature in the past few years. These studies stress in particular the need for a system of explicit guarantees, preferably through the establishment of a separate fund, with limited compensation to depositors.[52] As to the source of funding, some authors would tend to advocate a government-sponsored system in developing and transitional economies, as mere bank-funded systems would not necessarily ensure depositor confidence.[53] It should be noted that most systems put in place in CEECs in recent years adhere to a mere bank-sponsored fund. This is also the policy option adopted in the European Union's Deposit Guarantee Directive. In a recent study, Miller[54] advances the possibility of creating a deposit guarantee system based on the use of an assessment system, under which the banks themselves are fully liable for compensation to depositors in case of failure of a peer bank. Practically speaking, payments would be made in the first instance by public authorities, and recovered *ex post* with the banks, *pro rata* to their relative importance. According to Miller, such a system would overcome the possible underfunding of protection funds, and also stimulate active monitoring by banks of the risk profile of other banks, which they would be in a good position to accomplish. They would also have a strong incentive to monitor other banks, and to correct any deficiencies early on, as they would bear the brunt of the costs if a bank were to fail. This could therefore be considered as a valuable alternative for a fund-based system in transitional economies during the transformation process. This assessment based system will in fact underscore the protection regime in Slovenia (see below).

Against this background, the question arises whether mere transplantation of the Deposit Guarantee Directive is likely to create the conditions for sufficient depositor confidence, and hence may be considered as an adequate instrument in creating a sound regulatory environment. More specifically, the higher vulnerability of the banking systems in the course of transformation requires greater attention for the non-harmonised aspects of deposit protection which equally bear on the credibility of protection schemes. The presumed higher probability of bank failures during the transformation should be reflected in stronger financial arrangements and the formulation of clear objectives as to the funding capacity of the protection schemes.

With respect to deposit coverage, recent amendments to the banking laws in the CEECs examined have increased the level of deposit coverage ceilings such as to bring them more in accordance with the EU Deposit Guarantee Directive. As appears from Table 3.5, the coverage ceiling in the Czech Republic is significantly higher than the EU minimum, while in Hungary it is still clearly inferior to it. The limit set by the new Slovenian Law on Banking is close to the EU limit. Convergence with the European directive also appears from other modalities of the protection schemes, as recently amended. For instance, both Czech and Slovenian law have now extended the protection to deposits made by legal persons, whereas they were previously restricted to deposits made by natural persons.

The funding arrangements of the protection schemes in the Czech Republic and in Hungary are based, as in most EU countries, on regular contributions to be paid by credit institutions in relation to their deposit base (see Table 3.5). In the Czech Republic a fixed contribution is imposed by law, the amount of which slightly exceeds the average found in EU countries. The Hungarian scheme has a more flexible approach: as a rule, the annual contribution is determined by the NDIF at a rate which cannot normally exceed 0.2 per cent of the deposit volume of an individual bank, which also corresponds to the average level of contributions in the EU member states. However, the NDIF can impose different premium rates according to the risk profile of credit institutions. For instance, in 1996 the NDIF levied a slightly higher premium on banks where the average size of deposits was higher than the maximum coverage offered by the protection scheme (1.9 per cent) compared to those where the average of deposits was lower (1.6 per cent).[55] On the other hand, the law enables the NDIF to increase the annual premium for an individual bank to up to 3 per cent of the deposits, depending on the risks incurred by the bank's activities.[56]

Table 3.5: Deposit guarantee systems in selected CEECs

	Structure of deposit protection scheme	Admini-stration of deposit protection scheme	Deposit coverage ceiling (in national currency)	Deposit coverage ceiling (in EUR)	Annual contribution to guarantee fund (% of total deposits
Czech Rep.	Public	Deposit Insurance Fund (DIF)	400,000	10,700	0.5%–0.1% (building savings banks)
Hungary	Public	National Deposit Insurance Fund (NDIF)	1,000,000	40,100	Max. 0.2% (risk-adjusted)
Slovenia (from 1 Jan. 2001)	Public	Central Bank	3,700,000	18,940	Commitment proportional to relative share of deposits

The Slovenian protection scheme, as introduced by the 1999 Law on Banking and intended to replace the system of unlimited explicit state guarantee for deposits, will be fully effective as of 1 January 2001.[57] The protection scheme will be based on commitments by member banks, who can be called upon by the Bank of Slovenia in case of a bank failure. Uncommonly, the law does not set any ceiling on the commitment of an individual bank. Each bank must guarantee the payment of deposits of a failed bank to an amount equal to the relative importance of the deposits held with the former in the total amount of deposits held with all banks.[58] In order to be able at all times to execute the guarantee, an individual bank must have sufficient liquid assets. Therefore, the law requires each bank to invest assets in government or central bank securities at an amount determined by the Bank of Slovenia.[59]

As shown in Table 3.6, the coverage capacity of the protection schemes in Hungary and the Czech Republic appears to be relatively high when compared to the situation in EU member states. Before drawing general conclusions from this, additional elements should be introduced in the assessment: first, the presumed higher probability of bank failures in the process of privatisation and transition calls for a relatively strong protection system as a catalyst for depositor confidence. This certainly holds true in light of the policy objective to avoid further government backing of failed banks.

Table 3.6: Coverage capacity of the deposit protection schemes in selected CEECs

	Amount available in the deposit protection fund (mn EUR) (actual contributions + commitments	Amount of non-bank deposits (in mn EUR)	Coverage capacity of deposit protection fund (%)
Czech Republic[a]	69.628	32420	0.214
Hungary[b]	31.21	10215	0.305
Slovenia[c]		7258	

Notes:
[a] As of 31.12.1998;
[b] As of 31.12.1996;
[c] As of 31.12.1997.

Sources: Annual Reports of central banks; OECD, *Bank Profitability* (1998): amount of non-bank deposits.

Furthermore, the coverage capacity of the protection schemes should be viewed in light of the average size of (retail) deposits, which in turn will depend on the average per capita income. Assuming that the average in CEECs is lower than what is commonly found in most EU states, the protection schemes in CEECs will have to be more strongly capitalised, as fuller coverage of deposits will have to be granted in case of a bank failure. On the other hand, the coverage ceiling must be fixed at a level which is adequate for ensuring consumer confidence, and precisely taking into account the average size of deposits.

In this context, it is interesting to note that the Hungarian deposit protection system adopts a risk-adjusted approach, imposing a higher contribution to the protection fund for those credit institutions where the average size of deposits is inferior to the limit of coverage per depositor. Moreover, as the overall average size of deposits seems relatively low (HUF 169 000 or EUR 677), there is no absolute necessity to increase the coverage ceiling to the minimum imposed by the EU Deposit Guarantee Directive. Compared to per capita income, the coverage granted indeed appears to be relatively high.[60]

The elaboration of the Hungarian protection scheme seems to be more balanced, and hence confident, as it appears to be based on a rational assessment of the domestic economic environment. This system could be more effective in ensuring depositor confidence than systems which simply transplant the European directive and which do not base their funding and protection arrangements on the particularities of the domestic liabilities and deposit structure of the banking sector.

The situation in the Czech Republic over the last few years illustrates the risk of rapid 'consumption' of a deposit protection fund in the case of a major bank failure, and the difficulties for the public authorities in eliminating the implicit guarantee for bank deposits. In fact, the fund intervened on only one occasion, namely after the failure of Ceska Banka. However, all resources available in the fund had to be used to grant compensation to depositors.

In all other cases of compensation to depositors, the intervention came directly from public authorities, and compensation was up to 40 times higher than the coverage limit existing within the deposit protection fund. This public intervention was in some cases attributed to political factors, such as the desire to avoid social tensions before the parliamentary elections of 1996, but the official explanation was the (legitimate) fear of a generalised run on banks. Since 1997, the fund has been slowly recapitalised, with the contributions to be paid by banks to the fund being relatively high (0.5 per cent of deposits).

No further details can be provided for Slovenia, as the new system is not yet in operation. However, it may be doubted whether the existence of funding arrangements based exclusively on unlimited commitments is an appropriate policy for ensuring the credibility of the system. This deposit guarantee system is likely to be perceived by the public as a persistence of an implicit state guarantee in the absence of transparency as to the commitment capacity of the banks. In contrast, most EU countries have at present a system of actual contributions, or at least a mixed system with only a minor proportion of commitments to pay. The setting up of a separate fund with actual contributions to be made by the banks may be considered to enhance depositor confidence, due to the existence of separately held funds specifically effected for deposit guarantee.[61]

CONCLUSIONS

As the theory of comparative law and legal history amply demonstrates, transplantation of laws has, with variable degrees of success, been effected since antiquity. In this perspective, the 'export' of the *acquis communautaire* to Central and Eastern European economies should not be regarded as a unique historical process. Moreover, the legal transplantation of rules of economic law seems at first sight to be less burdensome than the 'export' of more fundamental legal practices which are more closely tied to the cultural and sociological specificities of a nation, such as family law.

This is not to say, however, that the legal transplantation of the *acquis communautaire* to CEECs, as exemplified in the field of banking, is a non-issue. From the side of both the European Union and Central and Eastern European countries, the almost mechanical incorporation of the *acquis communautaire* has been regarded as a mainly political move towards the possible future EU accession of the latter. It would however be wrong to view the incorporation of the *acquis communautaire* as strictly a formal and abstract process. Introducing economic law, and banking legislation in particular, cannot be isolated from the underlying economic substance: the rules should be adapted to the market structure in which they will have to operate.

This does not mean that the objective of transplanting the *acquis communautaire* should be put into question. In effecting the transplantation, specific attention should be paid to the specificity of the transitional economies. For an economy in transition, building a sound banking system could for instance in some circumstances require clear transitional rules instead of a mere formal incorporation of high supervisory and protective standards in the lawbooks. Furthermore, it has been stressed that in setting up the supervisory framework for banking supervision, the market should be confident in the quality of supervision.

The case of deposit guarantee harmonisation in the European Union, and its possible transplantation to CEECs, has further demonstrated the limits of transplantation: the European directive was mainly the result of a compromise between member states which had long-established deposit protection schemes operating in a relatively sound banking environment. Some essential aspects of the organisation of the protection systems were not harmonised, but are nevertheless essential in setting up a strong and sound protection scheme. In transplanting the directive to CEECs, these organisational aspects must not be overlooked.

Moreover, the utility of the EUR 20,000 coverage limit may be questioned in some circumstances, given the present economic environment in some member states. Here again, some applicants for accession could be better off with a clear transitional regime than with a formal system which eventually would not be able to fulfil its obligations under the transplanted directive. The case of deposit guarantee demonstrates that legal transplantation may not be viewed exclusively in political terms. If legal rules are to be effective, they will have to be shaped so as to be operationally functional.

NOTES

1. European Commission (1997), p. 138.
2. European Commission (1997), pp. 57–58.
3. For a general overview, see Maresceau (1997), pp. 6–7.
4. OJ, 1994, L 359/2 (Slovak Republic) and L 360/2 (Czech Republic). This coincided with the conclusion of Europe Agreements with Bulgaria and Romania in the same year.
5. For the text of the proposal, see: COM(95) 341 final.
6. OJ L 344/3 of 31 December 1996. The Agreement entered into force on 1 January 1997.
7. Balász (1997), p. 358.
8. Balász (1997), p. 373.
9. Müller-Graff (1997a), p. 16; Müller-Graff (1997b), p. 34.
10. Cremona (1997), p. 196.
11. For more information on the early stage of bilateral economic co-operation, see Maresceau (1989), pp. 6–11.
12. Annex XIIa Europe Agreement EU–Hungary; Annex XVIa Europe Agreement EU–Czech Republic; Annex Ixc Europe Agreement EU–Slovenia. The list may be amended by decision of the respective Association Councils (e.g. Art. 49 Europe Agreement EU–Hungary).
13. The notion of 'setting up' does not only includes the *creation* of a legal entity, but also extends to the *acquisition* of an existing company in the host state, as a result of which it becomes a subsidiary of the acquirer. This extensive interpretation is particularly important with respect to privatisation issues.
14. In the Europe Agreement EU–Slovenia, the notion of 'national treatment' has a broader definition than in the other Europe Agreements, taking as a reference the better treatment offered in either the host state or a third country as the basis for 'national treatment'. This approach in fact combines the notions of 'national treatment' in its traditional understanding, and the principle of 'most favoured nation'.
15. Art. 44, 1 (i) Europe Agreement EU–Hungary; Art. 45, 1(i) Europe Agreement EU–Czech Republic; Art. 45, 1(I) Europe Agreement EU–Slovenia.
16. Art. 44, 6 Europe Agreement EU–Hungary; Art. 45, 5 Europe Agreement EU–Czech Republic; Art. 45, 6 Europe Agreement EU–Slovenia.
17. Art. 44, 1 (ii) Europe Agreement EU–Hungary; Art. 45, 1(ii) Europe Agreement EU–Czech Republic; Art. 45, 1(ii) Europe Agreement EU–Slovenia.
18. Art. 55, 1 Europe Agreement EU–Hungary; Art. 56, 1 Europe Agreement EU–Czech Republic; Art. 53 Europe Agreement EU–Slovenia.
19. See in particular the case law of the Court of Justice with respect to the direct applicability of the freedoms of the EU Treaty: case 33/74, *van Binsbergen*, judgment of 3 December 1974, ECR 1974, p. 1299.
20. Art. 61 Europe Agreement EU–Hungary; Art. 62 Europe Agreement EU–Czech Republic; Art. 64 Europe Agreement EU–Slovenia.

21. Art. 62, 2 Europe Agreement EU–Slovenia.
22. Art. 83 Agreement EU–Hungary; Art. 84 Agreement EU–Czech Republic; Art. 85 Agreement EU–Slovenia.
23. COM (95) 163 final of 3 May 1995.
24. Müller-Graff (1997), p. 20.
25. Gaudissart and Sinnaeve (1997), pp. 45–46.
26. White Paper, Chapter 13, pp. 281–304.
27. European Commission, COM(85) 310.
28. European Commission (1997), p. 48.
29. European Commission (1997), p. 51.
30. European Commission (1997), p. 118.
31. For an overview, see Soveroski (1997), pp. 20–22.
32. The inclusion of the single-licence/home-country control principles was not initially envisaged in the draft law. See Bank of Slovenia (1997), pp. 45–46.
33. For an overview of the modifications, see Czech National Bank (1997), pp. 11–13.
34. The elaboration of most technical rules is delegated by the law to the Czech National Bank, acting by way of 'provisions'. For instance, a provision of 17 June 1999 imposes, as from 1 April 2000, new rules on the management of market risks by credit institutions, taking over the requirements imposed by the EU Capital Adequacy Directive.
35. P. 2, No. 6.
36. See for instance, Czech National Bank (1996), p. 2.
37. This is the case in the United Kingdom, Germany, France and the Netherlands. In Belgium, the minimum level, denominated in BEF, corresponds to EUR 6.2 M.
38. This was the case with the Czech banking crisis of 1995–96 (see Anderson and Kegels 1998, p. 207).
39. In Germany § 6(3) Kreditwesengesetz (full exemption of liability); in the United Kingdom: section 1(4) Banking Act 1987 (exclusion of liability under statutory law); in Luxembourg: Art. 20(2) Law of 23 December 1998 on the creation of the 'Commission de surveillance du secteur financier' (limitation of liability to gross negligence).
40. In France the case law of the *Conseil d'Etat* (limitation to 'faute lourde').
41. This is for instance the case in Belgium.
42. Law on Banking.
43. Krizaj (1999).
44. Art. 9 Second Banking Directive.
45. See also Anderson and Kegels (1998), p. 286.
46. Mutual recognition is however limited in a double way, mainly in order to prevent systemic distortions as a consequence of competition between deposit guarantee systems of different member states: first, the directive prohibits, by way of transitional provision, a credit institution from exporting its home state guarantee system to another member state where a lower coverage level would exist ('export cap'). On the other hand, a member state must allow a credit institution authorised in another member state which has a lower coverage level, to 'upgrade' its coverage in the host country guarantee system for its branch activities in that member state (so-called 'top-up option').
47. Recital 12 of the Preamble to the Deposit Guarantee Directive.
48. Paragraph 23, preamble to the Deposit Guarantee Directive.
49. ECJ, case C-233/94, *Germany v. European Parliament and Council*, judgment of 13 May 1997, ECR, 1997, p. I-2405.
50. For an overview including other CEECs, see Borish, Ding and Noël (1997), pp. 106–8.
51. Anderson and Kegels (1998), p. 262.
52. In particular, see Miller (1999), p. 51, with further references to other studies.
53. Talley and Mas, cited in Miller (1999), p. 55, note 51.
54. Miller (1999), pp. 53–54.
55. National Deposit Insurance Fund, *Annual Report 1997*, p. 13.
56. Section 121(6) and (7) Act No. CXII. of 1996 on the credit institutions and the financial undertakings.
57. See in this respect Krizaj (1999).

58. Art. 155 Law on Banking.
59. Art. 156 Law on Banking.
60. Borish, Ding, and Noël (1997), p. 146: in Hungary the coverage rate would correspond to two years per capita income, while in Poland and the Czech Republic the corresponding figure would be one year. In view of the economic developments in these countries, the figures might however rapidly prove to be obsolete.
61. See in the same sense Miller (1999), p. 53.

PART II

Case Studies

4. Banking Regulation and Supervision in Associated Countries: A Case Study of the Czech Republic[*]

Roman Matoušek and Anita Taci

1. INTRODUCTION

When banking sectors in transition countries grow (not only in the Czech Republic but also in other Central and Eastern European countries (CEECs)), difficulties arise in finding the appropriate way of controlling commercial bank activities, such as setting up rules eliminating or limiting imprudent behaviour. This discussion asks what sort of policy and targets should be adopted and applied. A further question might be what makes banking supervision and regulation in the Czech Republic different from similar activities in EU countries.

The banking supervision policy carried out in emerging markets – CEECs – takes into account a range of specific phenomena. Indeed, the key distinctive factor of banking supervision and regulation in these economies was the until recent absence of a market-oriented banking system. This meant that banking supervisors actually had to establish 'the rules of the game' and ensure 'a level playing field' for all participants in a given financial market. In the Czech Republic, this period in banking supervision could be labelled as a 'learning by doing' process. A further condition for a sound and efficient banking sector is the creation of a macro- and micro-economic environment which will be consistent with, and help promote, the widening financial activities of the commercial banking sector. Therefore the main priorities lay in developing an institutional framework, including: bankruptcy law, corporate law, laws protecting creditors instead of debtors, and prudential accounting standards. These issues were faced by all transforming economies.

Banking supervision and regulation is adopted as a set of measures preventing banks from operating in an imprudent way, while at the same time ensuring the

[*] This research was undertaken with support from the European Union's Phare ACE Programme P96-6009-R. The views and opinions expressed in this study are those of the authors and are not necessarily those of their institutions.

stability of the system as a whole. In our analysis, banking regulation and supervision is a system consisting of several related elements, each of which has a direct impact on the efficiency and stability of the banking system. The principal problem is deciding which type of bank regulation is optimal in terms of the degree of intervention, and finding a level of a regulation that is not counter-productive to the establishment of a market-based economy. These points are closely related to the problem of deciding the desirable methods for achieving another important objective, the efficiency and stability of the financial system. The results of this analysis should also be focused upon the design of systems of banking regulation and supervision that will be appropriate for the emerging single European financial market.

The crucial factors that will be discussed in the course of our analysis are the following: a legislative framework for bank prudential regulation, barriers to entry, exit and forced exit from the banking sector, and deposit insurance schemes. All these aspects of banking regulation and supervision in transition economies must reflect EU banking directives, since most of the Central European countries are at the threshold of a negotiation process regarding future membership. Therefore, in creating a banking sector the gradual harmonisation with EU directives is essential.

2. THE ROLE AND PLACE OF BANKING REGULATION AND SUPERVISION

In regard to the role of bank regulation in Central and East European countries, the issues faced by policy-makers at the beginning of banking reforms were: what could be and should be the pace of reforms to liberalise and restructure the financial and banking system (enhancing their functional efficiency)? How can the objective of functional efficiency be reconciled with that of stability and soundness? What degree of intervention in the banking system is admissible?

A regulatory body must first decide what the main objectives of banking supervision are. The principal objective of regulation might be seen as the mitigation of the potential instability of the banking system – in the limitation of systemic risk. The growth in the number of commercial banks, the share within a market, the complexity of the applied technology, and new products contribute to the increase in hostility in the environment in this sector; competition pressures and inexorably rising costs jeopardise a bank's success. The potential causes of systemic risk can be classified as follows (see Hviding, 1995):

- the vulnerability of banks to runs by depositors,

- the risk in the payment system, as when a large participant fails to meet clearing obligations, arising from 'pro-cyclical' (and potentially destabilising) trading practices.

In order for efficient banking regulation and supervision to be performed, the regulator has to clearly state the objectives of, and accountability for, its activities. The failure of several small-sized commercial banks in the Czech Republic demonstrates the importance of this principle. The CNB, as the banking supervisory body, faced criticism of its accountability for the current stage of banking in the Czech Republic. Further criticisms have been that interventions and rescue activities have come too late and had an uncertain impact at best.

In fact, this situation could have been be prevented by the CNB setting a clear and transparent policy for the banking system. Certainly, there are those who have argued that in the framework of the Czech National Bank Act the role and accountability of the CNB is clearly defined, whether or not the goals of banking supervision are clear and transparent. One can agree with this explanation, i.e. that the CNB is responsible for the stability of the banking system. However, this definition is too general. We assert that if the banking supervisory body (CNB) had declared its main aims, the CNB would not be blamed for the problems that some banks faced in the early transition.[1] Therefore, in order to avoid a repetition of this situation, the regulator must make clear its policy goals for the banking sector. In other words, the priorities of regulation should be clearly stated, such as the stability and soundness of the banking system and the protection of retail clients. These priorities can be listed as follows:

- The regulator has to prevent failures and systemic externalities of the banking system. This measure can be achieved, for example, via a financial support. This is, of course, accompanied by significant costs but in many cases is less expensive that the costs incurred by a series of systemic failures within the sector.
- Meeting the objectives of optimal resource allocation. This means above all applying a licensing policy that will eliminate 'capture banks'. These banks are characterised by providing credits to their shareholders, with little if any regard for the creditworthiness of such lending.
- Providing instruments of control and conducting monetary policy. If the regulatory body is a part of the central bank, the monetary policy department can better set their policy targets, since the stability of banks is essential for a sound and efficient monetary policy.
- Protecting depositors via setting prudential rules and deposit insurance schemes.

2.1   Banking Regulation and Supervision – Legislative Framework

The legislative framework of the Czech National Bank – banking supervision –
has undergone substantial changes since 1990, when a two-tier banking system
was introduced. The CNB has gradually amended the legislative framework for
commercial banking activities in order to meet EU regulatory standards (EU
directives) as well as the recommendations of the Basle Committee on Banking
Supervision. The focus has been on incorporating EU directives into Czech
banking law.

The main directives that have had a substantial impact on the European
banking industry may be listed as follows (Mulineux, 1996):

- The Second Banking Co-ordination Directive (effective 1 January 1993).
  This directive, in conjunction with the Own Funds and Solvency Ratio
  Directives, enables EU banks to branch into, or provide services to, any
  other member state.
- The Own Funds Directive (effective 1 January 1993). This directive defines
  the bank's capital.[2]
- The Solvency Ratio Directive (effective 1 January 1993), defining the
  amount of capital that must be held for regulatory purposes.
- The Consolidated Supervision Directive (effective 1 January 1993). In
  accordance with this directive, supervisors are required to regulate
  banking groups on a consolidated basis, rather than undertaking solo
  supervision.
- The Deposit Insurance Directive (effective 1 January 1993), which imposes
  a minimum level of deposit insurance of 20,000 ECU for EU member
  states.
- The Money Laundering Directive (effective 1 January 1993), listing the
  obligation of credit and financial institutions to prevent money laundering
  from drugs, organised crime and other illegal activities.
- The Large Exposure Directive (effective 1 January 1994), limiting bank
  ownership in companies or groups.
- The Investment Services Directive (effective 1 January 1996). This
  directive gives the same passport to the EU non-bank investment service
  firms as the Second Banking Directive provides for banks.
- The Capital Adequacy Directive (effective 1 January 1996). This directive
  requires that risk-based capital be applied to non-bank investment firms
  and introduces consolidated supervision for these firms.

The principal task of the Czech National Bank is the implementation of the
White Paper (Stage I and Stage II) for the associated countries. The Czech
National Bank has thus far adopted into Czech banking law the First Banking

Directive 77/780/EEC, the Own Funds Directive 89/299/EEC, Directive 89/647/EEC regarding solvency ratios, Directive 89/646/EEC regarding the provision of banking services, and Directive 94/19/EEC on deposit guarantee schemes. However, there are still certain technical differences that should be removed in the following period. The measures of Stage II have been implemented only partly. Directive (86/635/EEC) on consolidated accounts and Directive (92/30/EEC) on consolidated supervision have not yet been incorporated into Czech law. The same applies for Directive 93/6/EEC on capital adequacy. These directives should be imposed by the Czech National Bank no later than 2000.

Table 4.1 compares the implementation of EU directives into the banking sector for Poland, Hungary, Slovakia, Slovenia and the Czech Republic. The rules of prudential regulation enacted by these countries have followed the standards recommended by the Basle Committee, and are approaching the implementation of later European directives. In the first phase of the banking reforms, however, the norms of accounting and portfolio classification were much more lax than in the EU, and existing banks were granted a transitional adjustment period to meet the required capital adequacy ratio of 8 per cent.

A common feature of the implementation of these directives is the different approach and criteria imposed on banks when performing the banking supervision function. A proposed timetable for implementing all measures of the White Paper is scheduled over four to five years. The Czech National Bank has recently enhanced its efforts to meet 'The Core Principles for Effective Banking Supervision'. The Core Principles have become an integral part of the banking regulation policy. The Principles are perceived as a bridge leading to the successful implementation of the set of the EU directives.

In order to meet the EU Directives, the CNB revised in the Banking Act of 1992 in two stages. The 'small amendment' (Banking Act No. 16/1998) was approved by Parliament in January 1998 and the 'large amendment' (Banking Act No. 165/1998) took effect in September 1998. These amendments dealt with three broad classes of problems:

- difficulties in detecting problem loans and their impact on the capital adequacy of banks, and in providing adequate provisions for such 'classified' loans;
- the influence on banks by owners whose purpose is to exploit depositor resources for their own gain;
- weaknesses in the applying of conservatorship and bank liquidation.

The small amendment addressed the following problems: the interconnection of banks with the corporate sector, the separation of investment and commercial banking, and the increase in the amount of coverage provided in the Czech

Table 4.1: A comparison of the legal system in the Czech Republic (CZ), Hungary (H), Poland (P), the Slovak Republic (S) and Slovenia (SL) with the EC banking directives

Area of regulation	EU directives	Comparison
Access to market	Directive 77/780EEC (First Banking Directive)	Partly harmonised. Different criterion of economic need when applying for the authorisation
Providing of banking services	Directive 89/299/EEC (Second Banking Directive)	Principal rules for providing banking services are harmonised
Pursuit of business	Directive 89/299/EEC on the own funds	Remaining discrepancies are of a technical nature
	Directive 89/647/EEC on solvency ratio	Roughly harmonised in CZ, H, S and SL. Partly harmonised in P, where asset quality is evaluated only in terms of loan portfolio quality
	Directive 92/121/EEC on large exposures	Principal rules are harmonised, some technical differences have remained
Supervision	Directive 92/30/EEC on consolidated supervision	In the process of harmonisation
Money laundering	Directive 91/308/EEC on money laundering	Harmonised
Deposit guarantee	Directive 94/19/EEC	Partly harmonised, different subjects and limits of guarantee

Source: Varhegyi (1997).

deposit insurance scheme. The main changes brought about by this amendment are as follows:

- The prohibition of banks from acquiring direct or indirect majority control over non-financial institutions. A bank's qualified interest in one legal entry must not exceed 15 per cent of a bank's capital and 60 per cent in total.

- The prohibition of the placement of bank board members and bank employees on the statutory body or supervisory board of another legal entity.
- The prohibition of insider trading related to credit and investment operations and trading on customers' accounts and on one's own account.
- The implementation of measures ensuring the separation of credit and investment transactions.
- The application for a banking licence by an institution must be accompanied by a test of economic need.
- An increase in the insurance limit for deposits CZK 100,000 to CZK 300,000 per depositor.[3]

The fulfilment of these new rules and obligations for banks has been implemented on a step-by-step basis rather than all at once. The rules dealing with ownership participation have been phased in over three years and changes regarding participation in statutory and supervisory boards over six months.

A fundamental change included within this amendment is the separation between commercial and investment banking. However, the Czech banking system was deliberately built up as a universal one resembling the German banking model. Therefore such a radical change after eight years brings up a principal question regarding the optimal banking system.[4] Undoubtedly, the German banking model has contributed to the so-called 'closed triangle' between commercial banks, investment funds and firms in the Czech Republic. The suggested changes or restrictions will have a direct impact on the business strategy of these banks, although opponents argue that only a few banks do not already meet these limits.

The second amendment involved further substantial changes in the legislative framework for commercial banks. The revision of the Banking Act above all enhanced the general confidence in the banking sector. The amendment includes measures which:

- improved the accountability of a bank's management and board by requiring that a bank's board of directors be composed of the top management of the bank and that the board of trustees must be chosen by a general meeting rather than by the employees of the bank;
- allowed the CNB flexibility in dealing with problem banks, through the authorisation of an administrator to liquidate a bank, and a provision for the mandatory removal of a bank's licence if its capital falls below one-third of the required rate;
- broadened the obligation of banks to provide relevant information to the public;

- provided further improvements to the deposit insurance system, with an extension and specification of the groups of persons who are not eligible for compensation, such as those with a special relationship to a bank;
- gave the CNB greater information regarding the shareholders of a bank, via a requirement that voting stock can be issued only in registered form;
- required CNB approval before the acquisition of voting rights exceeding 10 per cent by a single investor or group of linked investors.

The deteriorating situation in the Czech banking sector was a driving force for these changes. The failures and irregularities among small and medium-sized banks showed the absence of internal effective controls. At the same time, the former Banking Act did not enable the CNB to effectively deal with problem banks. Although the amendments go hand in hand with the EU directives, there are still shortcomings in the Czech legislative framework. For example, in the amended Banking Act there remains a conflict between discretionary policy (decisions) and rules. Since the CNB is responsible for the stability of the banking sector, clear rules on how regulators will deal with problem banks are a necessity.

2.2   Prudential Rules Imposed by the CNB

If the primary role of bank supervision is to reduce systemic risk, this can be achieved in part by setting up appropriate rules for the prudential behaviour of commercial banks. These rules would include the control of bank solvency and liquidity, the imposition of a minimal capital requirement, the limitation of risk exposures to individual borrowers, and limits on credit exposure. It can be argued, however, that these restrictions might bring about a decline in bank efficiency. Indeed, the above restrictions may prevent commercial banks from providing credit to highly performing clients, whose influence often has a direct impact on a bank's financial position. Although, on the positive side this sort of bank regulation does not create a moral hazard problem.[5]

Since the start of the transition to a market economy, deregulation and the introduction of new regulatory rules have taken place in the banking sphere simultaneously. While departing from the totally regulated system of a centrally planned economy, the former Czechoslovak monetary authorities installed credit volumes and interest rate ceilings to assist the implementation of their monetary and credit policies, given the constraints and imperfections of the existing environment. However, the more competitive and liberalised the environment, the more banks and their financial institutions are exposed to risk, and consequently, the more crucial prudential rules and guidelines for their behaviour become. Deregulation policies, which attempted to increase the functional efficiency of banking institutions, phased out forms of intervention which could be considered as 'anti-competitive', such as credit volume controls and interest rate ceilings. Given the non-competitive environment existing at the beginning of banking reform, the Central Bank imposed obligatory interest rate ceilings on commercial bank credit to avoid interest rates surging 'unduly'. These ceilings, introduced in October 1990, were modified over time and phased out entirely on 1 April 1992.

The extent and speed of interest rate deregulation was remarkable, even compared with the post-war experience of developed economies, and represented a clear signal of the determination of monetary authorities to create a market environment. Though the phasing out of interest rate regulation seemed to be replaced by 'window guidance' by the Central Bank to some extent, commercial banks have in principle been free to set their lending and borrowing rates since these ceilings were eliminated. This has given them the leeway to develop their own interest rate policies, to react to market conditions and to choose policies that reflect the differences in creditworthiness and riskiness of their clients and projects.

Deregulation and the introduction of rules for prudential regulation were related to the various dimensions of banking activity. Seen in this manner, the enactment of deregulation procedures alongside the introduction of new regulatory measures was thus not contradictory in nature, the two were complementary to each other.

2.2.1 Implemented rules for prudential behaviour of commercial banks

As elsewhere, the introduced rules of prudential regulation followed both EU standards and the recommendations of the Basle Committee for Banking Supervision and Practices. However, in their targeting and in setting of the time profile, the CNB had to allow for certain constraining factors, the legacy of the past financial and industrial structure in particular. Consequently, a stepwise approach was adopted for the most part.

In addition to the Banking Act, which provides the essential legislative framework governing the activities of commercial banks, the CNB issued various 'provisions'. The provisions are an integral part of the Banking Act. The advantage of these provisions is that they react flexibly regarding the situation within the Czech banking sector. In contrast, the Hungarian Banking Act includes all 'provisions' in the Act itself, and therefore any amendment requires the approval of Parliament. This may hamper prompt reaction to new circumstances within the sector. In the Czech case, it would be a misunderstanding to assume that these provisions have been misused by the CNB. Nevertheless, there has been some discussion among lawyers of the legitimacy of the provisions.

2.2.2 Capital adequacy

In CEECs, there was a broad discussion about capital adequacy ratios. Most of these countries accepted the BIS recommendation to keep the required minimum

Table 4.2: Comparison of the Czech legal system with EC banking directives

Area of regulation	EU directives	Czech Republic
Access to market	Directive 77/780/EEC (First Banking Directive)	Harmonised
Providing of banking services	Directive 89/646/EEC (Second Banking Directive)	Principal rules for providing banking services are harmonised
Pursuit of business	Directive 89/299/EEC on the own funds	Remaining discrepancies are of the technical nature
Minimum capital	ECU 5 mn (6US$6 mn)	CZK 500 mn (ECU 14 mn)
CAR	>8% risk-adjusted and Directive 93/6/EEC on capital adequacy market risk	Only >8% risk-adjusted
Investments in non-financial firms	<15% core capital in one firm; <60% core capital in aggregate	<15% core capital in one firm; <60% core capital in aggregate
Large exposure	<25% core capital	<25% core capital
Connected exposure	<20% core capital	<20% core capital
Aggregate large exposure	<800% core capital	<230% core capital
Deposit insurance	<ECU 20,000 (US$25,000)	CZK 400,000 (ECU 11,500)
Bank supervision	Directive 92/30/EEC on consolidated supervision	In the process of harmonisation
Licensing	Open	Open
Loan loss provisions	Tax-deductible	Total annual tax deductible provisions may not exceed 2 per cent of the average level of credits during the tax period

Source: World Bank, CNB.

risk-weighted capital/assets ratio to 8 per cent, with the exception of Estonia, where a ratio of 10 per cent was maintained. The rationale for higher capital adequacy, at least at the start of the two-tier banking system, was to ensure a sufficient 'buffer' which would prevent a banking sector from running into financial distress. In addition, banking supervision has not yet been performed on a consolidated basis in many CEECs. In the Czech Republic, the imposition of supervision on a consolidated basis is currently under consideration.[6] One consequence of consolidated supervision may be that banks will be forced to increase the amount of capital that they hold. The same is true regarding the inclusion of market risk in supervision, which will come into effect by the end of 1999. Therefore it would have been more appropriate to install higher barriers to entry for banks when the system was unfolding, rather than now.

The Czech National Bank requires that the minimum capital for banks must amount to CZK 500 mn. This amount is almost three times higher than Directive 89/646/EEC requires (ECU 5 mn). In implementing the standard capital/assets ratio, the required minimum risk-weighted 8 per cent was made obligatory only for new entrants, i.e. for those starting banking activities begun after 1 January 1991. The 'old' banks were granted a transitional adjustment period with the following interim minima: 4.5 per cent by the end of 1991; 6.25 per cent by the end of 1993; and the final target of 8 per cent not later than the end of 1996.

Parallel to this, the liquidity ratios of banks, rules for credit exposures and for open foreign exchange positions also allowed for gradual stages of adjustment. Since 1 June 1993, banks incorporated in the Czech Republic have been not to exceed their net credit exposure as follows:

- To one client (or an integrated group) the limit of 40 per cent of a bank's capital by the end of 1993, and 25 per cent by the end of 1995.
- To a bank in the Czech Republic and in OECD countries (or an integrated group of these banks) a limit of 80 per cent of the bank's capital by the end of 1995.[7]
- To legal persons, equity capital of which the bank owns to an amount of 10 per cent or more, or which it controls, a limit of 20 per cent of a bank's capital by the end of 1993.
- The cumulative volume of credit to a bank's ten largest debtors must be no more than 230 per cent of the bank's capital by the end of 1995.

According to Directive 93/6/EEC on capital adequacy, in EU countries banks will include market risk in their model for capital adequacy. However, in the Czech banking system bank capital adequacy is still calculated according to the standard Basle accord – from 1988 the Cooke ratio. The Basle accord requires capital to be equal to at least 8 per cent of the total risk-weighted assets of the bank. Capital consists of two components: Tier 1 capital (core capital) and

Tier 2 capital (supplementary capital) (Jorion, 1997). The new provisions regarding supervision on a consolidated basis and capital adequacy including credit and market risk are in the process of implementation. The question remains what impact these measures will have on the capital requirements for banks. At least for the Czech banking system one might envisage the increase of capital. This will mainly influence small and medium-sized banks suffering from a lack of external financial sources, but will also be felt at least partially by state-owned banks. The new concept of the regulator relying on banks' own systems to measure the risk of potential loss is still in the process of implementation not only in CEECs but also in EU countries. In addition, there are disputes among economists about the impact of this way of calculating capital adequacy.

2.2.3 Liquidity

Liquidity regulations set no explicit quantitative obligation affecting a bank's liquidity position. The regulation of liquidity is focused primarily on two objectives: the method of liquidity management and organisational requirements for liquidity management. The former objective contains instructions as to the separation of assets, liabilities and off-balance-sheet items according to their residual maturity, estimated development of fixed-term liabilities, experience with the behaviour of depositor, the liquidity grade of assets, etc. The latter objective contains organisational prerequisites for liquidity management. The banks have to follow the criteria in order to finance from stable resources, to diversify funds by their maturity, establish organisational measures leading to effective liquidity management, and to develop regular contingency plans containing the main directions of activities and measures of the bank in cases of critical situations endangering its liquidity.

Table 4.3: Liquidity

	1994	1995	1996	1997	1998
Quick assets* in % of total asset volume	12.14	20.69	16.05	17.15	20.85
Quick assets in % of total primary resource volume	n.a.	39.06	30.28	32.73	39.58

Note:
* Quick assets are defined as cash value, deposits and credits with the CNB, current accounts with banks and treasury and other bills.

Source: CNB.

Within Czech banking there is a significant amount of money market and interbank dependency for many banks. With the exception of Ceska Sporitelna (Czech Savings Bank), Investicni a Postovni Banka (IPB) and Komercni Banka, banks tend to possess a low level of retail banking, and therefore tend to have an insufficient deposit base to cover their lending activity. At the outset of the transition, newly established commercial banks were completely dependent on the interbank market.

2.2.4 Credit risk and bad loans

The current regulatory framework requires provisions against credit risk only, with other risks covered by general reserves. The banking sector is exposed to interest rate risk and, owing to the reliance of several banks on short-term interbank, this borrowing exacerbates the existing maturity mismatch between bank assets and liabilities.[8] Exposure to market and exchange rate risks has been limited. This is evident from the fact that the share of marketable securities in banks' portfolios is relatively small, as well as the imposed prudential limits on open foreign exchange positions. However, the vulnerability of banks to interest and market risk became evident in May 1997.

A poor portfolio adversely affects the soundness of the banking system. The identification of the extent of problem loans in the Czech Republic, and in other transition economies as well, is not straightforward. In the discussion of transition economies the term 'bad loans' has often been used with two different interpretations, which causes some confusion. In a wider sense it comprises all types of qualified credits, for which the Czech banking statistics used the term 'risk credits' and later on 'classified credits'. In a narrow interpretation it is confined only to the worst sub-category of problem loans, i.e. to non-performing loans. The second qualification refers to the amendments in classification that have been implemented several times in the course of the transition, the most recent one becoming effective in the second half of 1994. As a result, the identification of problem loans (classified credits) as well as their division into individual sub-categories has been changing. The third constraining factor is related to the available data themselves. Their quality and coverage have also undergone considerable changes. While at the start of transition only big banks were scrutinised by external auditors, over time all banking institutions have become subject to auditing procedures and to increasingly more in-depth and more sophisticated supervision both on-site and off-site.

From Table 4.4 one might observe a gradual decline of total classified loans to total credits. However, this decline should be explained by the fact that the CNB did not include banks under conservatorship. The data in Table 4.5 provide the identification of trends in the classified client credits of commercial banks in the Czech Republic in the period 1994–97. These banks are also confronted with the corresponding trends in reserves and loan loss provisions. Parallel to

Table 4.4: Loan classification

	Delay in servicing	Required total provisions (%)	Annual tax-deductible provisions/reserves* (%)
Standard	Up to 30 days	0	1
Watch	31 to 90 days	5	1
Substandard	91 to 180 days	20	5
Doubtful	181 to 360 days	50	10
Loss	More than 360 days	100	20

Note:
* Total annual tax deductible provisions may not exceed 2 per cent of the average level of credits during the tax period.

Source: CNB.

Table 4.5: Classified loans (% of total credits)

	1994	1995	1996	1997	1998
Total classified loans	36.53	33.04	29.33	26.98	27.10
Weighted classification	21.52	20.26	18.82	17.42	17.19
Classified credits adjusted for collateral	n.a.	17.01	14.72	14.55	16.90
Reserve and provisions surplus (+) or shortage (−)	n.a.	−0.28	0.10	−0.03	n.a.

Note:
Excluding Konsolidacní Banka and banks under conservatorship.

Source: CNB.

the volume of classified credits; there was also a corresponding increase in the amount of risk-weighted classified credits, i.e. in the amount of reserve requirements. The data indicate that despite the growing volume of reserves and loan-loss provisions, the ratio of actual to required reserves continued to diminish in the covered period.

The trends in both of these ratios suggest that these problem loans and the resulting vulnerability of commercial banks is the greatest burden for banks. This conclusion must, however, be qualified by at least three arguments:

- As discussed above, the interpretation of time series data must allow for the institutional changes which have materialised over time.
- According to the legal regulations in force up to mid-1995, the possibilities of writing off non-performing loans were severely restricted. As a result, commercial banks stockpiled classified credits on the one hand and non-used reserves and loan loss provisions on the other.
- The ratios of classified credits and of accumulated reserves and loan loss provisions varied widely across groups of banks.

Another phenomenon specific to the Czech banking system is that real estate is used as collateral for a great number of loans. However, the liquidity of that collateral is very doubtful, as is also its price, which is overvalued in many cases. Therefore, in July 1998 the CNB imposed a new measure that changed the rules for creating reserves and provisions for loss loans collateralised by real estate and overdue for more than two years. This measure will be phased in over three years. Commercial banks have to create reserves and provisions which fully cover the value of collateralised real estate. This measure will have a direct impact above all on Komercni Banka, the biggest bank in the Czech Republic, with the highest percentage of non-performing loans.[9] Another bank, Investicni a Postovni Banka (IPB), which was taken over by Nomura (a Japanese bank) also displayed a relatively high ratio of non-performing loans backed by real estate but most of them are now fully covered by reserves and provisions due to capital injections provided by Nomura.

3. THE CONDITION OF ENTRY INTO AND EXIT FROM THE CZECH BANKING SECTOR

3.1 Licensing Policy

When the Czech Republic began to establish a two-tier banking system, it was widely accepted that the more banks operating within the financial market the better, as it was assumed that this would result in the system as a whole being more competitive and efficient.[10, 11]

The Czech Republic (among other countries) had a unique opportunity to start building a banking system almost from scratch. At the beginning of 1990, there were a few large commercial banks carved out from the former Czechoslovak state bank – Komercni Banka (Czech Republic) and Vseobecná

Uverova Banka (Slovak Republic). In addition, Ceská Sporitelna (Savings Bank), Zivnostenska Banka, Ceskoslovenska Obchodni Banka (Czechoslovak Trade Bank) and Investicni Banka, all of which existed as specialised financial institutions in the old system, started operating as commercial banks in 1990. However, it does not appear that the composition of commercial banks has been optimal.

The rapid growth of new commercial banks in the period 1991–92 brought a certain degree of competition into the financial market but later the financial position of these banks was considerably impaired. From Table 4.6, one observes the growth of commercial banks in the period from 1990 to September 1998.

Table 4.6: Number of banks in the Czech Republic (as of the end of year)

	1990	1991	1992	1993	1994	1995	1996	1997	1998
Total banks	9	24	37	52	55	54	53	50	47
Large banks	5	6	6	6	6	6	5	5	5
Small banks	4	14	19	22	21	18	12	9	4
Foreign banks	x	4	8	11	12	12	13	14	14
Foreign bank branch offices	x	x	3	7	8	10	9	9	10
Specialised banks	x	x	1	5	7	8	9	9	9
Banks under forced administration	x	x	x	1	1	0	5	4	0
Banks without licences	x	x	x	x	1	4	6	10	5

Source: CNB.

There are several questions regarding the expansion and openness of the banking system. Commercial banks were carved out of the former Czechoslovak State Bank (Central Bank). This step was identical for most of the former communist countries undergoing the transformation of domestic banking sectors. But when the current situation within the segment of the biggest commercial banks is considered, it is possible to see several shortcomings in the applied measures.

For example, in Poland, several regional banks were established instead of one or two large banks. The advantage of such a policy is, at least for the first stage of development, to avoid creating 'capture banks' (see below). This approach to decentralisation also led to all major regions in the country being covered by the banking sector, and made monitoring of the allocation of credits easier, through better knowledge of debtors and regional conditions.

Developing a banking sector requires two policies to be carried out simultaneously: liberalisation of the sector and the prudentially regulated entry of new banks. The licensing policy applied by the Czech National Bank, that evolved from a lax to a tough one, was inappropriate, as evident from the licensing policy applied by the Czech National Bank and the Ministry of Finance.[12] At the outset of banking reforms the minimum amount of capital was CZK 50 mn. This amount was later increased by the CNB up to CZK 300 mn. Since 1994 the capital has been CZK 500 mn. A relatively low required limit on the bank capital, in the early stage, has undeniably helped the growth of so-called 'capture banks' or 'zero banks'.[13]

The almost free entry into the banking sector, which was mainly adopted because of the perceived benefits of competition, has in fact been detrimental. Partly unrestrained access has induced a situation where too many banks serve a limited market. At present the growth of operating banks is almost zero – the banking supervision stopped giving new banking licences in September 1993 in order to allow time for established banks to consolidate their positions.[14]

One argument that has justified ceasing to provide banking licences was grounded in the fact that the banking system had displayed symptoms of over-banking and that there were elements of instability at several banks. Therefore, when establishing a banking environment, stricter selection criteria for granting banking licences should be used than in the case of an established banking sector. However, the situation that developed, where 'first-class' foreign commercial banks applied for banking licences and either had their applications rejected or were asked to acquire banks that were in distress rather than being allowed to set up greenfield sites, is another extreme, which is discussed below.

3.1.1 Further developments

We are aware of the fact that the present status of the Czech banking system cannot be significantly changed. Experience has shown that when establishing a banking system, one should adopt thorough criteria for granting banking licences for domestic banks or banks which do not have a sufficiently long track record. On the other hand, when a number of highly regarded foreign commercial banks applied for banking licences, the CNB overruled their applications or suggested that they acquire banks which were already operating on the market (and usually in financial distress). One must take into account

Table 4.7: Share of banks in total assets (%)

	1993	1994	1995	1996	1997
Large banks	82.30	77.18	71.72	68.87	65.67
Small banks	8.90	4.44	4.92	5.21	4.72
Foreign banks/bank branches	7.20	11.67	16.46	18.84	22.28
Specialised banks	n.a.	1.47	2.11	3.09	4.29
Banks under forced administration	n.a.	5.24	4.78	4.00	3.04
Total	100	100	100	100	100

Source: CNB.

the remarkable deregulation process, which has been strengthened by the criteria of the Second Banking Directive in EU countries. Finally, we do not assert that foreign banks can necessarily increase the competitiveness of the banking sector, but they can provide stability within the financial system, unlike 'zero banks'. Furthermore, the biggest commercial banks play a crucial role in the Czech financial market, extending their activities over the entire Czech Republic. As a result of these activities, a number of small-sized banks, including 'zero banks', are finding themselves in difficulty. It is far more difficult for small banks to find a place in the market. One of the possible ways to remedy this situation is for these banks to become niche players, with their attention focused on special activities and banking services, which are not (or only marginally) performed by larger banks. A minor comfort, though hardly a practical consolation for the bank regulation authority, is the fact that some EU countries have also struggled with a similar phenomenon.

According to the IMF, the key factors in assessing the viability of a proposed bank are:

- The integrity and probity of shareholders, directors, and/or officers of the bank.
- The actual objectives pursued by the major shareholders of the proposed bank relative to its safety and soundness.
- The qualifications, experience, and judgement of all or some of the directors, members of the supervisory board, and other high-ranking officials of the proposed bank relative to the nature, size and sophistication of the proposed business.
- The presence of a financial buffer to absorb losses that may surface as the bank's business is conducted, which is dependent on the nature and scale

of the proposed bank relative to the nature and scale of the proposed business and the risk attached to the same.

- The quality of corporate governance and the distribution and segregation of duties and responsibilities within the bank.
- The quality of the policies, management system, internal controls and procedures in the bank, in particular with regard to risk management, pricing, provisioning and internal audit.

It should be underscored that most of these factors are applied by the CNB in the process of assessing banks. Nonetheless, the problem remains of how to proceed with banking licence policy in the future. Some lessons for the Czech banking sector can be developed. Clearly, the present situation is no longer sustainable. The CNB, which has advocated a restricted policy, argues that this is necessary to sort out current problems largely connected with the unfavourable position of small banks – this situation has lasted for more than two years and must be resolved. In spite of this policy, the situation as of 1996 has not improved. Instead it has deteriorated further, judging from the number of failed and failing banks.

Arguments supporting a policy of speeding up the process of restructuring and consolidating the banking sector should also be seen in the light of the Association Agreement between the Czech Republic and the European Community,[15] which came into effect in February 1995. The policy decisions of the CNB regarding entry into the banking sector need to continue in the spirit of the Second Directive. The provision of new banking licences to Czech banks must be scrutinised by the CNB very carefully, and banking licences should only be provided to domestic banks if there is 'more' than a 100 per cent guarantee that the bank will be able to meet the criteria of the EU directives.

Concerning banks from EU countries applying for a banking licence to operate within the Czech system, slightly different rules should apply. It is accepted that it is necessary to adopt a strictly selective policy in order to avoid a negative impact on the banking sector from newcomers. However, as noted, the entry of foreign banks has had only a marginal effect on the overall domestic banking system. Hence, if there is a queue of highly regarded foreign banks wishing to operate in the Czech Republic, no obstacles should be imposed by the Czech National Bank. Furthermore, the CNB, by this tough restriction on foreign banks, gives a negative signal to the European Commission, when subjects wishing to obtain licences do not know what criteria to meet. If it is allowed to continue, this situation can cause doubts as to whether this country will be able to meet one of the essential criteria involved in the Second Directive: the ability of a non-domestic credit institution to operate in any member country. Providing banking licences to foreign banks is appropriately expressed by Bonin et al. (1996, p. 10):

There should be no special restrictions on the entry of foreign banks (i.e., greenfield operations) or the purchase of existing banks by foreigners. Foreign entrants should be subject to the same capital adequacy and examination standards that would apply to any domestic entrant or purchaser.

To sum up this part of the analysis, it can be concluded that the regulator authority should provide a banking licence if it is completely convinced that the applicant will meet all criteria imposed by law.

3.2   Exit from the Banking System

If a bank fails to comply with the regulatory requirements or becomes involved in criminal activities, the authority responsible for regulation and supervision must make a decision about the future of that institution. The outcome of this decision is constrained above all by the legislative framework – the range of supervisory instruments. Broadly speaking, there are a number of measures that can be employed. If normal prudential regulations fail to prevent banks from imprudent behaviour, remedial measures are required to avoid the further financial deterioration of the bank in question. By remedial measures we mean the effort of the bank management and the regulatory body to improve a given situation. However, in many cases there is no consensus between management and the regulator about which measures to take in order to restore financial stability. In this situation there must be a legal framework and available instruments enabling a regulator to impose mandatory measures. And finally, when all else fails, the regulator should revoke the banking licence.[16]

According to the Banking Act (No. 21/1992), banking regulation and supervision had a limited array of instruments to cope with banks that are in financial difficulty. These legislative limitations were recognised during the turbulence in the Czech banking sector in 1995–96. For this reason, the current Banking Act (No. 21/1992) was revised and the legal instruments available to authorities were strengthened and widened. At the same time, the range of operating instruments for forced administration of a bank was limited, and the new Banking Act also redefined criteria for the suspension of banking licences.[17]

3.2.1   The failures of small and medium-sized banks

Since 1990, when a two-tier banking system was established, we have witnessed the failure of several commercial banks. These banks had obtained their financial resources largely via the interbank market, and the biggest banks in the Czech Republic are (were) the main creditors of these small and medium-sized banks in the market. It is not surprising that the big banks were involved in rescue activities when these events occurred. A particularly prominent role was played by Ceska Sporitelna (Savings Bank) and Ceskoslovenska Obchodni Banka (Czechoslovak Trade Bank). Although Ceska Sporitelna allegedly lost a huge amount of credits, especially to AB Banka and Bohemia Banka, there is no evidence of systemic risk, or rather systemic crises, in the banking sector as a whole as a result of these losses.[18]

Although the likelihood of failure of some commercial banks in the Czech Republic is still possible, we would not envisage that the decline of small banks could lead to an epidemic in the banking system as a whole. Even if this is a matter of *ad hoc* judgement, the reason for this assumption lies in the 'too big to fail', or more accurately, 'too important to fail' doctrine. The large banks are too important in the Czech banking system; it is presumed that they have such a strong footholds they are able to deal with whatever disturbances there may be within the banking system. In any case, as the state is a shareholder in these banks the government will support these big banks if a solvency problem arises.

No deterioration on the Czech banking system as a whole can be traced due to the failure of small and medium-sized banks. The total assets of these banks amount to 5 per cent of total assets within the banking sector, so the direct impact of their failure on the banking sector overall was negligible. Nevertheless, the decline of small banks cannot be neglected, since it has the potential to cause systemic risk (crisis) in this segment of the banking sector, and also the decline of confidence in the banking sector as a whole.

The main weaknesses of the small and medium-sized banks can be identified as follows:

- An insufficient capital base.
- A lack of primary deposits and overdependence on the interbank money market.
- A maturity mismatch between assets and liabilities.
- Little if any transparency in the structure of shareholders (the possibility a bank in this segment of the market being a 'capture bank' is much higher than in the rest of the sector).
- An adverse selection problem due to the relatively high interest rates charged by these banks.
- Inadequate management in many cases.

A glance at the above-mentioned problems supports the idea that one of the possible ways of resolving these problems would be a merger of these small banks with bigger, healthier banks. However, this solution has not been widely adopted in the Czech banking sector. Reasons to be sceptical may also be found in the experiences of other economies. First it is desirable to analyse the benefits of mergers among banks. As key factors leading to mergers the following are often mentioned:

- The willingness of a bank to become a member of a core bank group.
- The opportunity to secure unrealised economies of scale.
- The rationalisation of branch networks.
- The capacity to meet the demands of large customers.
- The ability to match the size of other banks in international banking.
- The ability to meet foreign bank competition in a bank's home country.

Applying these factors to the Czech banking sector, there is minimal incentive for mergers or take-overs by domestic banks. One possible explanation is that the advantages are not significant, at most marginal. The small banks mentioned have few or no branches and their clients are mainly small private companies, which are not good performers. The process of mergers and acquisition in the Czech Republic can be seen from Table 4.8. As of September 1998 there is no bank under forced administration imposed by the CNB.

Table 4.8: Small banks under liquidation, conservatorship and prepared for merger (as of September 1998)

Name of bank	Start of operating	CNB adminis- tration	Liquidation	Method
Agrobanka	01.07.90	17.09.96	–	Taken over by GE
AB Banka	01.04.91	–	05.03.96	Licence revocation (15.12.96)
Banka Bohemia	29.01.91	31.03.94	18.07.94	Licence revocation (18.07.94)
Bankovní dum Skala	13.12.90	–	27.11.97	Take-over by Union Banka, licence revocation (31.03.97)
COOP Banka	24.2.92	23.04.96	–	Take-over by Foresbanka, licence revocation
Ceská Banka	15.01.92	–	–	Licence revocation (28.06.95), bankruptcy (28.06.1996)

Ekoagrobanka	01.11.90	16.01.96	01.01.98	Take-over by Union Banka, licence revocation (31.05.97)
Evrobanka	01.10.91	–	–	Take-over by Union Banka, licence revocation (30.06.97)
Kreditní a Průmyslova Banka	01.10.91	30.09.93	–	Licence revocation, (02.10.95), bankruptcy (02.10.95)
Kreditní Banka Plzeň	01.01.90	–	01.10.96	Licence revocation (08.08.96)
Podnikatelská Banka	18.12.92	06.06.96	–	n.a.
První slezská Banka	12.01.93	–	24.07.96	Licence revocation (13.05.96), bankruptcy (20.11.97)
Realitbanka	01.11.91	10.07.96	–	Licence revocation (17.04.97), bankruptcy (24.03.97)
Velkomoravská	03.11.92	10.07.96	–	–

Source: CNB.

Nevertheless, the question remains how to proceed in future. One way of proceeding, which might eliminate undesirable banks, could be accomplished by increasing the minimum capital requirement for banks – a measure which would have a relatively fast and positive impact on the banking structure. Above all, it is desirable to emphasise the measure before taking this step; there is a need to make clear which size banks, in terms of capital levels, should be eliminated. Unfortunately, the secondary consequence of this step is that a number of small banks that do not have any difficulties at present would also have either to increase their capital or merge with a larger bank.

An indirect way of increasing capital has recently been applied in the Czech banking system by the CNB. Since a number of small banks have a great proportion of bad loans, the CNB decided, within the framework of a consolidation programme, to oblige these banks to increase their capital in order to cover their bad loans. If they are not able to do so, the CNB will put these banks under forced (special) administration and look for a strategic partner. If no other investor can be found relatively quickly, Konsolidacni Banka – a state-owned bank formed to consolidate debts left over from the previous regime – will temporarily take over the bank. During this period the authority will seek 'bridge banks': banks or other institutions which will ensure the stability of the bank in question. These operations have a positive effect, in the sense of avoiding a further deterioration in the financial position of the bank in question. It is worth noting that this method of forced administration is an operation often used as a temporary solution for failed banks in Western countries. For example, such a method was applied when Barings Bank (UK) failed in 1995. The bank was placed under the administration of the Bank of England and then sold to ING, the Dutch banking and insurance group (see Lastra, 1996).

The last, but not necessarily least, way of dealing with failed institutions is to revoke the banking licence of the bank in question. Such a step avoids the further deterioration of a situation. On the other hand, it should be said that this step could have negative consequences as far as the credibility of the banking sector is concerned. In addition, this solution can be costly. Therefore, any hasty decision on the part of the banking supervisory body or other authorities could be very harmful. But when a bank has failed owing to fraud, liquidation is the appropriate response.

4.   FAILURES OF COMMERCIAL BANKS AND DEPOSIT INSURANCE SCHEMES

If banking markets were complete and information between all agents was symmetric there would be no need to protect their users. In this case, intervention by the authorities, as discussed in the course of this chapter (law, regulations, supervisors), would be unnecessary. However, the real financial world (and not exclusively the financial one) is far from perfect and its users must be protected.

The existence of asymmetric information is far more perceptible in a retail market than in a wholesale market. One can argue that its moderation can be carried out via a fuller disclosure by banks, which would undoubtedly lead to a reduction in costs and in the extent of banking regulation,[19] but this may cause unreasonable costs for small depositors. Nevertheless, by no means is it argued that the information disclosure within the Czech banking system has been sufficient. Annual reports issued by the Czech commercial banks did not provide relevant information as far as their financial position is concerned, particularly small and medium-sized banks. Regarding retail customers, there are a number of legitimate questions as to whether protection should be provided. The reasons for protection are based on the following:

- The absence of repeat orders, which does not enable learning by experience.
- The suppliers and demanders are less equal in a retail market than in a wholesale one.
- Individuals are limited to monitoring the behaviour of the supplier of financial contracts.

As indicated above, the need for banking protection appears reasonable. However, it is also closely linked to a moral hazard problem because any protection, for clients or bankers, is likely to lead to riskier decisions being taken. A further negative consequence of protection is that it incurs costs. Therefore, an optimal scheme of deposit protection must be established, one that is neither too generous in its protection (mitigating the moral hazard problem) nor too limited, and one that favours the stability of the banking sector. Broadly speaking, generous protection discourages the prudent behaviour of bankers and depositors, although only partial compensation can have a negative impact as well. It follows that the best solution would be to set up a fairly priced deposit insurance scheme. But such a scheme is very difficult to establish and therefore most countries have deposit schemes based on fixed rates.[20]

In regard to deposit insurance, several different types of framework can be discussed. The main distinguishing feature is whether the insurance scheme works on a legal basis or as an informal arrangement. Further classifications relate to whether these schemes work on a voluntary basis or through compulsory membership, and whether the schemes are administered officially or privately. For example, in France, Austria, the Netherlands, Italy and Switzerland deposit insurance is compulsory and operates on an *ad hoc* levy. The system does not require annual contributions from member banks, but the realised losses of declining banks are divided *ex post* among participants. Norway, Germany, Spain, Belgium and Finland have a deposit insurance system which is financed through periodic premium payments. The representatives of the banks themselves manage these funds. Japan, Canada and the United States apply a deposit insurance system based on collecting periodic insurance premia from banks through a deposit insurance corporation managed by the government.

According to the Deposit Insurance Directive, the minimum level of deposit insurance for all EU countries is ECU 20,000. The task of this deposit insurance scheme is not only to protect deposits but also to discourage runs on banks. In addition, the home member country protects branch depositors, but branches have the option of joining the host-country scheme. The compensation amounts in the EU countries are as follows: Belgian coverage is BFR 500,000. The UK scheme covers only 75 per cent of the eligible deposit and maximum compensation is limited to GBP 20,000. In France the limits is FFR 400,000. A further important point to note is that the UK scheme covers only sterling deposits in the United Kingdom, whereas the German scheme covers deposits in any currency.

In the Czech Republic a question linked to depositor protection was raised after the first failure of the banks, mentioned in Section 3.2.1. The amount of compensation available is well below the EU average, but is quite sufficient for ensuring a certain degree of confidence in the banking sector. The Deposit Insurance Fund was set up in the Czech Republic to ensure compensation of depositors. Compensation amounts to 80 per cent of an account; however, the maximum amount of any compensation is CZK 100,000 per depositor per bank. The contribution paid by the bank amounts to 0.5 per cent of the volume of insured deposits as of 31 December of the previous year. In the second amendment of banking law the compensation increased to 90 per cent of an account but not more than CZK 400,000. A further significant change is that this compensation scheme includes all accounts and not only household savings accounts. However, this deposit scheme does not cover accounts in foreign currencies, only CZK denominated accounts.

However, even though a deposit insurance fund exists in the Czech Republic, it must be said that depositors were compensated only once through the above-mentioned schemes (in the case of Ceská Banka). In the other cases, retail deposits were compensated not through the fund but rather through support of the authorities. The compensation was CZK 4 mn per depositor. These measures could not only be understood as an effort to avoid social tension before parliamentary elections in 1996, but also as an attempt to mitigate potential runs on small and medium-sized commercial banks. However, due to their discretionary (rather than rule-based) nature, these measures can cause a considerable moral hazard problem. Both clients and managers of commercial banks may assume that they can depend upon repeat orders of such rescue activities from the authorities in the future, and take greater risks as a result.

5.   CONCLUSION

This chapter focused on the current issues linked to the goals of banking regulation and supervision. Although the present situation in emerging markets is far from that of standard economies, it has been argued that remarkable progress has been made in creating a legislative framework regarding the prudential operation of commercial banks since the beginning of the 1990s.

The CNB has amended the legislative framework regarding commercial banks, with the primary goal of implementing the EU directives. Even if there remains a gap between EU standards and Czech banking law, more than a gradual shift can be observed. The following directives remain to be implemented: Directive 86/635/EEC on consolidated accounts, Directive 92/30/EEC on a consolidated supervision and Directive 93/6/EEC on capital adequacy. Nevertheless, the CNB has begun the process of incorporating this directive into Czech banking law.

The role and objectives of banking supervisors must be clearly spelled out; otherwise they can have a negative impact on the authority performing these activities in particular cases. Such a situation occurred in August–September (1996), when the CNB was made accountable for the situation in the banking sector. However, it would be naïve to believe that supervisors are better at identifying the weaknesses of banks in comparison with the incumbent bank management. In fact, sophisticated and efficient internal control (audit) mechanisms protect banks from financial distress more effectively than intervention. At the same time, the Czech National Bank must perform and adopt such policies (regulation) that do not allow moral hazard problems to be created. In other words the shareholders and bank management have to bear the costs linked to the financial distress of a bank. Taxpayers should be involved only if there is a danger of systemic risk.

As to the entry of new commercial banks into the Czech banking sector, it seems convenient to adopt a strictly selective policy. However, the decision to restrict the entry of foreign banks does not appear to be particularly rational. Empirical studies have proven that foreign banks have only had a marginal effect on the domestic banking system for the most part. Hence, if there are highly regarded foreign banks wishing to operate in the Czech Republic, no obstacles should be constructed for them by the banking supervisory body. These banks will not worsen the situation within the banking system. In addition, these tough restrictions on foreign banks give a negative signal to the European Commission as to whether the Czech Republic will be able to meet one of the essential criteria involved in the Second Directive.

The former Banking Act (No. 21/1992) had a limited array of instruments enabling supervisors to deal with problem banks. In particular, the range of operating instruments for the forced administration of problem banks was limited. In the course of our analysis we have suggested options which might be adopted by banking supervision to eliminate 'undesirable' banks. One way would be to increase the minimum capital requirement. As was shown in the course of our discussion, such a measure would have a relatively speedy and positive impact on the banking structure. Unfortunately, this measure is not selective and thus may also affect well-performing banks. The Czech National Bank has applied this measure in a slightly different way, by deciding in the framework of a consolidation programme that these banks must increase their capital in order to cover bad loans. If they are not able to do so the CNB will put these banks under forced administration and look for a strategic partner. The necessity of such measures was brought about by the problems of the small and medium-sized banking sector.

As for the protection of depositors, our discussion shows that without guarantees the banking sector could face liquidity problems. By no means do we argue that deposit insurance schemes can completely avoid runs, but they can contribute to an increase in the confidence within the banking system. As for the volume of compensation, experience has shown that it is crucial to avoid a moral hazard problem. It must be emphasised that deposit insurance schemes work until the banking sector no longer faces systemic risk. In these cases, authorities usually provide financial support (as found, for example, in the Scandinavian banking crisis). As for the compensation amount, the CNB increased this volume from CZK 100,000 to CZK 400,000.

Finally, although the legislative framework for efficient conduct of banking regulation and supervision has not been fully harmonised with the EU directives, we can see that substantial progress has been made since 1990.

NOTES

1. The credibility of the CNB declined when a number of small and medium-sized banks faced financial crises.
2. The directive is identical with the capital definition set by BIS.
3. From September 1998 this amount is CZK 400,000.
4. This question will be covered in much more detail by Lavrac and Borak in Chapter 5.
5. Moral hazard is defined as: 'The presence of incentives for individuals to act in ways that incur costs that they do not have to bear' (Bannock et al., p. 295). This can cause severe distortions in economic activity. It can be argued that by imposing prudential standards on commercial banks the above rules can help to reduce the likelihood of a moral hazard problem arising.
6. The CNB has prepared provisions for supervision on a consolidated basis, but only for financial institutions.
7. This rule was changed and the net credit risk exposure towards a bank in the Czech Republic and OECD countries or towards a group of connected debtors made up solely of such banks must not exceed 125 per cent of a bank's capital.
8. The Czech banks have kept their medium- and long-term credits at 25 per cent of short-term deposits and liabilities with a residual maturity of up to one week exceeded 30 per cent of total liabilities in 1997.
9. Komercni Banka announced an accounting loss of CZK 9 billion for the first half of 1998. The bank increased reserves and provision to cover non-performing loans.
10. However, it cannot be said that providing new banking licences was out of control. The ratio of banking applicants to those granted a licence was approximately ten to one.
11. The argument widely used by the private sector was based on the false idea that foreign banks could strengthen competitive pressures within the banking sector. There has been no evidence in EU countries that foreign banks have substantially influenced competitive pressures on domestic banks.

12. According to the former banking law the Ministry of Finance also had to agree with the granting of new banking licences.
13. These banks are characterised by providing credits to their shareholders above all.
14. Recently two foreign banks obtained licences from the CNB – Midland Bank and Westdeutsche Landesbank (the banking licence of West Deutsche Landesbank was revoked since the bank did not start operations).
15. In addition to the Czech Republic, Hungary, Poland and Slovakia also have reached Association Agreements with the EU, while Slovenia has entered into an interim agreement while the Association Agreement is debated in Parliament.
16. It is suggested that in many cases early regulatory intervention and closure when serious undercapitalization appears, i.e. closure before technical insolvency, can help reduce the contagion effects of the collapse of an individual bank (Lastra, 1996).
17. The CNB can remove a banking licence when bank capital falls below one-third of the required rate. The time period for removal of a banking licence in the case of a bank that does not take deposits or start operations was reduced from 18 months to 12 months.
18. In the interbank market, the largest lender is Ceská Sporitelna (Czech Savings Bank).
19. The issue of fuller disclosure is an important topic in New Zealand, where no protection of depositors exists.
20. The United States and Finland have tried to adopt fair deposit schemes.

REFERENCES

Akerlof, G. (1970), 'The Market for Lemons, Quantitative Uncertainty and the Market Mechanism', *Quarterly Journal of Economics*, 84, 3, 488–500.

Bannock, G., R.E. Baxter and E. Davis, *The Penguin Dictionary of Economics*, 5th edn. London and New York: Penguin Books.

Begg, I. and D. Green (1996), 'Banking Supervision in Europe and Economic and Monetary Union', *Journal of European Public Policy*, 3, September, 381–401.

Blommestein, H.J. (1996), 'Transformation of the Banking Sector in Central and Eastern Europe Policy Assessment and Next Steps', paper prepared for the joint OECD/WIIW seminar 'The Progress of Bank Restructuring in Bulgaria, Romania, Slovakia and Slovenia', Vienna, 9–10 December.

Bonin, J., K. Mizsei and P. Watchel (1996), 'Toward Market-oriented Banking for the Economies in Transition', Task Force Reports, The Institute for East West Studies, Czech Republic.

Broker, G. (1989), *Competition in Banking*, Paris: OECD.

Caprio, G. and D. Klingebiel (1996), 'Bank Insolvency: Bad Luck, Bad Policy, or Bad Banking?', Paper prepared for the World Bank's Annual Bank Conference on Development Economics, Washington, DC: 25–26 April.

Dewatripont, M. and J. Tirole (1994), *The Prudential Regulation of Banks*, Cambridge, MA: The MIT Press.

Gardener, E.P.M. (1978), 'Competition and Regulation of Banks', *Bangor Occasional Papers in Economics*, No. 14.

Hoening, M.T. (1996), 'Rethinking Financial Regulation', *The Economic Review*, Federal Reserve Bank of Kansas City 81.

Hviding, K. (1995), 'Financial Deregulation', *OECD Observer*, No. 14.

Jorion, P. (1997), 'Value at Risk: The New Benchmark for Controlling Market Risk', *IRWIN*, London.

Lastra, R.M. (1996), 'Central Banking and Banking Regulation', London School of Economics, mimeo.

Molyneux, P. (1994), 'Europe's Single Banking Market and the Role of State Authority', *The Review of Policy Issues*, 1, 1, 33–41.

Quinn, B. (1991), 'Techniques for Dealing with Problems Banks', in P. Downes and R.Vaez-Zadeh (eds), *The Evolving Role of Central Banks*, Washington, DC: IMF.

Rose, H. (1995), 'Financial Regulation: Underlying Issues', *Journal of the Institute of Economic Affairs*, 15, 7–11.

Tirole, J. (1994), 'On Banking and Intermediation', *European Economic Review*, 38, 468–87.

Tobin, J. (1984), 'On the Efficiency of the Financial System', *Lloyds Bank Review*, 153, July, 1–15.

Tuya, J. and L. Zamalloa (1994), 'Issues on Placing Banking Supervision in the Central Bank', in J.T. Balino and C. Cottarelli (eds), *Frameworks for Monetary Stability*, Washington, DC: IMF Institute, pp. 663–90.

Varhegyi, E. (1997) 'Overview: Reforms and Development of the Banking Systems in Transition Economies', mimeo, Budapest.

White, L.J. (1994), 'On The International Harmonisation of Bank Regulation', *Oxford Review of Economic Policy*, 4, 10, 94–105.

5. An Outline of the Banking Regulatory and Supervisory System in Slovenia

Neven Borak and Vladimir Lavrač

1. INTRODUCTION

Ten years ago Slovenia, then part of Yugoslavia, had no capacity for the prudential regulation of its own banking system. As will be discussed in the following section, a banking supervision department with adequate personnel existed within the former National Bank of Yugoslavia and within the national banks of Yugoslav republics and provinces. However, this supervisory apparatus did not conduct policy in line with banking supervision in a market economy. Rather, its purpose was simply to ensure compliance with the monetary, credit, and foreign exchange policies decided upon by the Yugoslav government, and implemented by the National Bank of Yugoslavia.

To accomplish these tasks, a process of reviewing reports submitted by banks and conducting on-site inspections to determine compliance with various credit allocation schemes was in place. This task was supplemented by the activity of the Social Accounting Service, which audited banks for the purpose of preparing financial statements. In neither case were banks properly examined specifically to determine their financial position or solvency. The objective of ensuring the safety and soundness of the banking system was not part of the National Bank's mandate.

Indeed, the legal framework relating to banking and prudential supervision itself was deficient. As Yugoslavia moved towards market-oriented reforms and widespread liberalisation occurred, new laws were drafted in order to ensure prudential regulation and to impose constraints on the level of risk assumed by a bank. Included in these measures were limits on a bank's exposure (both to a single client and in terms of the amount of an individual loan), capital ratios, enforcement process, requirements for banking licences, and limits on trading with insiders. After disintegration of the Yugoslav state, these tasks became the tasks of newly emerged states which proceeded with market reforms.

Taking into account that banks dominate the financial sector, banking sector restructuring has been in the forefront of Slovenian economic reforms. After

1991 this sector underwent profound changes that are still in progress. Two main changes should be mentioned: (1) the resolution of the bad debt problem which resulted from soft budget constraint built into the very foundation of the previous system, and (2) the adoption of Western standards of prudential regulation enforced by an independent central bank. Both changes were introduced simultaneously.

2.   A SHORT OVERVIEW OF BANKING SECTOR REFORMS IN COMMUNIST YUGOSLAVIA

2.1   Banking Reforms, 1945–76

The banking sector in Communist Yugoslavia had a long record of reforms, and several periods should be examined (Golijanin, 1979). Characteristically, these waves of banking sector reforms were synchronised with broader political and constitutional changes.

The first period was from 1945 to 1952, a period of great debate regarding the role of banks in a socialist economy. This culminated in 1952 with the centralisation of the whole banking sector in a single (mono) bank, called the National Bank of Yugoslavia, with both the powers of a central bank and the responsibilities of other kinds of commercial banking intermediaries. Only the negligible savings bank structure was left outside the newly formed monobank. This structure, with the monobank serving as central bank and the creditor of enterprises and the savings bank system servicing households, was a common feature of a command economy, and is fully covered in Western literature.[1]

However, in 1954–55, Yugoslavia introduced a self-management system, and the decentralisation of the banking sector began with the legal abandonment of the monobank system.[2] Local communal banks, local co-operative savings institutions, and the Post Office Savings Bank were established, with offices throughout the country. However, the central banking system remained in control of financing enterprises.

The second distinctive period was from 1961 to 1965, when the next important step towards decentralisation was undertaken. After 1961 a new banking system was designed to finance socialist enterprises through local communal banks, republican banks and specialised federal banks. Such a breakdown of the banking system in fact mirrored the administrative structure of the country, in which the state appeared on three levels: federal, republican and communal. Of course, the powers were left to the National Bank of Yugoslavia, which was a central bank, and to the federal banks specialised in the financing of foreign trade transactions, long-term investments and the agriculture sector. In 1962 the payment transactions were transferred from the National Bank of Yugoslavia to a new specialised institution, the Social Accounting Service, which was responsible for smooth payment transaction through deposit money accounts and for ensuring the legality of transactions. In 1963, some operations of the federal specialised banks were transferred to republican and communal banks.

The third period was from 1965 to 1971. In 1965 communal banks were allowed to operate throughout the country as banks for short-term financing of enterprises and banks for long-term financing. In addition, socialist enterprises, government and other socialist entities also became the founders of new banks. These banks were business banks – investment banks, commercial banks and savings banks. It was in this period when the founder-bank relations (banks being owned by their largest customers), which have been recently criticised, were established.

The fourth period, from 1971 to 1976, was a period of deep constitutional reforms that saw the transformation of the National Bank of Yugoslavia into a system of national banks across the federal units. The system of national banks which now collectively comprised the National Bank of Yugoslavia consisted of the eight national banks of republics and provinces. The system worked as a uniform central banking system which was responsible for the execution of the common monetary and credit policies and foreign exchange policy formulated and negotiated in the Yugoslav federal assembly and decided by the Yugoslav federal government. When policy decisions were made, the central bank system, being in fact an organisational mechanism, prepared measures and instruments for their implementation.

The governing body of the central bank system was the board of governors, composed of the governors of the national banks of the eight republics and provinces. The chairman of the board was the governor of the National Bank of Yugoslavia. Voting power was equally distributed among board members. The national banks of the republics and provinces, being part of a single monetary system, were made responsible for carrying out the decisions made by the board of governors of the National Bank of Yugoslavia, and were also to a lesser extent responsible to the governments of republics and provinces.

Also during this time period, former business banks were renamed as commercial banks and made further steps towards assuming full commercial bank activities. As the strict division between short-term and long-term financing transactions, and the banks involved in these activities, was abandoned, they obtained additional scope to transform towards fully fledged banking intermediaries.

From 1974–76 onwards, while other CEECs debated the introduction of a two-tier financial system (the break-up of the monobank into separate central and commercial banking institutions), the banking system of Yugoslavia exhibited some features of a three-tier system, with a national central bank (and republican and provincial central banks), the Social Accounting Service which operated the payments mechanism, and various separate commercial banks. However, this system was far from ideal, with a non-independent central banking system subservient to the Yugoslav government (and with a growing quasi-fiscal deficit), and with this central bank, the commercial banking system and the payment service institution all working in an environment aptly described as a 'soft budget constraint' by Kornai (1986).

2.2   Results of the Reforms

Despite many decades of reforms, there was initial confusion about the proper role of a banking sector in a society in which social engineering remained highly significant. Learning by doing was a constant characteristic of reforms that were more reforms for redistributing political power and control and less a deep economic reform. Money and credit in a socialist economy were from the very beginning tied to the role of the state in resource mobilisation and capital accumulation. They were part of a shortage economy in which finance was given a similar role as raw material.

Despite all the changes, ranging from a crude centralisation to several attempts at decentralising the monetary and credit system, the prevailing and almost constant doctrine over time was a type of socialist real bills doctrine, or elastic currency, requiring that the domestic currency should meet the needs of trade through some kind of stable relationship between the expansion of business activity and the expansion of the credit of commercial banks backed by the refinance activities of a central bank (Zecevic et al., 1979, pp. 9–10). Combined with the never completely abandoned differentiation between fixed capital and working capital financing[3] that revealed the fundamental weaknesses of the enterprise sector, such a doctrine initiated a constant pressure towards the centralisation of the monetary and credit system despite the proclaimed legal decentralisation.

In addition, enterprises had become the founders of banks and were also their largest net borrowers. This alone ensured that enterprises faced a soft budget constraint, as these banks existed in order to grant credits to their founders. At the same time, the presence of considerable government activity in the sector, such as 'priority industry' crediting schemes and selective credits extended by the central bank according to social plans and social agreements, both of which were used as main instruments of policy formation, furthered this soft budget constraint, and also gave the Yugoslav system some similarities with the financial system of less developed countries. Coupled with repressed interest rates, such a pattern encouraged the demand for credits and discouraged financial savings.

Despite the removal of territorial limitations on banks' operations, the constituencies and operations of banks in fact remained regional, and interlocked regional networks of enterprise founders, banks and state structures emerged. Together with the principle of unlimited guarantee by the founders of banks for all its liabilities, this became a significant obstacle to the interregional mobility of financial resource. Taken as a whole, the reform path was in fact socialist and non-market-oriented until the end of the 1980s, when banks were transformed into joint stock companies (corporatisation) and former founders became stock-holders.

3. DEVELOPMENTS IN THE BANKING SECTOR SINCE INDEPENDENCE

At the beginning of the transition process, the Slovenian banking system, which was organised as a two-tier system more than two decades ago, was dominated by Ljubljanska Banka Group (13 commercial banks), which by the end of 1991 accounted for 82 per cent of the total assets of the banking system. The remaining 18 per cent of total assets were shared by two bigger banks and a group of 13 banks, having 10 and 8 per cent respectively.

At the beginning of the 1990s Slovenia's banking system was (as elsewhere in former Yugoslavia) burdened by the bad debt problem. It was estimated by the Slovenian authorities that 30 to 40 per cent of loans were non-performing. Additional problem were liabilities of Slovenian banks and banks from other former Yugoslav federal units towards households stemming from the foreign exchange savings accounts where the former National Bank of Yugoslavia was at the top of the saving scheme. The banking sector, being unable to collect claims from loans and to fulfil obligations towards households, was in fact technically insolvent.

To resolve this heritage the authorities used the issuance of government debt as the main leverage of change. The resolution of the bad debt problem was a part of the package consisting of non-performing loans to borrowers located in Slovenia, of non-performing loans to borrowers from other parts of former Yugoslavia and of the claims of Slovenia's banks on the former National Bank of Yugoslavia for foreign currency deposits of households held by this bank.

The Slovenian financial structure is still very shallow. Financial deepening proceeds at a moderate speed. In 1992 the ratio between the total assets of the banking system and the country's GDP slightly exceeded 60 per cent to reach almost 74 per cent in 1998. In 1992 M3 aggregate to GDP was 31 per cent but went up to 51 per cent at the end of 1998. Thus the financial deepening of the economy remains significantly below the level of industrialised Western countries.

In 1992, 13 out of 26 banks, accounting for more than 70 per cent of deposits, had losses. In the period 1993–94 three banks (Ljubljanska Banka, Kreditna

Banka Maribor and Komercialna Banka Nova Gorica), which at the time comprised over 50 per cent of total assets, were put under rehabilitation. The process conducted by the Bank Rehabilitation Agency (BRA) started with nationalisation of bankrupt banks, writing off banks' losses against their capital and by replacing their non-performing loans by BRA's 30-year DM denominated bonds that were later substituted by government Tolar denominated bonds with shorter maturity and lower interest rates. A total of DM 1.9 billion of bonds was issued, equivalent to about 10 per cent of 1993 GDP, to remove two-thirds of the bad assets of the banks. Just a year later both Ljubljanska Banka and Kreditna Banka Maribor (which by the decision of Bank of Slovenia took over Komercialna Banka Nova Gorica) were each split by Constitutional Law into two entities, with the two old banks taking over all claims and liabilities to the entities from former Yugoslav federal units, and the two new banks Nova Ljubljanska Banka (NLB) and Nova Kreditna Banka Maribor (NKBM) retaining the remaining sound part of assets and liabilities. In mid-1996 an agreement between Slovenia and the London Club of Creditors was reached which released Slovenian banks from the joint and several liability obligation under the 1988 agreement between former Yugoslav debtors and commercial banks.

Consolidation of the banking sector has taken place since 1994. Although the four banking groups were established in 1997, by the end of 1998 only two groups were still existing. At the end of 1998, 24 banks were operating (with the above-mentioned additional two established pursuant to the Constitutional Law). Banking activity is dominated by a few bigger banks, with the top three holding over 50 per cent and the top seven holding more than 70 per cent of total assets (Table 5.1).

Table 5.1: Balance sheet totals and market share of the largest banks

Bank	Balance sheet total in billion SIT			Market share (%)		
	1996	1997	1998	1996	1997	1998
NLB	490.3	549.2	649.4	28.4	27.2	27.6
NKBM	197.2	237.7	285.0	11.4	11.8	12.1
SKB Banka	206.6	241.0	281.2	11.9	11.9	12.0
Banka Koper	99.3	120.3	137.2	5.7	5.9	5.8
Banka Celje	89.5	109.2	135.1	5.2	5.4	5.7
Abanka	88.3	103.0	123.1	5.1	5.1	5.2
Gorenjska Banka	71.8	90.7	108.0	4.2	4.5	4.6
Total – top 7 banks	1243.0	1451.2	1719.1	71.9	71.8	73.0
Total – all banks	1729.1	2022.0	2351.2	100.0	100.0	100.0

Source: Bank of Slovenia.

An improved banking supervision has been instrumental in building a sound banking sector. The Bank of Slovenia, acting as the banking sector supervisor from 1991, had adopted a number of regulations introducing BIS capital standards relating to capital adequacy, risk-weighted assets and provisions and had built up its supervisory capacities. These regulations have been under continuous process of upgrading, aiming to achieve compliance with international supervisory and prudential standards. Banks are required regularly to supply data for off-site and on-site inspections. The 1996 failure of one of the smaller banks revealed weaknesses in existing supervisory practices as well as in external auditing practices and additional regulation of liquidity was introduced and information system requirements were tightened.

The mission statement of the banking supervision in Slovenia adopted by the Bank of Slovenia's supervisory department stresses the need for supervision to be designed to ensure the highest possible level of safety and full-scale compliance with the regulations ruling the banking industry provided that banks meet all stipulated requirements. The strategy of the Bank of Slovenia spells out the principal developments and priorities to be attained. At the top of the list of the banking supervision long-term priorities is the task of procuring continuous, high-quality supervision of the banking system and comprehensive supervision of individual banks. To reach this objective a schedule of regular full-scope examinations for each bank to be scrutinised at least once every two years was drawn up irrespective of the fact that each bank reports in the statutory manner to the Bank of Slovenia, based on the CAMEL system (Capital, Assets Quality, Management, Earnings, Liquidity). Simultaneously the system of analytical assessment of collected data was built and is constantly being upgraded. The banking supervision process was till the end of 1998 organised around three main task-units: issuing of licences, analysing banking operations and supervising banking operations.

Granting licences includes:

- preparation of by-laws regulating granting of licences and authorisations;
- processing applications and preparation of reports on licences and authorisations granted;
- preparation of decisions to grant a licence and providing grounds for the decision;
- control over the enforcement of the adopted decisions, decrees, etc.

Bank operations analysis includes:

- drawing up foundations for supervision;
- follow-up of recommendations made by relevant international institutions;
- counselling on the enforcement of the legislation regulating the financial sector;

- instructions on use of accounting standards and advice on accounting;
- supervision of the operating activities of banks carried on statutory reporting requirements;
- implementations of measures to remedy detected irregularities in the operations of banks;
- analysis of banks' performance;
- preparations for the on-site examinations of banks.

On-site supervision of bank operations includes:

- planning of on-site examinations;
- direct checks of business operations of banks;
- measures for improvement of irregularities;
- follow-up of the enforcement of the measures taken against banks;
- advising on improvement of banks' operations;
- close watch on banks;
- co-operation with foreign auditors and chartered accountants;
- identification and assessments of conditions for pre-rehabilitation procedures, bankruptcy procedures and liquidation procedures;
- enforcement of pre-rehabilitation measures against banks;
- assessments of financial performance of banks and the evaluation of conditions for rehabilitation;
- placing banks in the bank rehabilitation procedure;
- governing and managing banks in special cases, etc.

The most frequent and the most common irregularities observed in the banking industry as found by external examinations performed in banks and reported by the Bank of Slovenia are the following:

- inadequate classification of clients and poor provisioning for the industry with a failure to suspend recording related income;
- inappropriate accounting policies;
- inadequate valuation of business exposure;
- inadequately secured loans;
- flawed updating of credit files;
- sub-standard recovery of past-due liabilities;
- violation of restrictions on large exposure;
- irregularities in setting up and computing lending interest rate;
- violation of restrictions regarding net debtors;
- inappropriate internal control structure;
- faulty information technology.

Although the asset quality (Table 5.2) and financial performance of Slovenian banks (Table 5.3) have improved significantly over the years, the country's banking sector is nevertheless faced with a number of actual and potential problems and challenges. The main obstacle to further strengthening of the industry is the lack of external competition. The Slovenian banking sector has been protected from foreign competition and the pace of restructuring is dictated by weak internal forces. Slovenian banks are not yet prepared for the challenges of EU accession and those of financial services liberalisation. The sector is not internationally competitive in terms of product variety and costs. It remains small in both absolute and relative terms.

Table 5.2: Classification of credit exposures (balance and off-balance sheet, percentage)

Category	1993	1994	1995	1996	1997	1998
A	81.1	86.1	89.4	89.5	90.1	89.6
B	6.6	5.7	4.8	4.2	4.4	5.0
C	4.7	2.5	1.9	2.4	2.3	2.1
D	3.2	2.6	2.1	2.2	1.8	1.8
E	4.3	3.1	1.8	1.6	1.4	1.5

Source: Bank of Slovenia.

Table 5.3: Financial performance (%)

	1993	1994	1995	1996	1997	1998
ROA	0.0	0.4	1.2	1.1	1.1	1.2
ROE	0.2	4.0	10.2	10.2	10.3	11.2
Net interest margin		3.7	4.9	5.6	4.9	4.5
Labour costs on average assets		3.2	2.0	1.9	1.9	1.7
Other costs on average assets		1.7	2.0	1.7	1.8	1.8

Source: Bank of Slovenia.

4. HARMONISATION WITH EU REQUIREMENTS

4.1 The White Paper

The Essen European Council adopted in December 1995 a document named the White Paper, in which a part of the pre-accession strategy for associated countries of Central and Eastern Europe was formulated with the purpose to provide guidance to the countries preparing themselves for operating under the requirements of the EU's internal market. The White Paper (1) identifies the key measures in each sector of economy and suggests the sequence in which approximation could be tackled and (2) describes the structures which will be necessary to make the approximation of legislation by CEECs effective.

A well-developed financial sector in general, and the creation of an efficient banking system in particular, are recognised in the White Paper as one of the cornerstones of successful transformation from a centralised economy to a market economy. At the time when the EC started its co-ordination of the financial sector all member states already had well-developed financial systems. The co-ordination which has taken place was therefore more a question of fixing minimum standards for the industry in preparation for the internal market rather than an attempt to develop the financial sector itself. The task that CEECs have to deal with is rather different. Approximation in the field of financial sector legislation in general presupposes the existence of a basic legislative environment, mainly the regulations concerning the establishment of companies, regulations concerning accounting and rules for controlling or auditing the companies. For the banking sector in CEECs those preconditions of alignment mean that the most important first step will be the establishment of a supervisory authority to oversee the banks with the tasks of making rules for granting authorisations to banks and rules on prudential requirements and then to ensure that the banks fulfil these requirements (especially solvency).

In defining the key measures which are an integral part of a correctly functioning financial sector the White Paper included all directives and grouped them in Stage I Measures and Stage II Measures. The directives chosen to form the first-stage measures are those which introduce the basic principles for establishment of financial institutions (Table 5.4).

Table 5.4: Stage I measures

Credit institutions (banks)	
First Banking Directive (77/80/EEC) (OJ L 322 of 17.12.1977)	First Council Directive of 12 December 1977 on the co-ordination of laws, regulations and administrative provisions relating to the taking up and pursuit of the business of credit institutions
Own Funds Directive (89/229/EEC) (OJ L 124 of 5.5.1989)	Council Directive of 17 April on the own funds of credit institutions

Solvency Directive (89/647/EEC) (OJ L 386 of 30.12.1989)	Council Directive of 18 December 1989 on a solvency ratio for credit institutions
Deposit Guarantee Directive 94/19/EC (OJ L 135 of 31.5.1994)	Directive of the European Parliament and of the Council of 30 May 1990 on deposit-guarantee schemes

Securities

Directive on Public Offer Prospectus (89/298/EEC) (OJ L 124 of 5.5.1989)	Council Directive of 17 April 1989 co-ordinating the requirements for the drawing up, scrutiny and distribution of the prospectus to be published when transferable securities are offered to the public
Directive on Stock Exchange Listing Particulars (77/279/EEC) (OJ L 66 of 16.3.1979)	Council Directive of 17 March 1979 co-ordinating the conditions for admission of securities to official stock exchange list
Directive on Notification of Major Holding (88/627/EEC) (OJ L 348 of 17.12.1988)	Council Directive of 12 December 1988 on the information to be published when a major holding in a listed company is acquired or disposed of
Directive on Insider Dealing (89/592/EEC) (OJ L 334 of 18.11.1989)	Council Directive of 13 November 1989 co-ordinating regulations on insider dealing

Investment funds

UCITS Directive (85/611/EEC) (OJ L 375 of 31.12.1985)	Council Directive of 20 December 1985 on the co-ordination of laws, regulations and administrative provisions relating to undertakings for collective investment in transferable securities

Horizontal directive for the whole financial sector

Money-laundering Directive (91/398/EEC) (OJ L 166 of 28.06.1991)	Council Directive of 10 June 1991 on preventing of the use of the financial system for the purpose of money laundering

Source: The White Paper.

As soon as one of the above-mentioned financial sectors has implemented its first stage programme it should continue to its own specific second-stage measures without waiting for the other sectors. The measures in the second stage will aim in particuar to strengthen the prudential regulation for the firms in order to bring them up to international standards. Some of the key directives proposed for the second stage will include provisions directly related to the creation of the Community internal market, such as the freedom of establishment and the freedom to provide cross-border services without further authorisation, and the principle of home-country supervision. Those provisions should be disregarded in the second stage (Table 5.5).

Table 5.5: Stage II measures

Credit institutions (banks)	
Second Banking Directive (77/80/EEC) (OJ L 322 of 17.12.1977)	Second Council Directive of 15 December 1989 on the co-ordination of laws, regulations and administrative provisions relating to the taking up and pursuit of the business of credit institutions
Annual Accounts and Consolidated Accounts Directive (86/635/EEC) (OJ L 372 of 31.12.1986)	Council Directive of 8 December 1986 on the annual accounts and consolidated accounts of banks and other financial institutions
Capital Adequacy Directive (93/6/EEC) (OJ L 141 of 11.6.1993)	Council Directive of 15 March 1993 on the capital adequacy of investment firms and credit institutions
Large Exposures Directive (92/121/EEC) (OJ L 29 of 5.2.1993)	Council Directive of 21 December 1992 on the monitoring and control of large exposures of credit institutions
Consolidated Accounts Directive (92/30/EEC) (OJ L 110 of 28.4.1992)	Council Directive of 6 April 1992 on the supervision of credit institutions on a consolidated basis
Securities	
Investments Services Directive (93/22/EEC) (OJ L 141 of 11.6.1993)	Council Directive of 10 May 1993 on investment services in the securities field

Capital Adequacy Directive (93/6/EEC) (OJ L 141 11.6.1993)	Council Directive of 15 March 1993 on the capital adequacy of investment firms and credit institutions

Investment funds

UCITS Directive (85/611/EEC) (OJ L 375 of 31.12.1985)	Council Directive of 20 December 1985 on the co-ordination of laws, regulations and administrative provisions relating to undertakings for collective investment in transferable securities

Source: The White Paper.

4.2 The Association Agreement

Alignment with the internal market should be distinguished from accession to the Union which involves acceptance of the *acquis communautaire* as a whole. The White Paper represents only one strand of the pre-accession strategy set out in the Essen conclusions. That strategy relies on two main instruments: the Europe Agreements and the structured relationship between the associated countries and the institutions of the European Union, the first taking the form of bilateral association agreements and the second taking the form of multilateral framework for strengthened dialogue and consultation. The associations established by the Europe Agreements should help the CEECs to achieve the final objective of becoming members of the Union. They include the objective of progress towards realising the economic freedoms on which the Union and its internal market is based. They foresee specific efforts towards alignment with the EU and include provisions concerning the approximation of legislation.

The Europe Agreement Establishing an Association between the European Communities and their Member States, Acting within the Framework of the European Union, of the One Part and the Republic of Slovenia, of the Other Part recognises that the major preconditions for Slovenia's economic integration into the Union is the approximation of Slovenia's existing and future legislation to that of the Community. Banking law and financial services are included in the areas to which the approximation of laws shall be extended. Furthermore, the Agreement requires both parties to co-operate with the aim of establishing and developing a suitable framework for the encouragement of banking, insurance and financial services sector in Slovenia. The co-operation shall focus on:

- the adoption of a common accounting system compatible with European standards;
- the strengthening and restructuring of the banking, insurance and other financial sectors;
- the improvement of supervision and regulation of banking and other financial services, and technical assistance to the establishment and the operations of an insurance supervision body in Slovenia;
- the preparation of translations of Community and Slovenian legislation;
- the preparation of terminology glossaries;
- the exchange of information, in particular in respect of proposed legislation;
- the developing of efficient audit systems in Slovenia following the harmonised Community methods and procedures.

4.3 The 1999 Banking Law

The Association Agreement came into effect on 1 February 1999. With the new Banking Law (Official Gazette of RS No. 7/99) that came into effect on 20 February 1999, Slovenia introduced all Stage I and to a large extent Stage II measures of the EU in this area aimed at providing the overall legal framework and at addressing fundamental principles and procedures governing the sector. This was a big step towards harmonisation of legislation with the First Council Directive, the Own Funds Directive, the Solvency Ratio Directive, the Directive on Deposit-Guarantee Schemes (effective as of 1 January, 2001), the Directive on Money Laundering and to a large extent the 25 Core Principles for Efficient Banking Supervision adopted by the Basle Committee on Banking Supervision in 1997. The principal characteristics of the law are the following:

- Establishment of a bank and definition of financial services in line with EU directives. The law defines taking of deposits from the public and giving credits based on such deposits by a bank in its own name and for its own account as banking services in addition to all other services which, pursuant to other laws, are to be provided by banks only. Limited banking licences are abolished and minimum capital required is set at SIT 1 billion (approx. EUR 5 million).
- Common standards for banking licence. It is up to the Bank of Slovenia to determine the terms and conditions as regards management, organisation and technical support.
- In line with the Second Banking Directive the board of management shall have at least two members who have been demonstrated to be fit, proper and experienced; they will be held accountable for compliance of the bank operation with prudential rules and other stipulations of the law. Accountability of the management is specified in detail.

- Foreign banks can establish branches in Slovenia subject to the Bank of Slovenia's licence, and are not allowed to provide banking and other financial services directly until Slovenia has become a full member of the EU. The Bank of Slovenia may require endowment capital in the form of deposit or other guarantee for settlement of any liabilities of such a branch deriving from its operations in Slovenia. Branches of foreign banks shall be subject to supervision by the Bank of Slovenia. In the transition period and until Slovenia has become a full member of the EU the stipulations concerning branches of foreign banks shall apply also to banks of EU member countries. After Slovenia becomes a full member of the EU, banks licensed for banking operations by the respective home (member) country authorities will be allowed to provide banking services in Slovenia either directly or through branches; their operation in Slovenia will be subject to supervision by the Bank of Slovenia to the extent determined by the Second Banking Directive.
- The difference in treatment of domestic and foreign investors acquiring an ownership share in domestic banks is abolished. Under the old law, approval of the Bank was necessary for domestic persons acquiring an ownership share exceeding 15 per cent of voting rights, and for foreign persons acquiring any stake (percentage) in a domestic bank. The new law stipulates that approval of the Bank of Slovenia is needed for acquisition of a 'qualified participation' (meaning a direct or indirect holding of 10 per cent of voting rights or of the capital). Approval by the Bank of Slovenia is needed for any further acquisition of shares of the same bank if such acquisition results in a 20 per cent, 33 per cent or an ownership share of 50 per cent of voting rights of the capital and in a controlling position of such an investor.
- Prudent and sound operation of banks is safeguarded by appropriate capital (in the old law regulatory capital) scaled to the scope and type of operations performed by a bank, and by management of risks in compliance with the law. The minimum capital requirement and the capital adequacy ratio of at least 8 per cent are in line with the 'capital directives' (Council Directive on Own Funds of Credit Institutions – 89/299/EEC) and the Council Directive on Solvency Ratio for Credit Institutions – 89/647/EEC) and have remained basically unchanged in relation to the old law.
- Identification, measurement and management of credit risk and provisioning for bad assets are in line with international rules and standards. New are non-mandatory reserves for general banking risks aimed at cover of any losses resulting from risks deriving from all banking operations.
- The stipulations on large exposure to a single borrower or to a group of related persons, on maximum single exposure (25 per cent of the bank capital) and on maximum large exposure (800 per cent of the bank capital)

are in line with the Large Exposure Directive (92/191/EEC). The law introduces the definition of related persons and enables supervision of credit institutions on a consolidated basis.

- The stipulations on management of liquidity risk, interest rate risk, currency risk and other market risks mean partial implementation of the CAD Directive; in line with the Second Banking Directive they limit investment of banks in equity and in real estate.
- Supervision of banks on a consolidated basis enables supervision of risk management activities of a whole banking group. The new definition of a banking group is broader and comprises other financial intermediaries, financial holdings and companies active in ancillary banking services. One of the features of the banking group is direct or indirect majority ownership participation of at least 20 per cent (against 40 per cent in the old law) of voting rights or capital (controlling stake and prevailing influence). The stipulations on consolidated supervision are in line with the EU Directive 92/30/EEC on consolidated supervision of credit institutions.
- Off-site control and on-site examination in line with international supervisory standards. The new law enables the Bank to supervise legal persons related to a bank if deemed necessary for thorough supervision of a bank or in case the Bank reasonably suspects that such legal persons conduct banking activities without having obtained the Bank's licence. The new law brings all credit institutions providing banking services under the jurisdiction of the Bank of Slovenia. Accordingly, the credit co-operatives have become subject to the Bank of Slovenia supervision and are obliged to comply fully with provisions of this new law after a transition period of five years. The minimum capital required for savings banks is set at an exceptional SIT 186 million.
- The Bank of Slovenia shall co-operate with other domestic and foreign supervisory authorities by means of exchange of information and direct examinations. According to the Post BCCI Directive, confidentiality and protection of confidential data and of business secrets are preconditions for such co-operation.
- In line with EU Directive 94/19/EC aimed at protection of small depositors and through that at stability of financial systems, a new deposit insurance scheme is to be implemented as of 1 January 2001. The scheme shall cover deposits of natural and of legal persons, with a deposit by an individual depositor limited to SIT 3,700,000. Exemptions from such a general deposit scheme are listed in Article 153. In case of bankruptcy proceedings in a bank, other banks shall be made liable to depositors and shall meet their obligation; to that end banks shall have invested the amount prescribed by the Bank into first-class securities (issued by the Treasury and by the Bank of Slovenia).

- The Bank of Slovenia plays a key role in the case of bank bankruptcy proceedings. Unlike under the old law, there is no rehabilitation, and no so-called special administration envisaged if a bank fails to comply with the requirement on regulatory capital and the Bank considers that further operation of the bank could endanger its liquidity and solvency. The special administration is envisaged for a period not exceeding one year.

5. CONCLUSION

In recent years Slovenia has made significant progress in building a market-oriented banking sector ruled by Western supervision and prudential standards. As Slovenia is keen to join the EU in the first round of enlargement, convergence with EU (and BIS) standards for banking and the financial sector is given highest priority. Based on the new banking law prepared in line with EU banking sector directives, the new batch of implementing rules and regulations was adopted by the Bank of Slovenia. The overall regulatory framework sets up constraints and guidelines that have a decisive impact on the risk management of banks. Provisions with strings attached will automatically come into force as of the day Slovenia becomes a fully-fledged member state.

The legal harmonisation of the banking sector presents only one part of the modernisation of the sector as a whole. The second, and more important, part is the real economic harmonisation and convergence of the Slovenian banking sector with banking abroad. It is precisely this part of the problem where the features of transformation, mainly the continued domination by the state, are most visible. Two radical steps are required to prevent legal harmonisation from being just an exercise in the window-dressing of the domestic system: opening the sector to foreign competition and the privatisation of state property in the banking sector.

Both requirements are clear signals that continued improvements in strengthening the Slovenian banking sector are beyond the possibilities of domestic players. According to prevailing Western views (WB, 1999; OECD, 1997; IMF, 1998), domestic efficiency improvements can be expected only if foreign banks or their branches and foreigners as owners penetrate the Slovenian banking sector. Less explicit in this argument is the fact that little room is left for any expectations that foreign influence will increase the international competition of Slovenian banks abroad. The Association Agreement between the EU and Slovenia leaves all responsibility for its financial stability to Slovenia alone, while simultaneously demanding full balance of payments liberalisation. These two requirements could be fully compatible only by chance.

NOTES

1. The list is far too long to be complete, but Garvy (1966 and 1977), Grossman (1968), Peebles (1991) and Zwass (1979) are all seminal works that examine in detail the banking structure found in socialist economies.
2. However, the changes to the system were not as great as was claimed. This is discussed further in Section 2.2.
3. Fixed capital was the amount of investment capital for each bank and enterprise, as determined by the government. Working capital was the amount of credit needed to finance production. An inadequate amount of this was distributed to firms prior to the production cycle; any additional funds had to be requested from the banks. This gave central planners a way of micro-managing the production process. See Podolski (1972).

REFERENCES

Bank of Slovenia (1992–1998), *Annual Reports, 1992–1998*, Bank of Slovenia, Ljubljana.
Bank of Slovenia (1997), *Report on Supervision of Banking Operations in the Year 1996 and the First Half of 1997*, Bank of Slovenia, Ljubljana.
Bank of Slovenia (1998), *Report on Supervision of Banking Operations in the Year 1997 and the First Half of 1998*, Bank of Slovenia, Ljubljana.
Commission of the European Communities (1995), *White Paper: Preparation of the Associated Countries of Central and Eastern Europe for Integration into the Internal Market of the Union*. 3.5. 1995, European Commission, Brussels.
European Union (1999), *Europe Agreement Establishing an Association between the European Communities and Their Member States, Acting within the Framework of the European Union, of the One Part and the Republic of Slovenia, of the Other Part*, OJ L 51, 26.2.1999.
Garvy, G. (1966), *Money, Banking, and Credit in Eastern Europe*, Federal Reserve Bank of New York, New York.
Garvy, G. (1977), *Money, Financial Flows and Credit in the Soviet Union*, National Bureau of Economic Research, Cambridge, MA.
Golijanin, M. (1979), *Bankarstvo Jugoslavije* (Yugoslav Banking), Privredni Pregled, Belgrade.
Grossman, G. (ed.) (1968), *Money and Plan: Financial Aspects of East European Financial Reform*, University of California Press, Berkeley.
IMAD (1998), *Strategy of the Republic of Slovenia for Accession to the European Union: Economic and Social Part*, IMAD, Ljubljana.
IMF (1998), *Republic of Slovenia: Selected Issues*. Staff Country Report 98/20, IMF, New York.
Kornai, J. (1986), 'The Soft Budget Constraint', *KYKLOS*, 39:1, 3–30.
Ministry of Finance (1997), *Financial Sector Review of Slovenia*, Ministry of Finance, Ljubljana.
OECD (1997), *OECD Economic Surveys: Slovenia*, OECD, Paris.
Peebles, G. (1991), *A Short History of Socialist Money*, Allyn & Unwin, Sydney.
Podolski, T.M. (1972), *Socialist Banking and Monetary Control: The Experience of Poland*, Cambridge University Press, Cambridge.
World Bank (1999), *Slovenia: Economic Transformation and EU Accession*, Volumes I and II, World Bank, New York.

Zecevic, M., B. Mijovie, M. Golijanin and N. Knecevic (1979), *Banks and Other Financial Institutions in Yugoslavia*, Privredno Finansijski Vodiè, Belgrade.

Zwass, A. (1979), *Money, Banking and Credit in the Soviet Union and Eastern Europe*, Macmillan, London.

6. Hungarian Banking in Transition*

Karl Petrick

1. INTRODUCTION

From the beginning of the transition in Eastern and Central Europe (ECE), the transforming countries have used existing Western regulatory standards as a benchmark for their own rules and regulations. In the banking sector, the Basle Guidelines for bank solvency was a standard adopted early on. Shortly after, the *acquis communautaire* and the conditions set out in the Europe Agreements made between individual ECE countries and the European Union (EU) also gained prominence. However, both the Basle rules and the *acquis* were created with the functioning of a long-standing market economy in mind: the unique situation found in ECE, as these countries sought to transform from an economy with long-standing and pervasive state ownership and control, was not well reflected in the Basle rules and the *acquis*. As stated by Michel Tison in Chapter 3 of this volume, simply adopting these standards was not practical: they had to be adapted to the circumstances of each individual ECE country.

This chapter discusses the structural changes in the Hungarian banking sector that made the adoption of the *acquis* possible. It begins with a brief look at the New Economic Mechanism (NEM). These measures pre-date the transition by nearly twenty years, however they can be seen as laying some of the groundwork for the reforms that began in 1986. They also provide some understanding of the pre-reform Hungarian banking sector. We then move on to examine the initial problems encountered in the commercial banking sector: undercapitalisation, a large amount of irrecoverable debt, and the pre-existing relationship between banks and their industrial clients. The resolution of these problems, occurring at the same time as the adoption of the *acquis*, led to the privatisation of the majority of the commercial banking sector and was a pivotal part of the overall transition from a command economy towards a market economy in Hungary.

* An earlier version of this chapter was contained in K. Petrick, 'The Role of the Banking System in the Transitional Economies of Hungary and the Czech Republic', unpublished PhD thesis, Leeds University, September 1998. My thanks to Hugo Radice, Mike Collins, Malcolm Sawyer and Jan Toporowski for their comments on that draft. All remaining errors are my responsibility.

2.   THE HUNGARIAN BANKING SECTOR, 1968–86

In 1968,[1] Hungary began to undertake economic reforms that can be seen as the planting of the seeds for the eventual transformation of this country. The New Economic Mechanism (NEM) devolved a degree of decision-making to individual enterprises. In terms of investment, however, decisions made at the enterprise level were limited to 'dynamic reproduction' (investment needed to repair and replace equipment), while the central authorities controlled any investment over that amount.[2]

Although the NEM in its final form kept financing decisions largely centralised in the hands of the state, the financial sector had not been forgotten in the debates leading up to the programme's implementation. In fact, there were two distinctly different views on this matter.[3] One side of the argument stressed the inadequacies of combining central and commercial banking activities in one institution, as expressed by one of the officials involved in the NEM, Istvan Haglemayer:

> In practice, the NBH (National Bank of Hungary) does not fulfil its central banking tasks (regulating the volume of credit in the economy), whereas in its credit-granting activity it operates without business risk and quantitative, institutional constraint. The 'central banking seed' of the sole bank has not had – and cannot have – any influence on the volume of credit.[4]

Due to the perceived inadequacies of the NBH, this school advocated the development of a 'two-tier' banking system, with the NBH 'devoted to influencing the business cycle' and a group of commercial banks pursuing 'business policies under conditions controlled by the central bank'. Nonetheless, this proposal was only for limited reforms – the commercial banks were to be split by industrial sector, with no interbank competition for business.

Despite its shortcomings, this plan was a radical one for a centrally planned economy at the time. Even so, some of the researchers who agreed with the need for a 'two-tier' banking system warned that the limited reform proposed would be unable to reach the expectations associated with it. They argued for a comprehensive structural reform, which included capital markets and long-term profit motivation. However, the authorities did not take up this proposal for a much broader reform.

The second view in the debates, as advocated by another of the officials involved in the NEM, Miklos Riesz,[5] argued that a centrally controlled financial system was an advantage, even to the extent that it would play a greater role in the 'more market-oriented economic management' that the NEM was promoting. Riesz also attacked the idea of sectoral banking being of limited practical use, as any state investments that affected more than one sector would require a centralised investment financing institution.

Within the view taken by Riesz and like-minded colleagues, due to the potent ability of the NBH (as a monobank) to monitor industrial performance, its continued monopoly on industrial deposit and loans was necessary, even as the planners moved towards more indirect economic management. Although doubts can be raised regarding the accuracy of Riesz's views on the ability of the monobank to perform its duties, nonetheless his criticism of the shortcomings of the plan to segment the banking structure by industrial sector was a valid one. In fact, the argument against creating a commercial banking sector in this manner would have more validity once the transformation began in 1986.

Initially, banking reform was seen as a 'second stage' to the NEM. However, due to the changed political climate throughout Eastern and Central Europe after the failed 'Prague Spring' reforms in Czechoslovakia, the NEM was never fully implemented. As a result, no reform of the banking sector was undertaken at this time, and 'the financial system remained dysfunctional both on macro (credit supply control) and micro (indebtedness) levels'.[6] Enterprise and state investment grew quickly, but 'meeting the demand of the then (still) rapidly growing economy was hindered by the limited borrowing possibility of the enterprise sector. Thus their demand for money was covered by the budget'.[7]

Institutions for long-term capital and official capital flows between enterprises were missing, so the only source for external funding was through budgetary funds, either directly or through the NBH. The continued 'mass enterprise indebtedness', and the lack of external finance possibilities, meant that the planning authorities had no choice but to accommodate credit demand or force the entire industrial sector into bankruptcy. This is consistent with the points raised in Part I, Chapter 2, of this book.

In the late 1970s, the need for a 'semi-two-tier' banking system began to be discussed. This meant the formal separation of the central banking and commercial banking activities of the NBH, but not, however, the dissolution of the NBH into separate institutions. All banking activities were to remain 'in house'. The NBH would have more autonomy from planning and the state budget. As such, credit policy would not follow central guidelines in detail, rather the NBH would be allowed some discretion.

There was, however, disagreement over whether the implementation of a semi-two-tier system was the end of the financial sector reforms or simply a mid-stage in the creation of a genuine two-tier-system. Those in favour of ending the reforms with semi-two-tier banking argued that 'preserving the bank's organisational framework, as well as avoiding competition, [was] necessary because credit-granting [was] not simply a business activity, but [was also] an instrument for implementing economic policy preferences in an indirect way instead of a direct one'.[8] In any case, a semi-two-tier banking system was not implemented at this time.

From the implementation of the NEM in 1968, more and more decisions were placed in the hands of enterprises, although this autonomy waxed and waned depending on the way the political climate in Hungary (and elsewhere in Eastern and Central Eastern Europe) changed. Throughout this time, events in the financial sector did not mirror events in the productive sector. Other than some cosmetic changes, the structure of the banking system remained largely the same.

This changed in 1982–83, when a liquidity crisis forced authorities once again to contemplate the need for a new financial structure. Once again, the debate was between separating the commercial and central banking activities of the NBH or to continue working within the existing organisational structure. The final decision, 'after hot debates, and influenced by shifts in the power relations of the concerned institutions',[9] was to decentralise the banking system by creating a two-tier system.

3.   TWO-TIER BANKING: THE ENTERPRISE BANKING SECTOR

The transformation of the Hungarian banking sector began in 1986, with central and commercial banking activities being formally separated within the national monobank. In 1987, three large state-owned commercial banks were created to serve the corporate sector. These were the Hungarian Credit Bank (by far the largest of the three), the Hungarian Trade and Credit Bank (K&H Bank); and Budapest Bank. These banks were created from the commercial banking departments of the monobank, thus ending the practice of one institution operating both as a central bank and commercial bank.

In addition, the Hungarian Foreign Trade Bank, a pre-existing state-owned bank that specialised in promoting foreign trade, was allowed to undertake commercial banking activities. These 'Big Four' were charged with providing banking facilities for the corporate sector. Until restrictions between enterprise and retail banking were abolished in 1989, these banks could not offer banking services to households. From the beginning of the transformation, these four banks have had a powerful oligopolistic presence in the corporate banking sector, and after 1989, only a relatively limited presence in the retail market.

3.1   Two-Tier Banking: The Household (Retail Banking) Sector

The National Savings Bank (OTP) and a confederation of savings co-operatives (Co-operative Bank) served the household sector. This confederation consisted of 260 separate banks, operating 1800 branches between them. However, many of these branches were run in a manner similar to Giro banks in Western Europe, rather than as fully operational bank branches. Takarekbank, based in Budapest, acted as the wholesale bank for this confederation.

OTP was the only bank which could claim a nationwide branch network (which it already had pre-transition), with 40 per cent of all bank branches in the country belonging to OTP. The Co-operative Bank also had a large network, although since this bank was split between 260 members, they operated as banks for individual regions rather than as an unified, nationwide bank.

Also, due to the limited nature of the operation of their bank branches, the Co-operative Bank members could provide only limited competition for OTP. Postabank, operating out of post office branches, quickly established a sizeable branch network, although not as large as that of OTP or the Co-operative Bank. For commercial banks, with small branch networks operating mainly in Budapest, attempting to create a greater presence in the retail market meant establishing new branches (at great cost) in rural areas that had previously been served by OTP and Takarekbank. They were unable greatly to affect the dominant position of OTP in the retail market. Similarly, OTP's forays into the corporate market after 1989 were also limited. This is not necessarily a weakness of OTP, once the amount of bad debt in the corporate sector is considered.

Despite the restrictions between corporate and retail banking being lifted in 1989, the situation remained largely the same, with no significant change in the amount of the retail sector being controlled by these three banks. Likewise, the corporate sector remains controlled by the 'Big Four'. The segmentation between the corporate and retail banking sectors was not unlike the situation found pre-transformation.

3.2 The Structure of Loans and Deposits

The new commercial banks were also created with a sizeable gap between loan portfolios (399.2 bn HUF) and deposits (117.9 bn HUF).[10] In contrast, retail banks such as OTP had a balance sheet composed of a large amount of deposits and only a small loan portfolio. This is due to the past activity of these banks. Pre-transition, OTP and the Co-operative Bank had collected the deposits of households, while the NBH operated as a monobank, extending credit to enterprises without attempting to match these amounts with deposits. OTP had also been the only bank providing some retail and small-sized loans, both for private citizens and small, privately owned businesses.

As a result of the past institutional structure, the banks that were created out of the NBH inherited a much larger loan portfolio than a deposit base, while the household banks inherited the opposite. Under the old system, this discrepancy was not a problem, as all excess funds in the household banks would have been deposited into the monobank.

Something that quickly arose from this uneven market segmentation was a thriving interbank market (although this market remains neither wide nor deep), with OTP and other retail banks using their deposits to cover loans made by the commercial banks – at a substantial price. The 'Big Four' were (and are) the most dependent on this market for funds. It is interesting to note that this situation was not unlike the one found pre-transition, the difference being that during the transition, the savings bank provided this service voluntarily, and collected a sizeable fee income in doing so.

4.   INITIAL PROBLEMS

As identified above, one of the main features carried from the pre-transition banking sector into the transition was the continued separation between enterprise and household banking. This is not surprising – after all, OTP held all household deposits pre-transition, and the various enterprise accounts had been held among the various departments of the NBH that became commercial banks.

Even though banks were allowed to serve both sectors, they initially remained in their respective specialities. More recently the corporate banks have begun to enter the retail market with more vigour, and OTP has begun to extend services to industrial clients. There is no quick solution to this market segmentation, although as banks compete for an increasingly knowledgeable and sophisticated pool of clients, this split between the two sectors will continue to diminish, although most banks may remain specialised to an extent. However, this market segmentation did heighten the effects of some other problems in the banking sector, as will be discussed.

More importantly, the way that the commercial banks were created gave rise to several different problems for the transition of this sector. The first arose due to the separation of the banks by industrial sector. This caused a considerable amount of concentration in both the lending and deposit portfolios of the newly formed banks, creating a considerable amount of 'creditor's dependence', as banks could not afford to let their largest clients fail.

In addition, the banks inherited a large portfolio of debt that could not be repaid once the transition began. As stated in Chapter 1, lending decisions were based on political, not commercial, criteria. The consequences of this were felt once market criteria were applied to banking practices. This problem was already suspected of existing pre-transition, but the absolute magnitude of this bad debt portfolio could not be appreciated until after the transition had begun and accounting practices began to reach international standards. As a result, the newly created banks were badly undercapitalised from the outset. The three interrelated problems of concentrated bank portfolios, the bad debt burden, and undercapitalisation would profoundly influence the development of the banking sector, as well as its ability to act as a catalyst for change in the productive sector.

5. BANK–CLIENT RELATIONS IN THE CORPORATE SECTOR

The NBH was the only bank serving the corporate sector before transition. In Hungary, the industrial banks that were carved out of this monobank were created along sectoral lines, with loan and deposit portfolios, along with initial staff being moved from the NBH into the newly created banks. It is interesting to note that the idea of creating banks along sectoral lines can be traced back to the debates concerning financial sector reforms in the NEM, as discussed in Section 2.

Due to the creation of industrial banks along sectoral lines, a marked feature of reform was not only a separation between retail and enterprise banking, but also a considerable market segmentation between the banks servicing the productive sector. Hungarian Credit Bank's clients were mainly involved in heavy industry, K&H Bank's clients were based in agriculture and food processing, while Budapest Bank inherited a portfolio that made it virtually the only provider of credit to Hungary's very troubled mining industry.[11] In addition, there was a considerable amount of concentration in each bank's lending portfolio by company, with between 40 and 50 per cent of a given bank's total lending being concentrated in less than 1 per cent of the bank's clientele.[12]

Due to the way in which they were created, all these banks continued to serve industrial clients that they had a relationship with pre-transition. The continuity between bank and client had some apparent advantages, not least of which was expertise in servicing a particular industrial sector. However, this continuity between the old and new systems can perpetuate inefficient behaviour of both banks and clients. Furthermore, in a situation of broad systematic change, as the transition is, the pre-existing links with clients probably did little to help the banks: the rules that they operated under in the new regime had nothing in common with the rules under the old regime. As a result, the apparent expertise that a bank had in serving a particular industrial sector was not as advantageous as it would appear.

From the outset of their existence, the commercial banks were expected to apply market criteria to their lending decisions. This would be difficult for experienced banks at a time of rapid systematic change. In Hungary, each bank was new and inexperienced at applying such criteria, as the concepts of creditworthiness and bankruptcy had been devoid of meaning under the old system. Moreover, decisions on a given firm's creditworthiness were immensely difficult at a time when even pre-existing firms had no 'proven track record' due to the changes brought about by transition.

However, the highly concentrated loan (and deposit) portfolios inherited by the banks constituted a major problem regarding the application of market criteria to banking decisions. Such concentrated portfolio distribution locked both bank and borrower into pre-set relations, not all of them ideal from a commercial bank's point of view. For instance, these portfolios created a large degree of creditors' dependence for the banks.[13] Due to the concentration of clientele, both by company and by industrial sector, the banks had very little portfolio diversification, and were themselves thus very exposed to any downturn, not only in the market sector that they serviced, but also in the fortunes of their largest clients.

This created a situation where these banks could not cut off lending to uncreditworthy clients, as the bankruptcy of such clients would also cause the collapse of the bank. This is illustrated by the fact that after three years of transition, nearly two-thirds of loans classified as either doubtful or irrecoverable were ascribed to the 50 largest debtors of the three large banks.[14] This made it difficult, if not impossible, to cut off any chronically non-paying customer without threatening the solvency of the banks, which were already undercapitalised to the point of insolvency, as will be discussed in Section 6.

The productive sector itself suffered from a high degree of concentration. Pre-transition, each industrial sector had been set up largely as a vertical monopoly, with each enterprise providing supplies to the next link of the productive chain. Each firm was reliant upon the firm that it supplied. As a result, 'the financial ruin of a few large enterprises would jeopardise the production of not just the given enterprise but also that of the entire sector. Against such a high degree of concentration, banking instruments were powerless.'[15]

Although the Hungarian government pursued a restrictive monetary policy at the onset of transition in an attempt to halt inflation, the credit activities of the newly created commercial banks initially increased. For example, in 1990, even though investment credits (long-term debt) saw a slight decrease (minus 2 per cent in real terms), working capital credits (short-term debt) increased by 10 per cent (in real terms). Mid-term and long-term placements were seen as too risky (both by bank and by client), while the demand for short-term loans (less than one year) increased. The increased reliance on short-term debt is understandable given the pervasive uncertainty as the rules changed during transformation, along with high and rising inflation.

Also, pre-transformation, short-term credit was just about the only type of credit available, since long-term projects were commonly paid out of budgetary funds. In this light, the lack of longer-term debt can also be seen as a legacy from the past. The commercial banks had little experience in granting any debt with more than a year's repayment, and they were sticking to what they knew best.

6. THE BAD DEBT PORTFOLIO AND UNDERCAPITALISATION PROBLEMS

Their concentrated loan portfolios made the enterprise banks dependent on the continued existence of their clients. In addition, the gap between their loan and deposit portfolios made these banks dependent on the retail banks for funds. In addition, these two facts exposed two interrelated shortcomings of the enterprise banks: each one held a considerable portfolio of non-performing loans, and each one was very badly undercapitalised.

As the president of the National Bank of Hungary, Ákos Balassa, stated in 1994, 'The equity capital with which the commercial banks were established after the reform of the banking system in 1987 was inadequate. Furthermore, a substantial part of the loans that they had inherited from the National Bank of Hungary was doubtful (at the time of the 1987 reforms).'[16]

Of course under the old system the amount of bad debt was zero: shifting funds from firms with a surplus of capital covered non-payment by other firms. However, it was recognised by the Hungarian government that some pre-existing debt would not be serviceable by the industrial firms once the banks began applying market criteria. What took everyone – the Hungarian government, bankers, and industry bosses – by surprise was the magnitude of the level of bad debt. As accountancy methods moved closer to the standard found in the West (and as regulations regarding the classification of loans also moved toward this standard), the level of pre-existing debt classified as bad grew.[17]

OTP and the Foreign Trade Bank were both affected much less by the rapid increase of irrecoverable loans in this sector, as they were less exposed to begin with. Partially because of this, of the three banks created out of the monobank, only Budapest Bank, which inherited a smaller and relatively more favourable portfolio than the other two, was rated higher in capital asset soundness than the Foreign Trade Bank a decade after banking reforms began (*The Banker*, September 1997).

However, no bank had a balance sheet completely free of bad debt. Pre-transition, the Foreign Trade Bank, in addition to its financing of foreign trade, also financed some large-scale infrastructure projects (the building of roads, etc.). These were long-term loans, and not all of them were recoverable after the start of the transition. Likewise, much of the bad debt in OTP's portfolio was from loans to small businesses, stemming from OTP's being the only bank in this market pre-transition.

The magnitude of this problem became apparent as the amount of reported problem loans outstanding grew from 2.7 bn Hungarian Forints (HUF) in 1987 to 6.5 bn in 1988, 21.2 bn in 1989 and 38.8 bn in 1990. This problem was worsened by the fact that banks also lacked adequate risk rating techniques, as well as having little, if any, experience in risk management.

A large amount of this bad debt (nearly two-thirds of the amount in 1990[18]) was inherited bad debt from the old system. Initially, regulations regarding loan qualification were lax, making it easy for banks to understate the level of their bad debt portfolio. As auditing laws began to move toward the standards found in market economies, the banks had to classify a growing amount of their existing debt as either substandard, doubtful, or bad.

As loan qualification standards changed over time, an ever-increasing amount of debt was classified as non-performing as rules tightened. In addition, Hungary, as well as the entire region, went into recession in the early 1990s. As a result, more and more firms had difficulty in servicing their debts.

The first major shift toward Western-style accountancy standards was enacted in December 1992. From laws enacted at that time, and put into practice in 1992, the classification of loans is as follows: substandard debt was classified as claims against companies operating in 'crisis sectors/branches', for example, mining. Doubtful loans were claims with more than 60 days of non-repayment registered, or outstanding loans to a debtor that has had losses in its annual balances for two consecutive years. Loans were classified as bad if they had registered more than 360 days of non-repayment.

In addition to the inherited stock of problem loans, an ever-growing amount of non-repayable debt was 'newly created'. This stemmed in part from an initial period of 'easy credit' at the onset of the transition: many of these loans were granted without adequate consideration, and proved to be irrecoverable. In addition, questionable loans were also forced upon the newly created commercial banks due to their concentrated loan portfolios. As was discussed in Section 3, commercial banks were not financially strong enough to cut off lending to their large non-paying borrowers, as the failure of these firms would have also caused the collapse of the banks.

By 1991, the amount of non-recoverable debt was estimated to be at least 50 bn HUF, more than twice the total capital stock of all banks. This is an optimistic estimate – some estimates of the amount of problem loans were several times higher. As Hungarian accounting regulations regarding the classification of debt were not completely compatible with international norms until 1993, the 1991 estimates were most likely an understatement. Table 6.1 illustrates how quickly the amount of bad debt grew.

In addition, there was the problem of inadequate loan provisioning. Initially, taxation laws enabled banks to set aside loan provisions out of their after-tax profits. As a result, banks set aside very little capital for this.

Table 6.1: Comparison of the loan portfolios of Hungarian commercial banks (31/12/91 and 30/09/92)

	31/12/91	30/09/92
Bad loans	HUF 36 bn	HUF 125 bn
Doubtful loans	HUF 82 bn	HUF 36 bn
Sub-standard loans	HUF 30 bn	HUF 41 bn
Total	HUF 148 bn	HUF 262 bn

Source: G. Csaki (1996).

7. THE EFFECTS OF NEW BANKRUPTCY LAWS

The magnitude and concentration of the bad debt portfolio prevented this finance constraint from becoming a hard one: first, banks could not force firms into bankruptcy without also potentially causing the collapse of the bank. A bankruptcy law had been enacted in 1991, designed to improve the payment behaviour of enterprises.

This law was the most stringent one enacted in Eastern and Central Europe. In fact, as the law required debtors to declare bankruptcy as soon as debts were outstanding longer than 90 days, regardless of the amount due or the intentions of their creditors (which left the creditors with no choice but to initiate liquidation procedures), it was also considerably more stringent than the bankruptcy laws found in many Western economies.

Placed alongside the issues of 'creditor's dependence' and bank under-capitalisation discussed above, the original bankruptcy law was bound to fail. No bank could afford to initiate bankruptcy proceedings on any but its smallest debtors, and possibly not even them. Given the level of dependency not only of banks, but also of other firms on the continued existence of the largest firms (which also appeared to be the most likely to be in arrears to both banks and other enterprises, as outlined above), no creditor could afford to begin bankruptcy proceedings against a debtor.

Furthermore, this law was enacted just as the productive sector lost many of its traditional markets, as trade between Eastern and Central European countries, and with the Soviet Union (as it was still called at the time), rapidly declined as all Eastern and Central Europe countries went into recession in the early stages of the transition. As a result, the number of bankruptcy and liquidation procedures in Hungary increased rapidly in 1992. This law was curtailed in mid-1993, ending the obligatory bankruptcy after 90 days of delinquent payments and requiring the consent of creditors before liquidation procedures were initiated.

8.   INTER-ENTERPRISE DEBT IN THE TRANSITION[19]

In addition to the non-payment of bank debt, the inter-enterprise credit market also grew in the early transition. The amount of inter-enterprise arrears quickly grew, as did the number of firms involved. This is shown in Table 6.2.

Table 6.2: Inter-enterprise arrears, 1987–93

Year	Arrears (HUF bn)	Arrears (% of GDP)	No. of firms
1987	14	1.0	82
1988	46	3.2	208
1989	73	4.3	314
1990	91	4.4	432
1991	159	6.8	1021
1992	104	3.7	1097
1993[a]	103	–	N.A.

Note:
[a] Third quarter

Sources: L. Szakadát 'Hungary's Ponzi Game', in L. Halpern and C. Wyploz (eds), *Hungary: Towards a Market Economy*, Cambridge University Press, Cambridge, 1998, p. 222 and R.W. Anderson and C. Kegels, *Transition Banking: Financial Development of Central and Eastern Europe*, Clarendon Press, Oxford, 1998, p. 109.

The figures above may be an understatement of the amount of inter-enterprise arrears. Speder (1991, p. 135) estimates the amount of 'unsettled debts' in the inter-enterprise market in 1989 as being over 127 billion Hungarian Forints and this figure was estimated as two or threefold that amount during the first half of 1990.[20] Likewise, the amount of inter-enterprise debt at the beginning of 1992 was estimated to be as high as 240 bn HUF, or equivalent to 23.8 per cent of banking credit to the private sector (Anderson and Kegels, 1998, pp. 108–9).

This was, at least in part, due to the high interest rate charged by commercial banks. As Speder (1991, p. 135) states, 'the nominally increased short-term credit supply of banks could not satisfy the enterprises' growing demand for money. The additional demand flowing into the inter-enterprise money market elicited a sudden lengthening of "queues" waiting for due payment'. He also notes that inter firm credit was highly concentrated among sectors (with engineering being the largest debtor) and among firms, with one-third of all uncovered payments being concentrated in barely 1 per cent of firms (25–30 firms), although nearly every firm was affected to an extent.

Speder's conclusion was that 'the enterprises that enjoy monopolistic positions and are incapable of structural adjustment react to reduced liquidity with this peculiar way of money creation' (Speder, 1991, p. 136). All of the problems stated above cast considerable doubt on the ability of the newly created commercial banks to behave much differently than they had pre-transition.

The effects of this inter-enterprise credit on the ability of outsiders to monitor enterprises was also similar to the effects pre-transition. A firm could still be well run but in financial trouble due to non-payment from other firms. As such, the financial position of a firm could not be used in the same manner as in a market economy: in and of itself, the fact that a firm was insolvent did not mean that it was not well run or potentially profitable – but it also didn't mean that the firm wasn't a hopeless, loss-making case. In addition, many firms had been created in order to supply particular enterprises – without this market, these firms would have had no sales at all. In that situation, these firms could do little else but produce, supply, and hope for the best.

This caused a serious problem for the Hungarian authorities (who were committed to privatising the productive sector), as well as for prospective investors: any attempt to decide on the market value of a firm was little more than a conjecture. Likewise, attempting to determine the viability of a firm based on its financial statements was nearly impossible. In this light, the achievements made in privatising both banks and firms are remarkable indeed.

In conclusion, although the reforms had attempted to create financial incentives for both bankers and enterprise managers, the actuality was that in the early transition, these incentives were not that powerful. Or, to put it in terms such as those used in Chapter 1, the finance constraint for industry remained soft, despite attempts to harden it.

9.   NEW REGULATIONS FOR BANKS AND ENTERPRISES

At the end of 1991, Hungary entered into an Association Agreement with the European Union (EU). As part of this Agreement, Hungary was required to begin to harmonise domestic laws and regulations with EU standards. Alongside this Agreement, and as a first step towards harmonisation, several new laws were enacted at the end of 1991 in order to move the Hungarian financial system and accountancy laws towards Western standards (Acts on Financial Institutions, Accounting, Bankruptcy and Corporate Taxation, respectively[21]). The various aspects of the Association Agreements that the EU has reached with various transition countries have already been covered by Michel Tison in Chapter 3. However, the laws that were enacted began a profound shift in Hungarian law towards Western, and especially EU, norms. These will be examined in turn below.

The Act on Financial Institutions (commonly referred to as the Banking Law) was intended to bring Hungarian banking practice in line with Western regulations. As such, it stressed the obligation of banks to be prudent in their lending practices. The Banking Law also separated commercial and investment banking. Commercial banks that wished to undertake investment banking activities, such as dealing in securities and managing investment funds were required to set up subsidiaries dedicated to these activities. This separation of commercial and investment banking goes against the idea of universal banking enshrined in EU guidelines, where a bank can undertake both activities without needing to set up a separate subsidiary.

While this was no doubt influenced by Western advisers, who stressed the Anglo-Saxon model of capital markets as the 'correct' banking system (as opposed to the Germanic universal banking model), this decision was nonetheless based on two practical concerns:

1.   If banks were allowed to operate as universal banks, they would gain control over the newly established securities market.
2.   Bank deposits should not be exposed to the high risks involved in trading securities.

Given the relative power of the commercial banks in the financial sector, along with the fact that the securities market in Hungary was neither wide nor deep (nor terribly liquid) at the time, the first concern is justified. Also, as the entire economy, and that of the surrounding region, was undergoing rapid, systemic change; the newly created (and very inexperienced) commercial banking sector was very vulnerable to changes in this uncertain environment. The decision was made partially to protect commercial banks from these risks by restricting their banking activities. This was a wise choice, and was consistent with the main focus of the law, namely prudent banking practices.

The eventual control of banks by private ownership was also enshrined in the Banking Law, with the vote of the government on an individual bank's board of directors limited to no more than 25 per cent by 1995, and with the requirement of the government to limit its ownership of a particular commercial bank's shares to no more than 25 per cent (later reduced to 15 per cent) by 1997.[22] In addition, the amount of bank shares held by non-bank corporations was also limited to 25 per cent. By doing this, the government hoped to avoid the case of banks being owned by their largest debtors.

The accountancy and corporate taxation laws were designed in part to help banks determine the financial position of debtors, both in screening potential borrowers and in monitoring current debtors. The practice of reporting unrealised income as an asset on a firm's balance sheet (thus inflating income figures) was ended, making the balance sheets of firms (including banks) more transparent. For banks, the criteria for qualifying loans as either performing or non-performing were considerably tightened.

In step with this, required loan provisioning levels were based on the new assessment criteria. In addition, the practice of loan provisioning before taxes, rather than after taxes, was also established. As a further incentive for banks to have adequate provisions, any additional amount that banks set aside for this was exempt from income tax.

Also in December 1991 the Hungarian government began to address the bad debt problem of the three commercial banks created from the monobank. The following measures were taken:

1. Government guarantees were provided on the banks' non-performing loans that had been outstanding by end 1987 (amounting to 10.5 bn HUF).
2. As mentioned above, any additional provisions that banks might need for loan-loss provisions were exempted from income tax.
3. Dividend payments were restricted until the bad debt problem had been resolved.
4. New regulations allowed the large commercial banks to transform their inherited stock of non-performing loans for equity.
5. The government made plans to accelerate the privatisation of banks in order to draw in new capital.[23]

These steps were limited. Limiting the banks' ability to pay dividends might gain the attention of bank owners in a market economy, but the government was the majority owner in all of the banks affected. Similarly, announcing that privatisation was to be accelerated did not mean that banks would be sold quickly: first, suitable owners would have to be found. In addition, allowing banks to swap non-performing loans for non-performing equity was a Faustian bargain, at best.

Even the government guarantees, the linchpin of the plan, fell short. Since the total amount of bad debt in these banks was estimated at 50 bn HUF at the end of 1991,[24] it is clear that the government guarantees covered only a small portion of the portfolio.

The method of initiating the government guarantees was also problematic, as they were only callable when liquidation procedures were initiated on a debtor. As debtors were forced to consult their banks to gain approval for their restructuring plan, the emphasis was placed on the ability of bank managers to assess the ability of individual debtors to resolve their difficulties – hardly a strong point of the banks in the early transition.

In contradiction to the insistence that banks should decide which of their defaulting borrowers could be restructured and which could not, the stringent bankruptcy law took that decision away from banks. Under this law, any debtor who had not made debt payments within 90 days was declared bankrupt, regardless of the possibility of its restructuring. With firms having no choice but to declare bankruptcy after three months of non-payment, banks and other creditors had no choice but to begin liquidation procedures in order to attempt to recoup losses.

Although banks did respond to the new banking laws and accountancy practices by beginning to refrain from granting new high-risk loans, they also continued to extend new loans to debtors that were already in default, while asking for more loan guarantees from the government.[25]

These new loans to non-paying debtors were mainly loans for working capital (in order to pay wages, for example) rather than investment capital. As such, they ensured the continuation of the enterprise in question, without helping the firm to improve its situation. They can also be seen as money lent in order to enable the debtor to make payments on existing debt, and therefore avoid having to declare bankruptcy. New loans to pay old loans is not a prudential reason for lending, but necessary given the financial fragility of the commercial banks and their concentrated lending portfolios.

While the position of Hungarian banks regarding the level both of bad debt and equity capital showed improvement following the 1991 reforms, this proved to be short-lived. As the stock of debt was assessed under the new regulations, the level of existing bad debt classified as non-performing once again increased (see Table 6.3). In addition, the new accountancy and bankruptcy laws were enacted at a time when the old COMECON market had largely ceased to exist and the Western European market was in recession, further increasing the bad debt portfolio as previously good risk borrowers ceased to be able to service their debt due to a downturn in demand in the productive sector.

Table 6.3: Non-performing debt portfolio (HUF bn), 1992–94

	31/12/92*	31/06/93**	31/12/93	31/12/94
Non-performing debt	188	186	325	418
Bad debt	187	85	186	243

Notes:
* Before loan consolidation.
** After the loan consolidation programmes were completed.

Source: Csaki (1996).

10. THE CONSOLIDATION/RECAPITALISATION PROGRAMMES

Various loan, bank and debtor consolidation processes[26] took place between 1991 and 1995, although the majority of the work was finished by the end of 1994. The details of the various programmes are covered in much more depth in the following chapter, so only a quick overview will be provided here. The initial loan consolidation programme (1991–93) improved capital adequacy and debt provisioning levels in the short term, but did not address the undercapitalisation problem. Of the various schemes, the second programme of bank consolidation (mainly a series of bank recapitalisations) which took place in 1993 and 1994 was the most critical, as it did directly address the inadequate capitalisation of banks. In tackling this problem, it succeeded in stabilising the commercial banking sector, and enabled banks to reach acceptable levels of capital adequacy and liquidity.

The goals of the debtor consolidation programme (1994–95) were to improve the financial position of banks and firms on one hand, and end the reproduction of bad and doubtful loans on the other. This process did improve the debt portfolios of the participating banks, and can also claim to have improved the customer base of the banks. The debt burden of successfully participating firms was reduced, it is hoped enabling them to be both productive and profitable (and therefore enabling them to become good long-term bank customers). In addition, many firms that could not reach an agreement under this programme were liquidated, enabling banks to end their lending to these firms.

The consolidation process has been criticised for being ill thought out and often politically rather than economically motivated (Csaki, 1996 takes this view, and provides quotes from like-minded officials during the period). However, given the ever-changing nature of the transition process, in particular the changes in information as the Hungarian authorities moved toward the level of accountancy and disclosure found in the West, it is doubtful that any better programmes could have been conceived at the time.

In hindsight, the programmes of 1991–95 were successful in stabilising the commercial banking system, and this allowed a number of banks to be closed down without causing a run on the entire system, as will be discussed in the next section. Most importantly, in light of the rapid privatisation of the Hungarian banking sector in 1994–97 (also discussed in the next section), the consolidation programmes can be seen as a necessary step in achieving this.

11. BANK PRIVATISATION

From the outset of the transition, the stated goal of every East European economy was to reduce state ownership in both the real and financial sectors. One reason for this is that this was the main feature of a market economy as presented by advisers coming from the Western countries. Pre-transition reforms in Hungary had already lowered the central state ownership of some banks below 100 per cent by transferring some ownership to regional and local government units. The members of the Co-operative Bank were also a special case, being owned in principle by agricultural co-operatives and their members. Despite reorganising, with Takarekbank (based in Budapest) becoming an 'umbrella bank' for the entire confederation, the Co-operative Bank remained a mix of component banks, some well run and reasonably well capitalised, some not.

In the early years of the transition, the Hungarian government was able to reduce its direct ownership in the large commercial banks from 75 to 100 per cent direct ownership to below 50 per cent on average. However, this is not evidence of the success of popular capitalism. In the initial share offerings, between 30 and 50 per cent of the shares in individual banks were bought by large enterprises. This too created problems. Not only were the new shareholders the main clients of the banks that they partially owned (a large enough problem in itself given the already formidable problem of creditor dependency of the banks), they were also state-owned enterprises.

In effect, the state switched its direct ownership of the banks to a mixture of direct and indirect ownership, and was criticised for using state-owned enterprises as a veil for continued state ownership. This may partially be the case, but as sale of shares (of both banks and enterprises) to private citizens was not allowed until 1991, these enterprises were the only prospective domestic buyers. Moreover, the general lack of capital in the economy meant such enterprises were among the very few domestic agents capable of buying shares in any significant amount even after the restrictions on sale to individual citizens were lifted.

New legislation was enacted at the beginning of 1992 that was designed to provide an impetus to the privatisation of large enterprises. This legislation required the lowering of the capital holdings of state-owned enterprises – in effect, a forced confiscation of bank shares by the government.[27] In addition, the bank recapitalisation programme of 1993–94 also increased direct state ownership in commercial banks. As a result, an average of 75 per cent of all bank shares were placed back under state control, due to firms selling their stock holdings back to the government, and banks issuing new shares to the government.

Some bank shares were held in direct control through the Ministry of Finance, while the remainder were held under 'indirect' state control through the State Asset Holding Company (ÁPV), part of the Privatisation Ministry. The principal idea behind ÁPV was that it would be easier to privatise banks (and firms) if the majority of ownership were held by the government and then sold once a suitable large investor was found.[28]

OTP was an exception, as the sale of the national savings bank to a majority foreign owner was deemed by authorities to be too politically sensitive an issue. As a result, nearly a quarter of the shares in this bank were sold to the general public in a voucher scheme. OTP was the only bank privatised in that manner, and it was only a partial privatisation. This approach is in stark contrast to the 'voucher privatisation' approach favoured by the Czech Republic, which was designed to result in the ownership of shares being widely dispersed among the general public.

In hindsight, the Hungarian method has been a great success in privatising the Hungarian economy and providing banks and firms with an influx of new capital. However, the initial stage of recentralisation of ownership must have caused panic among the neo-liberals advising the Hungarian government.

Hungary had already proven itself to be the most receptive country for foreign direct investment in Eastern and Central Europe, through its laws and regulations regarding sales of firms to foreign buyers (this will be examined further in Chapter 9). Since the only domestic investors with the capital to invest in the large commercial bank were the main clients of these banks, it was decided that the banks would also have to be available for sale to foreign buyers. The provision in the Banking Law that declared that the state could hold no more than 25 per cent of an individual bank's shares by 1997 (covered above) was designed to provide a legal impetus to privatisation.

Both the Hungarian Foreign Trade Bank, which inherited a relatively strong portfolio, and Budapest Bank, which was the smallest of the newly created commercial banks and which had a reasonably strong portfolio (outside of the mining industry, its clients were mainly light industry, which fared better in the transition than heavy industry), attracted early attention from foreign investors. But for Hungarian Credit Bank and K&H Bank, and many of the newer commercial banks, there was no initial reason to expect a quick privatisation, due to their large portfolio of bad debt.

In fact, initially none of these banks was able to finalise a sale to a large foreign investor. This includes General Banking and Trust, mentioned earlier. Even though this bank was able to sell off 50 per cent of its ownership to various American and Canadian investors (the other 50 per cent being held by the Hungarian government) in 1993, it did not find a majority foreign owner until 1996.

For many banks, their burden of bad debt was a key factor in the difficulty of attracting a foreign investor. Thus, despite initial interest from several foreign banks, Budapest Bank was unable to finalise a sale, even though the European Bank for Reconstruction and Development (EBRD) was willing to be a partner in order to reduce some of the risk. These potential owners decided that, once

Western accounting standards were applied, the level of bad debt in this bank was too large to justify a sale.

Aside from government actions to both recapitalise the banks and reduce the bad debt burden, individual banks began to tackle this issue on their own by creating 'bad debt workout units' within the bank. This is in contrast to the Czech Republic, which created the Consolidation Bank as a bad debt workout unit for the commercial banking sector as a whole.

While the role of the government and ÁPV should not be underestimated in this, perhaps the main reason for the banks dealing aggressively with their bad debt was more pragmatic: they needed new capital to survive; the amount of capital needed could only come from foreign investors; foreign investors were unlikely in any large amount until the bad debt problem was resolved. Banks with relatively favourable loan portfolios, such as General Banking and Trust and the Hungarian Foreign Trade Bank, were able to acquire partial foreign ownership relatively quickly (in 1993 and 1994, respectively). However, banks with larger bad debt burdens were not so fortunate.

The need for change was forcibly shown to the domestic commercial banks once Hungarian firms were allowed to seek loans from banks outside Hungary. The possibility for foreign banks operating inside Hungary to 'skim' the best clients away from domestic banks was always present. But this was more a potential threat than an actual one, as these banks were small in number and cautious in lending to any firms aside from foreign firms and joint ventures operating in Hungary, if they lent to domestic firms at all. But once Hungarian firms were allowed to approach banks operating outside Hungary, successful firms found that they could gain access to loans with lower interest rates and lower collateral requirements (not to mention larger amounts of money) than Hungarian banks would (or could) offer.[29]

The amount of lending to Hungarian firms from banks operating outside Hungary should not be overstated – although continuing to grow, it remains a relatively small amount. However, the spectre of being left with all bad risk borrowers seems to have shaken domestic banks out of their complacency concerning their bad debt portfolio. With encouragement from the government, they started to deal with this problem on their own. As a result, bad debt workout units were created as subsidiaries in each large bank.

An example of this is the case of Risk Ltd, the bad debt workout unit for Hungarian Credit Bank, set up in 1994. Before Risk Ltd, the investment division of the bank, HCB Invest, was given the task of going through the bad debts and deciding which loans to sell off and which to restructure (a formidable task given the uncertainty of the transition and the lack of skill in this area for bank staff). In 1994, Hungarian Credit Bank, under new (government-appointed) management, separated its uncollectable loans outstanding into an affiliated asset management firm: Risk Ltd.

The orders regarding bad debt also changed: sell off all existing bad debt, at whatever the price. At the time of its creation, Risk Ltd inherited HUF 16 bn (net value) of non-performing loans. By July 1995, HUF 9 bn had been sold off (the initial goal was to sell HUF 5 bn), while by July 1996, 12.8 bn, equalling 80 per cent of the loan portfolio at Risk Ltd, had been sold. The remaining 20 per cent of the loan portfolio was primarily in real estate, for which the market was very limited (from interviews with Sándor Zelles, head of sales, Risk Ltd).[30]

Despite this success, Hungarian Credit Bank itself still had HUF 11 bn worth of bad debt, as well as HUF 70 bn worth of compensation bills. Nonetheless, the activity of Risk Ltd improved the balance sheet of Hungarian Credit Bank to the point where foreign investors began expressing interest, and the eventual privatisation of Hungarian Credit Bank looked likely.

Budapest Bank was successfully privatised in December 1995, with GE Capital and EBRD buying between them over half of the ownership of the bank. However, the story of Budapest Bank's privatisation was not initially one of success. Earlier in 1995, Credit Suisse, ING and Allied Irish Bank all initially offered a tender for the bank. Allied Irish withdrew its offer after being declared by the government to be third in the queue, with Credit Suisse being the first choice.

However, after examining the bank's books in more detail, both Credit Suisse and ING decided not to invest.[31] By the autumn of that year GE Capital emerged as an interested investor. It was able to acquire Budapest Bank at a substantially lower price than had been previously sought, leading to accusations of the government giving away assets. The truth was simpler – the only way to gain access to foreign capital was to accept a relatively low sale price.

Hungarian Credit Bank and K&H Bank also found foreign investors in late 1996 and mid-1997, respectively. These sales came as a surprise to many, as Hungarian Credit Bank had a very large bad debt burden, despite having begun an intensive internal restructuring, and K&H Bank was seen as a bank that had yet to begin restructuring its operations. As stated in Standard & Poor's 'Bank System Report: Hungary' (April 1996), 'Although both Hungarian Credit Bank and K&H Bank have been targeted for privatisation, they will need to improve their creditworthiness significantly to attract investors. The long-term viability of these two banks is questionable.' In addition, other banks that were expected to be unsellable, such as Mezöbank, also found investors in 1997.

The result has been that Hungary has substantially reduced its direct state ownership of banks by the end of 1997 (as shown by Table 6.4), a result that looked out of reach just one year earlier. And in selling blocks of shares to foreign investors, needed capital and expertise were also imported, something that the Czech Republic's voucher privatisation programme, with its dispersed ownership among domestic private investors, failed to do.

Table 6.4: Privatised Hungarian banks, 1994–97

Bank	Largest owner(s)	Year(s) sold
Foreign Trade Bank	Bayerische Landesbank (Germany), ERBD	1994
Budapest Bank	GE Capital (USA), EBRD	1995
Hungarian Credit Bank	ABN-Amro (Netherlands)	1996
General Banking and Trust*	Gazprombank (Russia)	1996
OTP Bank**	Various foreign and domestic investors	1995–97
K&H Bank	Kreditbank (Belgium), Irish Life Insurance	1997
Mezöbank	Girocredit (Austria)	1997
Takarekbank	Deutsch Genossenshaft (Germany)	1997
PK Bank	Atlasz (Hungary)	1997

Notes:
* 50% of this bank had been sold off in 1993. Gazprombank bought 100% ownership in 1996.
** The prospect of OTP being majority owned by foreigners was politically sensitive, so this bank was partially privatised through vouchers, the only bank in Hungary privatised in this way.

While the state continues to own minority shares in the above banks, many foreign owners have either increased their initial share-holdings or announced plans to do so. Not all of the foreign banks have been satisfied with their investment, however. After Dunabank (a retail banking subsidiary of Hungarian Credit Bank) had been allowed to go bankrupt and withdraw from the market, it was eventually bought by ING Bank. This was a strategic move on the part of ING Bank, not just as a way to gain access to the Hungarian market, but also as a way to capture Dunabank's successful credit card business, which was the only part of the bank with any value.

However, as a result of the deal, ING Bank also took on Dunabank's loan portfolio, and found itself looking after a large amount of small loans (which ING had neither the staff nor the inclination to monitor), many of them irrecoverable, and saddled with collateral such as three unflightworthy aeroplanes. It has since attempted to sell off its loan portfolio to other banks, but has not been able to find a willing buyer.[32]

The ultimate goal is for the state to own only a single 'golden share' in OTP and a few other large banks. Ultimately, the state will hold a 'golden share' in about 20 industrial companies, including Hungarian Telecommunications and MVM Electricity, which operates the national grid. Some companies, such as the postal service and railways, will remain state owned.

As of June 1997, 50 companies were wholly state owned, while the state retained shares in 60 other firms. This is down from over 1800 state-owned firms that the state privatisation agency (ÁPV) took over in 1990. And while in the early stages of privatisation there were no institutional investors well-capitalised enough to buy a commercial bank (excepting their large industrial customers), the purchase of PK Bank by Atlasz, the Hungarian insurance company, in 1997, suggests that that too is changing.

12.   CONCLUSION

Hungary has successfully undergone massive changes since the original monobank was first separated into commercial and central banking departments in 1986. The implementation of EU rules and Basle guidelines was a very important step in this transformation. However, neither the *aquis communautaire* nor the Basle rules were designed to deal with the situation that was found in Eastern and Central Europe: the ending of a long-standing control economy with pervasive state-ownership, a newly formed commercial banking sector that was as a consequence financially weak and inexperienced, and a huge amount of inter-enterprise debt. As a result, adopting these measures was necessary but not sufficient.

In order for the *acquis communautaire* to be successfully implemented, the Hungarian government had also to undertake significant macro and micro-economic restructuring, in order to deal with the problems stated above.[33] Without these reforms, the goals set out by the *acquis* would have been unobtainable. The end result of this restructuring is that Hungary, after over a decade of reforms, stands as one of the primary applicants to the EU, and is very likely to be one of the first countries admitted to a newly enlarged Union early in the twenty-first century.

NOTES

1. The reforms were decided upon by the Hungarian Central Committee in May 1966. For that reason, Hungarian economic literature places the start of the NEM in this year, although it took two more years to begin implementation (L. Szamuely and L. Csaba, 'Economics and Systemic Changes in Hungary, 1945–96' in H.-J. Wagener (ed.), *Economic Thought in Communist and Post-Communist Europe*, Macmillan, London, 1998, p. 176).
2. Due to the lack of change in the economy's institutional and organisational structure, it has been questioned whether the NEM represented a departure from central planning at all (from interviews with Laszlo Andor, lecturer at Economics University, Budapest).
3. From interviews with Rezsö Nyers, chairman of the commission that planned the NEM, now head of Hungarian State Banking Supervision.
4. Quoted in Antal and Suranyi, 'The Prehistory of the Reforms of Hungary's Banking System', *Acta Oeconomica*,1987, pp. 35–36.

5. Quoted in Antal and Suranyi, 1987, p. 36.
6. Antal and Suranyi, 1987, p. 38.
7. Ibid., p. 38.
8. Ibid., p. 45.
9. Ibid., p. 47.
10. F. Karvalits, 'Born for Distress: A Short History of the Two-Tier Banking System in Hungary and an Analysis of the Crisis Situation', Columbia University, mimeo, 1993, p. 11.
11. From interviews with Petér Bihari, Budapest Bank.
12. Z. Speder, 'The Characteristic Behaviour of Hungarian Commercial Banks', *Acta Oeconomica*, 1993, 44:1, p. 133.
13. This issue was a common theme in nearly every interview. The term 'creditor's dependence' is taken from an interview with Julia Kiraly, Director of Training at the International Training Centre for Bankers, Budapest.
14. Speder, 1991, p. 134.
15. Ibid., p. 135.
16. Á. Balassa, 'The Consolidation of the Banking System', National Bank of Hungary, mimeo, 1994, p. 1.
17. This is true of all the transforming countries.
18. From interviews with Mihály Kopányi, Head Economist of the World Bank (Hungary).
19. This topic was also a common theme brought out in interviews. However, the amounts disclosed varied, as do the amounts stated above.
20. From interviews with Mihály Kopányi, World Bank (Hungary).
21. For instance, the Accountancy Law implemented the EU's Fourth Directive in all its major aspects.
22. It is interesting to note that at the time of the research for Petrick, 'Problems and Prospects: A Survey of the Commercial Banking Reforms in Hungary and the Czech Republic, 1987–94', MA diss., Leeds University, 1994, this target for bank privatisation was seen as wildly optimistic by the officials that were interviewed. Even during further empirical work in 1995, the likelihood of this target being met in full seemed remote. Bank privatisation will be covered in Section 10.
23. These measures, and subsequent efforts of the Hungarian government to address these problems, are covered in more detail in the following chapter.
24. This estimate was made in 1991. Later estimates are considerably higher, as shown in Table 6.1.
25. Taken from interviews with Ákos Balassa (NBH) and Mihály Kopányi (World Bank); also covered in Á. Balassa, 1994, as well as in A. Thorne, 'Eastern Europe's Experience with Banking Reform: Is There A Role for Banks in the Transition?', *Journal of Banking and Finance*, 1993, pp. 208–21.
26. This section provides the major points of the recapitalisation processes. More detail on each separate programme can be found in Istvan Ábel's chapter in this book as well as (Chapter 7) Csaki, *Hungarian Banking System: After Consolidation – Before Privatisation*, Institute for World Economics, 1996, and É. Várhegyi, Gy Feno, K. Mohacsi, Z. Speder, *Improving Enterprise Finance by Reforming the Banking Sector in Hungary*, Financial Research Ltd, Budapest, 1996.
27. If socialism can be referred to as the slowest way from capitalism back to capitalism (Igor Filatotchev, 'Privatisation and Corporate Governance in Transitional Economies: A Review', *The World Economy*, 1997, 20:4, pp. 497–510), the early stage of Hungarian financial reforms can be thought of as the quickest way from direct state ownership back to direct state ownership. However, any shares bought by privatised companies were not affected, so state ownership in the banking sector remained less than 100 per cent.
28. From interviews with István Ábel, then managing director, financial institutions, at ÁPV, now deputy general manager of the monetary policy department, NBH.
29. From interviews with Júlia Király, International Training Centre for Bankers, Budapest.
30. Banks commonly took over real estate as collateral for non-payment of loans. As a result of the rapid growth in the amount of irrecoverable loans, the commercial banks quickly became the largest real-estate agents in Hungary, as Csaki (1996) points out.

31. This is reported in Csaki, (1996), pp. 20–21.
32. From interviews with Ferenc Flink and Petér Zoltán, officials at ING/Dunabank.
33. As well as simultaneous political restructuring.

PART III

Policy Issues and Implications

7. Real Dangers in Banking Crises: Examples of Failed Hungarian Banks

István Ábel

1. EXTREME REGIME CHANGES IN EASTERN AND CENTRAL EUROPE

In assessing the causes and consequences of bank failures in Hungary and in other transition economies, most analysts agree that both macroeconomic disequilibria and microeconomic distortions like poor management and regulatory and supervisory deficiencies have been at the root of banking crises, although some controversy remains about the importance of different factors (McKinnon and Pill, 1997; Mázsa, 1998).

Isolated bank failures are inevitable. What can be avoided is widespread systemic failure, whereby a large part of the banking system is placed in jeopardy. Increased or enhanced supervisory responsibility does not suggest that individual banks should be protected from failure, but it does have implications for the manner in which failures are allowed to happen (Randall, 1993a). Most importantly, the failure of one bank must not undermine the stability, or the public's perception of this stability, of the banking sector as a whole.

Widespread failures usually occur in periods of regime changes or during major changes in external or internal policy conditions (Demirguc-Kunt, 1989; Martin, 1977). The transition to a market economy, and the events which occurred in Eastern and Central Europe following the collapse of communist power brought about extreme regime changes in economic and social behaviour. Weakened social safety and public order, including crime control, a changing legal system burdened with ambiguities, and unprofessional and inadequate enforcement worsened the impact of shocks generated by collapsing institutions, values and former market networks.

Large formerly state-owned enterprises which were previously under-capitalised but also possessed an almost unlimited access to bank financing at subsidised rates were suddenly confronted with difficulties due to decreased access to, and increased costs of, external funding. At the same time the quality and creditworthiness of bank clients deteriorated as domestic and East European export markets shrank. As discussed in Rojas-Suarez (1998), most major systemic banking crises can be traced back to a regime shift, which also altered the nature, scale, frequency and correlation pattern of shocks. In these cases, the vulnerability of the financial system was increased by changes in the incentives faced by banks, increasing the riskiness of traditional behaviour, and/ or by the introduction of new and inexperienced players. This is also true in the banking sectors of Eastern and Central European countries.

2. CHARACTERISTICS OF THE REGIME CHANGES IN TRANSFORMING ECONOMIES

The transition in Eastern Europe has been characterised by ownership changes, increased competition and vulnerability, a decline of the traditional industrial and agricultural sectors, and an overall shortage of financing. Capital flight, although normally present in turmoil, is rarely observable in transition economies.

2.1 Ownership Change: Blessing or Curse?

The privatisation of banks is no less important for developing the infrastructure of the market economy than the privatisation of their clientele. Both areas, however, may lead to major disruption of bank–firm relations, which can cause serious problems. For instance, the new owners of companies may prefer to bring their own banking relationships. At the same time, the new strategic partners of the banks must decide upon, and adopt, approaches to local clients suitable for their needs. All of this can take a large amount of time in the best of circumstances. In the meantime, corporations suffer from a lack of flexible banking services and banks lose valuable current and potential future clients.

Bank privatisation, however, is a sensitive issue. If it is mismanaged, or if it is open to entry of actors which are not properly designated to keep prudential practices, the results can be catastrophic. And it is no less dangerous to sell smaller-sized banks in this way. Most of the failing small banks in Hungary had problems stemming from ownership. None of those that did not have a strategic owner (another bank to which reputation did matter) survived.

2.2 Increased Vulnerability as a Short-term Consequence of Financial Liberalisation

Past experience in transition economies and elsewhere has shown that the removal of interest rate controls and the liberalisation of entry in an uncertain macroeconomic environment leads to volatile interest rates. The complexity of the difficulties in managing risk under the circumstances of such an unstable and unpredictable environment is beyond the capacity of relatively inexperienced bankers. At the same time, additional pressures arise in the wake of competition resulting from the struggle for market share following liberalisation. This narrows interest rate margins, which can lead to unsound lending practices in order to attract customers: in a hurry to acquire new clients, banks offer higher rates to depositors and easier access (and lower rates) to borrowers. In Eastern and Central Europe, this practice proved to be not only unsustainable, but unjustified even under current (relatively stable) conditions, not to mention during the early transition, when major structural changes often had unexpected consequences.

2.3 A Rapid Decline of Traditional Industrial Sectors and a Delayed Emergence of Modern Sectors

These structural changes were not characterised by a process of modern sectors crowding out the traditional ones, but rather by a vacuum left behind by collapsing industries which lost their traditional markets in similarly declining Russia and other Eastern European countries. A significantly large part of bank clientele not only lost their export markets but also became unviable due to the newly prevailing domestic demand and prices.

The emergence of new and progressive enterprises was hindered by financial repression which led to a severe lack of financing. Banks remained in effect the hostages of customers inherited from the previous system, who were often both their largest and worst debtors. This inherited amount of bad debt created a great deal of 'creditor's dependence', and banks went bankrupt alongside their old customers unless they could find ways to bridge the gap and wait for more profitable newly progressing enterprises. However, facing certain failure unless they continued to lend to old customers at favourable rates, banks had little room to attract new firms, who also faced extremely high interest rates and collateral requirements if they attempted to borrow from banks. At the same time, the continued soft budget constraint faced by the old firms did not provide them with an incentive to restructure. One possible way to find escape from this circle was bank (and client) privatisation with a strategic partner.

2.4 Lack of Financing

German unification and the experience of East Germany bears some similarities with the problems of transition in other countries of Eastern Europe – at least in terms of needs and traps. In the case of Germany there was a well-established capital market in place, and the banking system was also one of the strongest in the world. Neither of these is true for other transforming economies. Still, the bulk of the financing for German restructuring came from the budget which, consequently, went deeply into the red, to the astonishment and denial of German taxpayers, who are noticeably more sensitive to such events than taxpayers in other parts of the world. A weak banking system and emerging, but still shallow and illiquid, capital markets made things even more difficult for other transition economies. A serious recession cut budgetary revenues, while at the same time soaring unemployment compensation tapped budgetary sources badly needed for restructuring. As a result of mounting needs and a limited supply of funds, financial repression emerged.

Under tremendous pressure, central banks pursued policies designed to enhance central bank profit transfers in order to support the budget. The most common alternatives to achieve this are the following: (a) monetary policy that maintains high reserve requirements, or (b) put an additional burden on financial intermediaries in the form of an implicit inflation tax. Konopielko (1997) examines reserve requirements as an implicit tax and calculates that this burden amounted to 0.81 per cent of GDP in Poland and 0.76 per cent in Hungary in 1992. This source represented 77.08 per cent of the National Bank of Poland's contribution to the budget and was 306.35 per cent of the Hungarian National Bank's profit contribution to the fiscal budget (Konopielko 1997, pp. 214–15). The calculations are based on the opportunity cost measure, which is the difference between the average loan interest rate of financing the budget by issuing bonds and the interest rate on reserves. This measure might be slightly biased upward as the imposition of required reserves might contribute to an increase in bond rates.

As an unintended consequence, this practice had an unfavourable impact on the development of the financial sector. Even in cases where this practice provided opportunities for the banks to earn high-margin business this expansion was achieved at the expense of the customer. Such developments are not sustainable in the long run without sacrificing growth potential.

2.5　Capital Flight

Abrupt change in the volume and direction of capital flows may cause major disruptions in asset prices and exchange rates. Both types of changes can cause systemic bank failures through generating losses in bank incomes and reducing the value of collateral. But even if the capital flows are smooth, the sterilisation of inflows by the central bank may require the maintenance of high reserve requirements, or if the sterilisation is done through passive instruments, it may hinder any possible reduction in interest rates.

3. CAUSES OF FAILURE

There is little debate on possible causes of banking failure. The list of measures to avoid widespread failures is as long as it is reasonable. It is based on emphasising the importance of macroeconomic policies, maintaining a sufficiently competitive environment, adequate regulation and supervision of financial markets and institutions, complete and sincere data reporting, and proper governance in banking, business and government. Few countries, however, are likely to live up to such standards. The list below reflects the weaknesses revealed by recent experience and borrows heavily from Honohan (1997). It is a fair assumption that future crises will reveal other weaknesses.

3.1 Macroeconomic Distortions

3.1.1 Lack of macro stabilisation efforts

Most financial systems can absorb macroeconomic shocks without suffering institutional failures. Some banks survive even severe macroeconomic shocks. These are typically banks which followed policies explicitly designed to insulate themselves from disturbances. In order for bank failures to take place, there certainly need to be microeconomic deficiencies in bank behaviour, as well as errors in macroeconomic or monetary policy management. The best that one can do in order to improve the status of the financial sector is to start with macroeconomic stabilisation policy.

3.1.2 Asset price bubble, or monetary overhang?

Crashing asset prices triggered the Asian banking crisis in 1998. Similarly, a collapse of corporate asset markets in transition economies contributed to the banking crisis. The falling value of collateral made formerly sound lending policies unsafe and irresponsible. However, as Honohan (1997) notes, no single bank is able to generate an asset price bubble on its own. An overall credit expansion is involved in generating asset price bubbles, as is an inadequate response by the sector to future changes in asset prices, which results in an over-abundant rate of base money creation in the system.

For the first two to three years of the transition, all of the Central and Eastern European countries in transition experienced deep recessions. The austerity programmes pursued in order to stabilise these economies reduced domestic demand significantly. At the same time, the liberalisation of prices added an inflationary shock. As the recession deepened, the tax base was eroded and transfer payments increased, plunging the fiscal budget into serious deficit. The budget deficit soaked up private savings that could have been channelled into financing the business restructuring and expansion necessary in order to initiate the supply response to price and trade liberalisation.

Monetary policy in these years was under severe pressure to ease monetary conditions. An abrupt credit crunch generated by a much more restrictive monetary policy would most probably have made financing the transition even more difficult, but at the same time it would have put an end to the practice of wasting depositors' money on unviable projects. The fiscal stabilisation policy implemented to cut transition hangover, however, had to be supported by a restrictive monetary policy to strengthen the credibility of these policies. In determining longer-run monetary policy strategies, conventional price stability objectives should remain in the context of financial stability, and these two have to be mutually consistent objectives. This also means that central banks in transition economies increasingly have to focus on the impact of policies on asset values and resulting balance sheet variations. Changes in the balance sheet of economic actors influence real economic activity, and consequently are important for determining macro policies.

3.1.3   Insufficient sterilisation of capital inflow

The privatisation and opening up of the economy to foreign investors in the early years of the transition generated massive capital inflows. Capital inflows, although vital for financing economic modernisation, may lead to excessive monetary expansion. Accelerating inflation at the same time increases country risk and reduces the attractiveness of a country for investors. That is why conducting appropriate monetary policy to sterilise the inflow and drain the base money is vital, although it may not be easy, especially if a tightening of monetary conditions increases interest rates.

High interest premia also may attract speculative financial investments, thereby encouraging further capital inflows. Speculative inflows may help financing temporarily, but as this type of finance is generally unstable and very sensitive to changes in the global financial climate, to rely on it is extremely dangerous. The best strategy to keep speculative inflows low is to keep interest premia low and encourage FDI and long-term financing.

3.2   Microeconomic Deficiencies

3.2.1   Managerial denial of known but uncontrollable potential risks

Systematic management errors are often mentioned as a reason for bank failures, but economic analysis should concentrate on the deeper causes of these errors. Whenever the environment for banking changes dramatically, 'manager's myopia' bears more risks for the financial system. After years of stability, bankers, supervisors and policy-makers tend to underestimate the potential for problems to arise, and continue previous practices even if it means not coping with new challenges. Learning for decision-makers cannot stop once a manager is promoted to his position. Institutions, corporations and their environment are changing constantly and their managers must adapt readily to these changes.

In addition, millions of office hours of officials and supervisors are wasted analysing past events in secrecy. However, reducing this secrecy would probably reduce the risk denial threshold of others and so help to prevent future crashes from occurring. Exaggerating the secrecy in financial issues reduces the immunity and self-correction capability of the whole system against so-called systemic risks. Current practices often put the interest of an individual bank ahead of the interests of the whole financial system.

3.2.2 Rigidities in adjusting costs
The liberalisation of banking markets, the removal of administrative controls on interest rates, and more liberalised entry following privatisation can all contribute to an increase in the volatility of prices, while increasing competition places pressure on profitability. At the same time, it is difficult quickly to adjust the cost structures which evolved under the protected old restrictions.

3.2.3 Excessive credit growth
Excessive credit growth which is not accompanied by appropriate equity growth predicts some crises. In such cases, the regulatory and supervisory system should follow a more refined complex operation of checks, including simple and sensible automatic (not negotiable) safety measures. Randall (1993b) proposes direct supervisory action against excessive risk taking by individual banks. Randall's proposal is intended to act countercyclically with respect to financial cycles. He argues that corrective market forces tend to have an impact too late, and even then they have a procyclical effect, aggravating the depressed phase of the cycle.

3.3 Institutional Traps

3.3.1 Weak enforcement of prudential regulations
A widespread banking crisis, which is often attributed to management, may be more accurately attributed to poor supervision and enforcement. Even if supervisory work is done professionally, failure strictly to enforce their resolutions may undermine the soundness of the whole banking system.

3.3.2 Political interference
Often the problem is not that supervisors didn't know or suspect, but that the bank owners were too well placed politically. As a result, any preventive actions taken by bank regulators were curtailed or derailed by political actors.

3.3.3 Denial of risks on the side of depositors
It is often stated that deposit guarantees remove the depositor's fear of default,

allowing management to adopt riskier strategies. The real problem, however, is that the denial of information concerning so-called bank secrets reduces this fear even further.

3.3.4 Fraud

Fraud has always been a problem in banking. The potential for fraud occurs at various levels, not only by banks against customers (via pyramid schemes, for example), but also often perpetrated by customers perhaps with the collusion of bank staff. Preventing the activities of a bank customer from causing damage to other customers is a difficult issue. We may need to learn to live with it until it is kept under control by proper regulations and until law enforcement is equally efficient inside and outside banking. We still have to learn not to differentiate between various forms of bank robbery.

4. BANK CONCILIATION IN HUNGARY

4.1 Banking System Rehabilitation – A Decentralised or Centralised Approach?

In the early years of the transition, as a result of the transition recession and poor management, the banking system in most countries in Central and Eastern Europe was on the verge of collapse and called for government intervention (Surányi, 1998; Abel and Szakadát, 1997). Governments could choose to take either direct centralised or decentralised actions:

(a) A *decentralised* approach was pursued in Poland and partially in Hungary. In this case, individual banks retain responsibility for loan recovery, relying on significant assistance from the state. The programme was called a loan consolidation programme.

(b) Governments could follow a *centralised* approach – as in the Czech and Slovak Republics, Slovenia and also partially in Hungary – by carving out bad debts, placing them in a centrally created agency for collection or liquidation. At the same time government money is used to recapitalise the banks.

In *decentralised* cases, reform programmes identified banks as lead restructuring agents because they were presumed to know the condition of debtor enterprises better than non-banks, and because they could serve as a vehicle for decentralised debt resolution. The government's knowledge about individual enterprises was assumed to be more limited than bank information about their clients. Government agencies were also known to be too bureaucratic, and incidental political considerations rendered them inefficient partners in decisions inherent in enterprise restructuring.

For these reasons, in Hungary banks were expected to play a comprehensive role in several aspects of restructuring, such as: (a) conducting an analysis of problem debtors to determine the level of debt owed, and how to best have principle repaid and interest serviced, (b) restructuring the debt of potentially viable enterprises, (c) participating in financing the physical restructuring of potentially viable enterprises, (d) exercising corporate governance over these enterprises, and (e) writing off the debts, curtailing new credits to, and in some cases liquidating non-viable enterprises.

In the *centralised* approach, however, the government took the lead in restructuring banks (and sometimes enterprises) through a series of recapitalisations. This primarily involved carving out bad debt from banks, but in a few cases also involved bank rehabilitation agencies. Every Central European country has recapitalised all its state-owned commercial banks at least once.

Different approaches to bank restructuring have resulted in changes in governance, management and operations at a time when the legal and regulatory framework changed equally dramatically. The government-led approach, although in some respects efficient, also has problematic implications for the future: namely it did not prevent similar problems from occurring later. The recapitalisation of banks in and of itself does not change the internal operations of a bank, and may also create a situation where banks expect to be automatically bailed out of future problems. However, active state participation in the bailouts has contributed to delays in faster privatisation, which could have attracted much-needed foreign investment in the banking sector. Centralised approaches appear to have worked well only in countries where the legal and regulatory framework has been adjusted to enhance open competition and transparency.

4.2   The Hungarian Consolidation Programme

At the end of 1991 the Hungarian government issued a guarantee covering up to 50 per cent of doubtful loans inherited by the commercial banks from the National Bank of Hungary. These loans originated before 1987. In 1992 the impact of new bankruptcy legislation and revised rules for asset qualification caused a sharp increase in the volume of bad and doubtful loans, as more debt was classified as non-performing under the new regulations. As a result, all of the state-owned commercial banks would have become technically insolvent without immediate rehabilitation.

4.2.1 Bank-oriented loan consolidation
By the end of 1992 it was clear that the rehabilitation of the banking sector could no longer be postponed, because without it the banks would have lost

their capital and also at least some depositors' money as well. The Loan Consolidation Programme was launched (Balassa, 1996). This partially centralised portfolio cleanup put in action by the government in December 1992 covered banks with a capital adequacy ratio lower than 7.25 per cent. Fourteen commercial banks and 69 savings co-operatives took part in the programme.

In March 1993, these banks were able to sell their claims on domestic business organisations classified as 'bad' to the state. Assets classified as 'bad' before 1992 were purchased at 50 per cent of par value, while those classified as 'bad' in 1992 were purchased at 80 per cent. Certain claims outstanding against certain specified companies were purchased at 100 per cent of par value. The government bought up loan and interest claims to a face value of HUF 102.5 bn (2.9 per cent of GDP) and paid for them with HUF 81.3 bn of loan consolidation government bonds specifically issued for the purpose of bank rehabilitation. These are negotiable, 20-year maturity, adjustable-rate bonds indexed to the market-determined interest rate of treasury bills. Interest payments have been credited once a year.

The state sold a package of bad loans totalling a face value of HUF 40 bn to the state-owned Hungarian Investment and Development Bank Corp. (MBFB). The MBFB had the option to reschedule debts, to swap them for equity, or to forgive them. The remaining portion of the claims was temporarily managed by the seller banks based on contracts renewed every three months until the middle of 1994. Claims still held by the Ministry of Finance were offered to business organisations (asset management companies) in 1994. The claims that could not be sold in this way have been managed by the MBFB based on a Ministry of Finance commission.

The portfolio clean-up programme carried out on the basis of the end-of-1992 status substantially improved the situation of the banks affected, and also the aggregate indicators of the entire banking system as well. By the end of 1992, the total problem loan portfolio of the banking sector declined from HUF 288 bn (9.8 per cent of GDP) to HUF 186 bn and the bad loans declined from HUF 186 bn to HUF 84 bn. Bank provisions decreased and the institutions reached a positive capital adequacy ratio. However, this rehabilitation effort left the organisation, management and operating systems of the banks essentially unchanged.

4.2.2   Enterprise-oriented loan consolidation

In the second half of 1993, the government bought the debts of 12 large, state-controlled enterprises, which were selected based on their strategic importance. To alleviate their financial burden, part of their debts outstanding against the state was forgiven or rescheduled. In addition, the government purchased a substantial portion of the claims of creditor financial institutions outstanding against these large companies by again issuing consolidation bonds (at 90–100 per cent of par value). The banks received HUF 57 bn worth of loan consolidation bonds during this phase of rehabilitation. The assets of enterprises whose majority owner was the State Property Agency (ÁVÜ) or the State Property Management Holding (ÁV Rt.) were acquired by the government at this time, and later they were sold to these two state agencies with the purpose that the assets be disposed of under the reorganisation plans for the enterprises concerned.

4.2.3 Recapitalisation of the banks

The amount of problem debt in the banking sector rose to HUF 352 bn (9.9 per cent of GDP) measured by the old accounting standards, out of which the amount of bad debts rose to HUF 186 bn by the end of 1993. At the end of 1993, with the amendment of the Banking Act, the rules on classification and provisioning were adjusted towards international standards. According to the new accounting rules the amount of bad, doubtful and substandard assets totalled HUF 418 bn (11.8 per cent of GDP) on 31 December 1993, of which the value of bad debts was HUF 243 bn. (Balassa, 1996, p. 13). This 30 per cent increase in bad debt reflects that the old rules seriously underestimated the magnitude of the problem. A huge amount of bad debt, however, was still the consequence of a continued economic depression and the fact that lending practice adjusted too slowly to the worsening conditions of the banks and their clientele.

Because of the expanding nature of the problem, another comprehensive rehabilitation programme became inevitable by the end of 1993. The poor result of the previous schemes forced the government to pay attention to critiques of these programmes, so the government decided to proceed in a more decentralised way, explicitly increasing the banks' involvement in bad debt workouts while also improving their flexibility in using the funds provided by the state. After the experience of the previous attempts to rehabilitate the banking sector, the government accepted the view that recapitalising the banks would be a more efficient way of handling the problem rather than simply cleaning up their portfolios. As a means to achieve this, the government again used consolidation bonds.

Recapitalisation was implemented in three steps. In the first step, at the end of December 1993, eight banks received capital injections (totalling HUF 114.4 bn) which enabled them to raise their capital adequacy ratios to above 0 per cent. A capital increase and subordinated loans were also provided for the National Savings Co-operatives Institution Protection Fund. In addition, a separate HUF 10 bn information technology project was financed by the state at the state-owned OTP Bank (National Savings Bank). Altogether, HUF 130 bn worth of consolidation bonds were transferred to financial institutions in the first step.

In the second stage, in May 1994 the government offered additional capital in the amount of HUF 18 bn to the banks participating in the restructuring, enabling them to reach a 4 per cent capital adequacy ratio. By recapitalising banks in this manner, the government's stake in seven of the eight banks participating in the programme reached or exceeded 80 per cent. This was criticised as a stealthy method of renationalising the banks, but this increased ownership share was used constructively by the state. The increased stake in the participating banks enabled the government to require (via a 'consolidation agreement' which was signed by each participating bank) that the banks modernise their systems of control, organisation and operation. Based on these programmes, among other things, the loan appraisal, risk and asset classification procedures of the banks were upgraded. It was expected that, along with the recapitalisation of the banks, this would help attract foreign strategic investors.

As the third step in the bank rehabilitation programme, in May 1994 subordinated loan was granted to four banks (including three large ones) in the amount of HUF 15 bn in order for them to reach the Basle Agreement standard, an 8 per cent capital adequacy ratio. To reduce moral hazard problems, the calculations determining each bank's share in the support were based on the status of the banks as of 31 December 1993. This transfer did not impose additional direct expenditure on the budget, since the banks paid interest to the budget at a rate identical to that of the consolidation bonds. The overall high level of the budget deficit, however, forced the government to put an end to its participation in the financial restructuring of the banks at the end of 1994.

With this consolidation programme, the participating banks were able fully to replenish their risk provisions and deal accordingly with the problem assets which remained in their portfolios. The financial institutions involved were obliged to set up a restructuring plan for these non-performing debts, and participate in the rehabilitation process of the bankrupt enterprises. Banks could either manage the bad loans themselves or transfer them to workout organisations specialised in the management of such claims. In fact, most banks created a subsidiary as a bad debt workout unit for themselves, set up as an independent company. Some of these were later sold or privatised, and remained in business after concluding the workout of those assets which were initially transferred to them.

These bad debt workout units were seen as essential to ensure the privatisation of banks. For example, the fast privatisation of the largest bank in Hungary, Hungarian Credit Bank (MHB) was a priority for the government. To assist in this task, its workout unit (Risk Kft.) had a definite time profile of three years for concluding the task. In the meantime, the privatisation process could progress undisturbed by the potential risks involved in this part of the portfolio. As an additional bonus, recovery from the workout reduced the cost faced by the

Ministry of Finance, which provided state guarantees backing Risk Kft. At the end of the three-year span, the unit had finished its task and was liquidated.

Hungarian Credit Bank also illustrates the effective use of the state's increased ownership share. When it was decided that top management was not acting quickly enough to resolve the bad debt and undercapitalisation problems, they were fired and a new management team was appointed by the government. The new management saw successful recapitalisation, portfolio cleanup and privatisation as top priorities, and much of the work of Risk Kft. was performed after this team was in place.

After the closing of the bank consolidation scheme – expressly not as a part of it – one of the largest banks (Budapest Bank) received an additional HUF 12 bn of consolidation bonds in order to avoid a capital reduction during its preparation for strategic sale. This contribution to the capital reserve was given in order to offset the bank's loan losses, with the condition that the bank should be privatised by the end of 1995. If it was not successfully privatised these bonds had to be returned to the government. The bank was indeed privatised at the end of 1995, and the government repurchased the bonds out of the proceeds of privatisation.

Early in 1996, two relatively large banks, Mezöbank and Agrobank, merged, and at the same time received an additional capital injection of HUF 9 bn. Also early in 1996, as a supplement to the consolidation scheme, the government offered guarantees for the net value of the claims transferred by two banks (the Hungarian Credit Bank and Mezöbank) to the workout companies.

Until the end of 1994, HUF 330 bn worth of consolidation government bonds were issued in the consolidation scheme (this is equivalent to 9.4 per cent of the 1993 GDP), which increased the net debt of the country by HUF 300 bn, as HUF 30 bn were transferred as subordinated loan. By mid-1996, the value of consolidation bonds issued reached HUF 360 bn as a result of additional actions. Although bank rehabilitation was expensive, it helped bank privatisation to start. From this point of view the rehabilitation programme was clearly successful. Various indicators of the banks' performance in the post-rehabilitation period also improved remarkably. The capital status, profitability and portfolio quality of banks participating in consolidation improved considerably overall.

4.2.4 Bank privatisation

The main consideration of a strategic investor in the case of a bank is *reputational risk*. His new acquisition must be successful; otherwise his own risk rating will suffer. For the bank being acquired, this is also an important consideration. In order for it to have a good reputation, it needs to attract top-quality investors. For reputational risk considerations, and for other reasons mentioned in Bonin et al. (1998) and Buch (1998), the best partner is a foreign strategic investor, preferably an AAA-rated multinational bank. However, in order to attract such investors, an important precondition is macroeconomic stability. In an unstable environment no financial institution can be safe and prosperous, as its clientele would be too risky. For this reason, the unfavourable macroeconomic conditions of the early 1990s severely hindered the privatisation of state-owned banks in Hungary (Várhegyi, 1998).

Out of the five large state-owned banks, Magyar Külkereskedelmi Bank (Hungarian Foreign Trade Bank) was the first institution offered for sale. This bank was seen as a good acquisition for foreign investors, as it had inherited less bad debt from the old system than other banks. Stakes of 25 and 16 per cent were acquired by Bayerische Landesbank and the European Bank for Reconstruction and Development (EBRD), respectively, in late 1994 and mid-1995. After purchasing the shares the two investors subscribed to newly issued shares as well. Later both EBRD and the state sold their shares to Bayerische Landesbank.

The large Hungarian savings bank, OTP Bank (National Savings and Commercial Bank) was privatised in successive stages. First, nearly 20 per cent of the bank's equity was offered for sale to Hungarian investors in 1994. A year later, 21 per cent of the shares were transferred to the Social Security and Pension Funds, and municipalities. Foreign institutional investors could acquire another 20 per cent and employees purchased 5 per cent in an initial public offering. The next 8 per cent were offered to domestic small investors in 1995. As a final stage of privatisation the remaining shares of OTP were sold in 1997 to both foreign and domestic institutional and private investors. The bank now has a very diverse ownership structure without a dominant investor. Its shares are also quoted on the Budapest Stock Exchange.

The European Bank for Reconstruction and Development also participated actively in the privatisation of another large Hungarian financial institution, Budapest Bank. Together with General Electric Capital, EBRD purchased a majority stake in the bank in December 1995. A year later, the Hungarian state had to buy back Polgári Bank (a retail banking subsidiary of Budapest Bank) from the new owners in the framework of the portfolio guarantees of the sales contract. Polgári Bank was later sold to another domestic bank (Pénzintézeti Központ Bank), with which it was merged in 1999.

The next largest bank to be privatised was Magyar Hitel Bank (Hungarian Credit Bank). ABN–AMRO purchased nearly 90 per cent of MHB's equity at about 225 per cent of face value, with an option to buy the remaining publicly held shares. Although MHB was in a very bad financial condition in the early 1990s and its portfolio cleaning cost a great deal to the taxpayers, the success of the restructuring was reflected in the favourable purchase price. Shortly after the sale, the new owner increased the capital of the bank, transforming MHB into a financially strong large ABN–AMRO representative bank in Hungary.

The sale of another large domestic bank, Kereskedelmi és Hitel Bank (K&H or Commercial and Credit Bank) was completed in 1997. In a two-round tender the consortium of the Belgian Kredietbank and Irish Life insurance company of Ireland obtained a 10 per cent stake in the bank for USD 30 mn, equalling 567.3 per cent of the shares' face value. As in the case of MHB, the new owners did not get any special portfolio guarantees from the government. The bank's capital was increased by USD 60 mn later in that year. The EBRD also took part in the transaction by converting its subordinated loan capital to registered capital in an amount of USD 30 mn. It is planned to introduce the remaining stakes of the state and the social security funds into the stock exchange later.

Less spectacular, but equally important in the privatisation of the Hungarian banking sector, was the sale of CIB Bank (Central European International Bank). The National Bank of Hungary had a 34 per cent stake in the majority foreign-owned institution, which had a special offshore status in Hungary. The central bank sold its shares to one of the foreign owners in 1997. At the beginning of 1998 all the former privileges of CIB Bank were revoked, and it became a domestically registered bank.

In addition to the sale of the large credit institutions, two medium-sized banks were also sold to foreign strategic investors in 1997. Deutsche Genossenschaftsbank purchased a 61 per cent stake in Takarékbank (Savings Co-operatives' Bank) at 532 per cent of the face value of the shares. Since Takarékbank is the 'umbrella' bank of Hungarian co-operative savings and loan institutions, strategic voting rights are provided for the co-operatives. The other medium-sized bank privatised in 1997 was Mezöbank (Agricultural Bank). This institution was sold to the Austrian Erste Bank, also well above the face value of the shares. In both cases the new strategic owners contributed a capital increase they pledged in the contract.

As these events clearly show, the topics of bank rehabilitation and privatisation were closely connected in Hungary. Dominant state ownership was a serious handicap to the formation of a truly competitive and flexible banking sector, but was also useful as a means to force banks to deal with their problems and prepare for privatisation. Following macroeconomic stabilisation in 1995, and continued microeconomic improvements in the internal situation of the state banks, these banks became an attractive target for strategic private investors. Table 7.1 shows how the ownership structure of the Hungarian banking sector changed between 1991 and 1997.

4.2.5 Bank mergers and liquidations

Liquidation is always the final option accepted in the case of banks, as its consequences are far reaching. The number of clients suffering losses as a result of a bank's failure may be too large, or the Deposit Insurance Fund, and

Table 7.1: Ownership structure of the Hungarian banking sector (in % by registered capital)

	1991	1992	1993	1994	1995	1996	1997
Domestic ownership out of which	78.4	75.9	86.7	83.5	63.8	49.0	37.0
Government and social securities	40.5	39.1	67.7	65.8	41.9	31.1	20.5
Foreign ownership out of which	15.8	18.5	12.4	16.0	35.7	49.2	60.8
Banks	13.1	15.7	9.9	13.9	26.8	38.9	52.5
Preference shares	5.8	5.6	0.9	0.5	0.5	1.0	1.4
Own shares	–	–	–	–	–	0.8	0.8
Total	100	100	100	100	100	100	100

Source: Surányi (1998).

potentially other banks, may have to contribute a large amount of money in order to pay back deposits. Either case could destabilise the banking sector as a whole. This is why there needs to be a very strong case for it before liquidation procedures begin. Indeed, in most of the cases in Hungary a criminal investigation was directly linked to the decision, with the management of seriously troubled banks charged with criminal activity.

In Hungary all of the banks liquidated or merged into larger banks were small or medium-sized banks. Most of these had no more than a ten-year history, the greater part of this time having been spent as specialised financial institutions in the old system, themselves established by a special organisation, such as the Industrial Development Fund (which set up a commercial bank, Investbank, established in 1983 and merged into Pénzintézeti Központ Bank in 1995), or the Fund for the Development of Industrial Cooperatives (Iparbankhaz, established in 1984 and liquidated in 1990). The Fund for Innovation in the Construction Industry established Ybl Bank in 1983. Corvinbank was also established by another innovation fund in 1984. Some smaller banks were established as a co-operative bank (Konzumbank was established by industrial co-operatives).

Various industrial ministries set up the specialised funds in the old system. Although they later certainly helped to decentralise the banking system, and in this sense contributed to the transformation of the financial sector, they also helped to ensure the continuation of a soft budget constraint for the firms which they serviced. This is why the original funds were set up in the old system, and the newly established commercial banks set up by these funds continued this practice. In all of these cases, there was no strong capital base, and no continuous support for expanding or even maintaining the position of these new commercial banks in a dynamically expanding business.

But the idea of owning a bank simply to provide credit for its owners is not only found in the case of Hungarian state-owned companies. Ybl Bank, one of the smallest, was liquidated in 1991, soon after the private group Hepta took control of it and replaced the management with their own people. The group used the bank for financing its own interests. The top management of the bank, mostly incompetent financiers, were sentenced for fraud.

The bank was bought from liquidation by Budapest Bank and was reopened as Polgári Bank in 1992. Polgári Bank was owned by Budapest Bank when it was sold to GE Capital in 1995. The new owner, however, decided to get rid of the mounting problems created by Polgári Bank. Using the guarantees offered by the Ministry of Finance in the Budapest Bank transaction, they sold it back to the state in late 1996, cashing the amount of the registered capital. In early 1997, the bank was offered for sale in an open tender and Pénzintézeti Központ Bank, another state-owned bank, bought it from the Ministry of Finance basically for an offer to increase the capital above the level of minimum capital requirements.

Pénzintézeti Központ Bank had itself been sold to Postabank in 1998 in a transaction still debated in the media. There was no other applicant for the bank, and the offer price for the share transfer was 164 per cent of face value of the registered capital sold. The new owner decided to merge Pénzintézeti Központ Bank and Polgári Bank under the name of Polgári Kereskedelmi Bank in 1999.

Agrobank was established in 1987 on the basis of the Agricultural Innovation Bank Depository Association. In 1992 several foreign investors took control of the bank through capital increases. The foreign investors were organised and also mostly owned by a Hungarian origin Australian citizen (living in England) who had left Hungary in 1949. The bank suffered huge losses in 1992 and 1993, and participated in the loan consolidation schemes. In addition to loan consolidation, as part of the rescue the Ministry of Finance increased the bank's capital. As a result of this capital increase the ownership structure was the following: 30 per cent Ministry of Finance, 57 per cent owned by four foreign corporations, and another 324 shareholders, combined ownership added up to 13 per cent.

The bank aggressively supported the existing credit programme, which provided subsidised loans for privatisation purposes. This policy attracted the attention of the authorities and prompted reviews by the National Bank of Hungary (10 March–25 April 1994) and Hungarian Banking Supervision. These examinations detected minor irregularities but silently approved the practices of the bank. However, on 15 November 1994 the CEO and the president (who was also the majority owner) were both arrested and detained for three days. This was enough to prompt a run on the bank.

After a series of supervisory sanctions against the bank, the foreign owners agreed to sell their shares to the Ministry of Finance for a nominal amount of approximately USD 100. In January 1996, the Ministry of Finance merged Agrobank into Mezöbank, itself a troubled mid-sized (and in this case state-owned) bank that served the agricultural sector. A judge cleared the criminal charges against the CEO and the president in June 1997, but the Supreme Court overruled this decision and convicted them in April 1998. There is a detailed description of the story in *Függöjátszma: Az Agrobank-Dosszié* (1998), which still leaves several questions open, even as to whether the chief executive was guilty or not.

Realbank was established as a specialised financial institution by Budapest Bank in 1989. In 1991 the bank issued bonds (Reallízing II). In 1992 Budapest Bank, unhappy with the practice of the management of this institution in connection with the bond issue, tried to change the management. Eventually they decided to sell its stake to a consortium controlled by the management of Realbank. The bank continued to issue bonds, and tried to separate the non-performing portfolio from the bank by selling it to satellite companies whose ties to the bank were not transparent. By 1998 the continued accumulation of bad debt, alongside the obscure practices that management used to hide the magnitude of the problem, led to more and more frequent supervisory sanctions, and eventually Banking Supervision took over the management functions in July 1998. Subsequent investigations concluded with the decision to close the bank in January 1999.

4.3   A SUMMARY OF THE MAIN CAUSES AND MISTAKES IN THE HANDLING AND RESOLUTION OF BANK FAILURES IN HUNGARY (1990–98)

Every bank failure is a unique event. Even if there are similarities between cases, it is often difficult to find uniformity behind the single phenomenon called bank failure. To make this task simpler, and also in order to find conclusions from the Hungarian cases described in the previous sections, the cases are summarised in Table 7.2. The characterisation and evaluation given in the table are the subjective judgement of the author. I often mention fraud as a main cause, even in cases where nobody was caught or convicted. This summary judgement is more a reflection of public sentiment and should not be interpreted as an offence against anybody personally involved in the cases. In fact, it is usually impossible to pin down the responsibility to a single factor.

Table 7.2: Main causes and resolution of bank failures in Hungary (1990–98)

Bank	Type of problem leading to the crisis (numbers refer to the points listed in Sections 2 and 3)	Single most important cause of the particular case	Resolution
Általános Vállalkozási Bank	2.1 3.2.1, 3.3.4	Fraud	Acquired by WestLB (1992)
Ybl Bank	2.1 3.2.1, 3.3.4	Fraud	Bought from liquidation by Budapest Bank and reorganised as Polgári Bank (1993)
Leumi Bank	2.1 3.2.1, 3.3.4	Fraud	Liquidated (1994)
Agrobank	2.1 3.2.1, 3.3.4	Fraud	Merged into Mezöbank (1996)
Iparbankház	2.3 3.1.5, 3.2.1, 3.2.2, 3.3.3	Manager's myopia	Liquidated (1995)
Konzumbank	2.3 3.1.5, 3.2.1, 3.2.2, 3.2.3	Excessive credit growth	Acquired by State Development Bank (1995) Konzumbank is offered for sale (1999)
Corvinbank	2.3 3.1.5, 3.2.1, 3.2.2, 3.3.3	Manager's myopia	Acquired by State Development Bank (1996) Merged with Konzumbank (1997)
ÁÉB	2.1 3.2.1, 3.3.4	Privatisation to non-strategic partner	Sold to Gasprom Bank (1995)
Dunabank	2.3 3.1.5, 3.2.1, 3.2.2, 3.3.3	Uncontrolled costs	Liquidated, parts sold to ING (1995)

Bank	Type of problem leading to the crisis (numbers refer to the points listed in Sections 2 and 3)	Single most important cause of the particular case	Resolution
Polgári Bank	2.3 3.1.5, 3.2.1, 3.2.2, 3.3.4	Fraud	Acquired by Pénzintézeti Központ Bank (1997) Merged with it as Polgári Kereskedelmi Bank (1999)
Budapest Bank, K & H Bank, MHB, Mezöbank Takarékbank (bank consolidation 1992–94)	2.2, 2.3, 2.4 3.1.5, 3.2.1, 3.2.2, 3.2.3, 3.3.2, 3.3.4	Lack of macro-economic stabilisation Excessive growth	Privatisation Budapest Bank – GE Capital and EBRD (1995) MHB–ABN–AMRO (1996) Mezöbank – Erste (1997) K & H – Kredietbank and Irish Life (1997) Takarékbank – DG Bank (1996)
Postabank	2.3 3.1.5, 3.2.1, 3.2.2, 3.2.3, 3.3.1, 3.3.3, 3.3.4	Excessive growth, Political interference	Management change and brought under the control of State Privatisation and Holding Company (1998)
Reálbank	2.3 3.1.5, 3.2.1, 3.2.2, 3.3.3, 3.3.4	Fraud	Brought under control of Deposit Insurance Fund (1998) and liquidated (1999)

The experience of Hungary shows that the main cause of banking failure in the larger banks was the economy-wide structural changes, which rendered a significant portion of their clientele either in desperate need of restructuring or unviable. This cause could hardly have been prevented, as it is part itself of the transition to a market economy.

Systemic management errors contributed to the course of events, and in most of the cases led to the collapse of an individual bank. This fact raises the issue of the responsibility of regulatory and supervisory agencies. Fraud was also very often present in these cases. No supervision setup can completely prevent fraud. However, certain minimum standard regulatory structures are vital in order to reduce the risk of escalating fraudulent practices. The responsibility of the regulators, however, is crucial in determining the responses to the crises. And this is where real dangers which have remained unnoticed due to poor supervision can lead to devastating consequences.

To the author's surprise, political interference played a much less important role than was expected in the case of Hungarian banking failures. As there are many parties, including the banks, their competitors and regulatory authorities involved in the mismanagement of banking crises, it is too easy to blame the inefficiency only on political interference. Most likely all of these parties try to enhance their own position by trying to get politics involved in their own interests.

5. CONCLUSIONS

Macroeconomic stabilisation is the key factor in establishing and maintaining financial sector health. This should not be derailed by a short-term fear of revealing financial sector weakness. Once this stability is in place, the micro-economic process of cleaning up and recapitalising individual banks can have positive results and lead to the successful privatisation of the sector. Without macroeconomic stability, however, even the most comprehensive microeconomic programme is likely to be ineffective at best. Included in this macroecomonic stabilisation is the need for a stable and clear legal environment, including banking, corporate, and bankruptcy laws, as well as effective law enforcement and well-defined property rights. These are all necessary preconditions for a sound bank–client relationship.

The longer the consolidation procedure lasts, the higher the expenses, mainly because of the moral hazard of involved parties. Costs should be properly identified in advance as much as possible. However, this does not indicate that the process should speed along at all costs. There was much talk in the early transition of 'shock therapy' and a 'big bang' approach to transition. The past ten years have shown that the process inevitably takes time. The consequences of a quick (and consequently sloppy) privatisation can be just as devastating as doing nothing. A fine line must be drawn between moving too slowly and too fast. And at different stages the speed of the transition must be adjusted accordingly.

Minimum standard regulatory structures are required for limiting micro-economic weaknesses. A supervisory agency must be equipped with adequate financial resources and a well-trained staff, and must have the power and authority to take corrective actions in due time. A close co-operation with bank auditors is also necessary for efficient intervention. In addition, banking supervisory agencies should be independent of the government and protected from political pressures. Political interference is the greatest danger to any regulatory system. In order to limit political attraction and improve regulatory enforcement, it is vital to increase the transparency and openness of financial reporting, and minimise secrecy.

Regulatory policy should foster a competitive market structure. It is possible to begin this even with continued state ownership in the early transition, but the focus must still be on privatisation and removing the state from micro-managing the economy. Bank consolidations ideally should come about due to market forces (although the successful merger between Agrobank and Mezöbank was decided by government fiat). These consolidations should be encouraged only when they form viable institutions, and discouraged whenever increased concentration is likely to reduce competition.

The consolidation of the banking sector should be linked with enterprise restructuring. Without strengthened financial discipline in the corporate sector, banking sector rehabilitation cannot be successful (Begg and Green, 1996).

In order to avoid expectations that future government support is likely, recapitalisation of banks should be linked directly to the privatisation process. Open competition among possible investors and the transparency of the privatisation procedure should be maintained until the last step of the transaction. Political or other interest groups, as well as rival banks, should be kept away from the privatisation process of an individual bank. The privatisation method should maximise the likelihood that the governance of the bank will be independent of the state, and of current bank management. This goal is most likely to be achieved if a strategic investor obtains a significant stake in the bank.

Increased globalisation introduces new risks, but also can be an advantage. Increased ownership links potentially strengthen the resilience of a small open economy's banking system. For this reason, along with those described above, foreign strategic partners should dominate bank privatisation.

Providing adequate information to the public, whether from private rating agencies or from auditors, offers favourable safeguards. A true assessment of problems requires good accounting practices. Improvements in the legal system must also enhance the enforcement of responsibilities in these activities. And banks must adopt international accounting and asset classification standards in their everyday operation.

REFERENCES

Ábel, István and László Szakadát (1997), 'Bank Restructuring in Hungary', *Acta Oeconomica*, 49 (1–2), 157–90.

Balassa, Ákos (1996), Restructuring and Recent Situation of the Hungarian Banking Sector, *NBH Workshop Studies*, No. 4.

Begg, Iain and David Green (1996), 'Banking Supervision in Europe and Economic and Monetary Union', *Journal of European Public Policy*, 3 (3), 381–401.

Bonin, John P., Kálmán Mizsei, István P. Székely and Paul Wachtel (1998), *Banking in Transition Economies: Developing Market-oriented Banking Sectors in Eastern Europe*, Cheltenham, UK: Edward Elgar.

Buch, M. Claudia (1996), 'Opening up for Foreign Banks, Why Central and Eastern Europe Can Benefit', *Kiel Working Paper*, No. 763.

De Juan, Aristobulo (1996), 'False Friends in Banking Reform', *Central European Banker*, September, 4–9.

Demirguc-Kunt, Asli (1989), 'Deposit-institution Failures: A Review of Empirical Literature', *Federal Reserve Bank of Cleveland, Economic Review*, fourth quarter, 2–18.

Függőjátszma: Az Agrobank-Dosszié (Suspended game: The Agrobank Dossier) (1988), Kornétás Kiadó.

Honohan, Patrick (1997), 'Banking System Failures in Developing and Transition Countries: Diagnosis and Prediction', *BIS Working Papers*, No. 39.

Konopielko, Lukasz (1997), 'Reserve Requirements as an Implicit Tax: The Case of Poland and Hungary', *Communist Economies and Economic Transition*, 9 (2), 209–18.

McKinnon, Ronald and Huw Pill (1997), 'Credible Economic Reform and Overborrowing', *American Economic Review, Papers and Proceedings*, May, 189–93.

Martin, Daniel (1977), 'Early Warning of Bank Failure', *Journal of Banking and Finance*, November, 1, 249–76.

Mázsa, Péter (1998), 'Bankválságok kezelése' ('Handling Banking Crisis'), mimeo, p. 50.

Randall, E. Richard (ed.) (1993a), *Safeguarding the Banking System in Environment of Financial Cycles*, Federal Reserve Bank of Boston, Conference Series No. 37.

Randall, E. Richard (1993b), 'Safeguarding the Banking System from Financial Cycles', in Randall (ed.) (1993a), pp. 17–64.

Rojas-Suarez, Lilian (1998), 'Early Warning Indicators of Banking Crises: What Works For Emerging Markets?', Inter-American Development Bank, mimeo.

Surányi, György (1998), 'Restructuring the Banking Sector in Hungary', National Bank of Hungary, mimeo.

Várhegyi, Éva (1998), 'Bankprivatizáció' ('Bankprivatization'), ÁPV Rt.

8. Western Rules for Eastern Banking

Neven Borak

INTRODUCTION

For the transforming economies, two facts should be stressed: first, regarding the transition of the financial sector the formidable tasks faced may be listed as follows: (1) the rehabilitation of the existing banking system, (2) the introduction of prudential regulation standards in line with those found in Western countries, (3) tightening the liberal licensing laws and low entry requirements found in the early transition period, (4) the creation of an independent central bank and (5) establishing the cost to banks in the rehabilitation process of enterprises. The combined results of this endeavour thus far are: high interest rates, both for lending and for deposits, a credit crunch along with credit rationing and government guarantee schemes – all of which affect the allocation of credit. These results are not unlike those found in Western countries after a financial crisis.[1]

Second, there is no adequate definition and measure of the properness of the banking system. As a matter of experience, definition and measure are *ex post* concepts connected with the dominant doctrinal view at the time the definition is given. What can be said is that the prevailing signal that the enterprise sector has received thus far is to rely heavily on self-financing, rather than bank lending, as a crucial drive for real investment.

The consequences of the second point are not so straightforward for the financial system. They fit within two competing banking models; the first of which is a framework that targets the establishment of a market-oriented, Anglo-Saxon banking system, and the second of which calls for the establishment of a universal banking system, such as that found in Germany and Japan. For transition economies, the essence of the argument is not the inflow of external funds into enterprises, but more importantly the inflow of influence exerted on enterprises in order to induce the necessary adjustments and restructuring. In fact, this aspect, coupled with privatisation, dominates the debate regarding the appropriate type of banking system. The search for a proper banking system is a search for an efficient device for transmission, and for a method for outsiders to exercise control on enterprises (Stiglitz, 1985; Goodhart, 1994). In other words, this is a debate regarding proper corporate governance.

However, the search for a proper model is a search for control on banks as well. The government has two instruments at its disposal for exercising control over banks: ownership and regulations. Both are understood to be powerful tools regarding the instrumentalisation of government policies. The ideas, practices and other modernising elements that are currently introduced into ECE countries, either through the advice of consultants or through the imitation of Western practices, concentrate on the transformation of bank–enterprise relations. However, while recreating this relationship along 'market-oriented' lines is necessary, it is nonetheless not sufficient for the completion of the transformation of the financial sector, for it is not the only relationship being changed. Equally important, the restructuring being undertaken must also concentrate on changing bank–government relations, as the state ends its reliance on central planning and commercial banks move from being instruments of the state into independent entities operating in a market economy. This explicitly means that the state gives up its dominant position as the *owner* of commercial banks and fulfils its role through the means of prudential regulation and supervision.

Although the state must withdraw from the ownership of commercial banks, it still has a large role to play in the successful transformation of the financial sector. From rehabilitation measures which include the restructuring of bank liabilities by (a) the recapitalisation of banks with both public and private equity (the latter being nearly unknown in current practice), and the restructuring of banks' assets by methods which may include (b) a 'loan hospital', (c) debt-for-debt exchanges, (d) debt-for-equity swaps, (e) a 'good bank–bad bank' structure, (f) a government restructuring institution, (g) loan swaps and (h) government bond-for-bank loans swaps, the dominant position is occupied by government-backed actions, not private initiatives.

Despite several disadvantages that must be stressed, such as the government's continued control over the banking system; the consequential transfer of the risk of banking losses to the government; a delay in the realisation of a privately controlled and operated banking system; additional regulatory forbearance for the government's banks; a propensity towards measures that transfer a portion of the costs of rehabilitation to banks that are not included in the rehabilitation process; and liquidity dependency of banks on the activities of the government,[2] the government's involvement in the rehabilitation of commercial banks was unavoidable, due to the nature of the system that each CEEC is transforming from. This will, however, also have a profound effect on the nature of the banking system that is being created. For that reason, even though Western rules and procedures are being adopted, the end result will be distinct, according to the circumstances of the transition: an Eastern banking model will emerge.

A CORPORATE GOVERNANCE PERSPECTIVE

Zysman (1983, p. 55) enumerates three different types of financial systems, with various consequences for the connections between the state and economy (enterprises, banks and other intermediaries). The first system is a system based on the capital markets, with resources allocated by prices which are established on the competitive markets where enterprises and financial intermediaries operate. The second is a credit-based system with critical prices controlled by the state. The third is a credit-based system dominated by financial institutions. The state may appear in all three roles simultaneously, even though this brings it into conflicting situations. One such conflict is between government debt financed by the subordination of financial intermediaries and financial regulation. The second interesting conflict emerges when the state opts for a monetary policy of targeting the quantity of money, aiming not only at price stability, but also at the subordination of financial intermediaries.

The three systems mentioned are an important element of the connections between enterprises and the state, and between the state and banks (and other financial intermediaries), and their governance. According to Zysman (ibid., p. 286) the model of adjustment in the first type of financial system described above is company-led, in the second type state-led, and in the third type negotiated.

Walter (1994) and Story and Walter (1997) offer similar insights into the role of the government and the structure of a financial system. They distinguish between the equity market system (Anglo-American), the bank-based system (German), the bank industrial cross-holding system (Japanese) and the state-centred system (France). In all these models, the financial system has a central role in the resolution of agency problems. From the corporate governance perspective they draw distinction between an outsider and an insider system.

The outsider system is closely related to Zysman's capital market based financial system. In this system there is a free market for shares. Through this market, individuals can be the direct owners of enterprises and banks, as well as indirect owners through investment funds (or institutional investors). Cross-holding of ownership between banks and firms is not allowed.

The insider system is suitable for both types of bank- or credit-based financial system discussed by Zysman. Typical of this type of system are inimical take-overs which affect the response of the managers of enterprises and force them to act according to the demands of owners. Cross-holding between banks and enterprises is allowed in this type of regulation. The banks perform both commercial banking and investment banking activities, and have control over enterprises. The capital market is not well developed. This type of system does not foresee hostile take-overs against the will of managers, which are practically unknown (in contrast, hostile take-overs are common in an outsider system). In each of the credit-based systems outlined above, the state and economic agents intertwine. The state may pursue a number of policies, within two extremes: a *laissez-faire* approach, where it provides for macroeconomic policy only (competitiveness policy and foreign trade policy leave all the rest to market mechanisms) to a partial or complete ownership over corporations, regulation of the credit system, and to the directives of central planning. Finally, in the state-led system, the government is very active on both the capital market and bank intermediation and is also the dominant focus of lenders and borrowers.

This actually means that the implementation of government force is needed in order to trigger changes in enterprises. In CEECs, this practice resulted in the actual stratification of rules adopted for dealing with different groups of enterprises and banks, and of the transformation process as a whole. At the heart of the matter was the debt overhang issue. Two main features of the whole process were partially give-away privatisation (enterprises sold at low prices) and the use of government debt as drivers, transferring previously incurred losses from the business sector to the government sector, and transferring net wealth to new owners. Yet the expected results of this restructuring: high outside pressure from newly established investment funds operating as 'real' owners, from banks acting as senior creditors, and from new bankruptcy legislation for enterprises and for the banking sector, have not materialised as clearly as was hoped. The results of all this activity are still ambiguous. This ambiguity is generated by the differentiation of newly created institutions and applied rules on the one side and by the possibilities of development of either state ownership or internally governed enterprises and banks, both generated from the previous socialist ownership, on the other side. The breaking up of the mono- or state bank resulted in the creation of a separate commercial banking system blended with a flavour of investment banking. Investment banking in Eastern European circumstances was predominantly understood to be in regard to the role of a bank in corporate governance. Basically, it emerged as a vehicle for ownership transformation (especially in voucher privatisation schemes) and not on an evolutionary basis.

Due to the actual needs of reforming economies, one of the most stressed features of universal banking was the establishment of a close relationship between commercial banks and borrowing firms. This marks the beginning of a bank's almost total involvement in an enterprise through short-term financing, fixed-capital financing and equity stakes.[3] The question is, of course, that of the relative importance and role of four interconnected factors: (1) historical factors, (2) regulatory framework, (3) economic policy and (4) behavioural responses. From the point of view of reforming economies the second and the third factors are the most important, as they are devices employed through the process of transition.

In addition, both factors are precisely those vehicles that enable the search for convergence between universal banking and narrow or core banking, irrespective of a country's historical heritage or the expected behavioural response of banking legislation. The monetary and exchange rate policies employed, the capital shortage of both banks and enterprises or a strengthening of the regulatory requirements for banks can lead to a contraction of the real sector through a credit crunch, and also to the reorientation of banks towards servicing the government[4] and the central bank.

Arguments in favour of German universal bank model (Steinherr, 1993; Kregel, 1992) are as follows: irrespective of banks' ownership, German universal banks provide a full range of both commercial and investment banking services. On the liabilities side, the banks accept short-term sight, time and savings deposits, long-term funds in the form of fixed-term deposits and issues of saving bonds and bank bonds. On the assets side, they grant short-term advances, and medium- and long-term loans. Banks also provide brokers' services, deal in securities, and accept seats on the supervisory boards of non-banking institutions. In actuality, this description accurately describes only the 'Big Three' German commercial banks – Deutsche Bank AG, Dresdner Bank AG and Commerzbank AG (Smith, 1994).

The exceptions to the general universal banking rule, although they may still fall under the coverage of a universal banking system, are specialised banks operating in narrower fields, such as the financing of mortgages, instalment sales, postal giro and savings banks, and other specialised functions. These banks are often either subsidiaries of a universal bank or are state-owned. However, only the central institutions of public and co-operative banking sectors are allowed to own equity capital in non-banking institutions. Private sector banks are involved in retail banking.

Universality in the German case covers at least three areas, and consequently German banks are involved in all markets for financial services. The securities markets consists of bonds and equity. Bonds extend relations to both public debt finance and to housing finance. Equity markets lead to complex relations between the business and the banking sector. In the third integrating area, banking meets insurance, with Allfinanz (a German financial holding company) being the result. According to Kregel (1992, p. 239), the main advantage of the German model is its reliance on a strict regulation of maturity matching and active monitoring of a detailed balance sheet. Its universality is based on capital adequacy rules, liquidity rules and exposure limits.

European integration, in which several CEECs are involved at least through obligations from Europe Agreements to form a free trade area, also envisions a single market of financial services, which will be achieved through the convergence of the banking systems in accordance with EU banking directives. Among the pillars of this process is a universal banking model. Financial intermediaries with different structures and characteristics, and regulated by different rules, will reshape towards a universal model. This is compatible with the concept of the credit institutions with a bank defined as an undertaking whose business is to receive deposits or other repayable funds from the public and to grant credits for its own account. This in turn is subject to the supervision and monitoring by authorities of its liquidity, solvency, deposit guarantees, the limiting of large exposures, administrative and accounting procedures, and internal control mechanisms.[5]

Activities that credit institutions perform are: (1) acceptance of deposits and other payable funds, (2) lending (consumer credit, mortgage credit, factoring, with or without recourse, and financing of commercial transactions, including forfeiting), (3) financial leasing, (4) money transmission services, (5) issuing and administering means of payment (credit cards, travellers' cheques and bankers' drafts), (6) guarantees and commitments, (7) trading on their own account or the account of customers in money market instruments, foreign exchange, financial futures and options, exchange and interest rate instruments, transferable securities, (8) participation in securities issues and provisions of services related to such issues, (9) providing advice on undertakings regarding capital structure, industrial strategy and related questions, and services relating to mergers and the purchase of companies, (10) money brokering, (11) portfolio management, (12) the safekeeping and administration of securities, (13) credit reference services, and (14) safe custody services.[6] The Second Banking Directive includes within it the concept of a financial institution other than a credit institution, which is defined as an undertaking that performs all activities listed above with the exception of deposit taking. So the European banking directives, which should be implemented by candidate countries for integration in the EU, explicitly introduce into these countries the concept of financial universality, and not just the concept of universal banking.

We shall now focus on the most relevant issues for Eastern countries: relations between banks and enterprises and between banks and the government. By EU law, credit institutions are allowed to have up to 15 per cent of their own funds in non-bank and non-financial entities. The total amount of all such holdings may not exceed 60 per cent of their own funds. Two points should be made. The first is related to debt-for-equity swaps as a way of introducing ownership and control of banks over enterprises. According to the Second Directive, shares held temporarily during a financial reconstruction or rescue operation shall not be counted as qualifying holdings for the purpose of calculating the above-mentioned limits, although the bank will be obliged to increase its own capital or to take equivalent measures. This directive was written for cases where exceptional circumstances created the need for the restructuring of a single or several institutions, not the reconstruction of the whole economy, as found in the transition economies. Nevertheless, it is interesting that the directive foresees a period of ten years for a bank to dispose of excess holdings.

The second point is related to credit, interest rates and market risks. This directive offers the possibility to exclude from its scope any credit institution that specialises in interbank and public debt markets, and that fulfils, together with the central bank, the institutional function of a banking system liquidity regulator, provided that: (1) the sum of its asset and off-balance-sheet items included in the 50 per cent and 100 per cent weighting must not normally exceed 10 per cent of total assets and off-balance-sheet items and shall not in any event exceed 15 per cent before application of the weighting, (2) its main activity consists of acting as an intermediary between the central bank and the banking system, (3) the competent authority applies adequate systems of supervision and control of its credit, interest rate and market risks.

In view of current Eastern bank rehabilitation methods and monetary policy practices, both of which influence the foreign exchange exposure of banks, exchange rate risk should be added to the list above. In other words, such a bank would not have loans to enterprises or equity stakes on the assets side. It would have to lend to the government, or to entities with government guarantees. Once again, what is meant as a special case within the directive is a dominant feature of banking in CEECs. Government rehabilitation bonds exchanged for enterprise loans and for the recapitalisation of banks dramatically improve their solvency ratios: a completely insolvent banking system becomes highly solvent after this method is initiated. Further, from the Second Banking Directive we can also assume that the answer to financial universality instead of multi-tier banking could be multi-tier prudential regulation.

A RISK MANAGEMENT PERSPECTIVE

The first important step in the reform of the financial sector in former socialist economies was the break up of the monobanking system and the introduction of a two-tier banking system in which the state bank (national bank) performed the activities of a central bank as defined in a market economy and became responsible for the conduct of monetary policy and monetary regulation, while the newly instituted (and still state-owned) commercial and specialised banks were assigned the functions of deposit mobilisation, lending, payment, and other commercial banking activities. The second important step that followed was the changes in the legal and regulatory framework, aimed at changing the incentive structures needed for building a sound banking system and good business practices. The first step just reorganised the intermediation between mobilisation and allocation of resources, the second one added the task of risk trading to intermediation.

Each of the transforming countries has used the Basle guidelines for risk management and the EU banking directives as a template for the reformation of their financial sector. One possible conclusion from this is that after a rehabilitation phase the banking system will be shaped to mirror the Western benchmark. However, neither the Basle recommendations nor the EU directives were established in order to create a model for reforming countries to copy: the Basle agreement was established in order to promote the soundness of banks involved in international business, while the EU guidelines support the creation of a single market in banking and other financial services for member countries. Both the Basle accord and the EU directives were written assuming the pre-existence of a market economy in the countries that abide by these rules. Thus, the situation foreseen by these guidelines is far removed from that found in an economy transforming from nearly 50 years of central planning.

The debate on a proper banking model for the former socialist countries was relatively short but intensive. It was a part of the debate on the comparative advantages of different financial and banking systems found in developed industrial countries, which included both functions of intermediaries – the mobilisation and allocation of resources and risk transformation. As usual, real life practice exceeded the conclusions of the debate. A brief overview of recent changes in the regulatory frameworks and interrelations between banks, enterprises and the state sector in CEECs is given in Table 8.1.

We can learn two lessons from the table. The first relates to the starting vintage of legislative modernisation of the banking sector at the beginning of the 1990s that introduced a new structure of incentives and announced a hardening of the budget constraint. Changes and improvements made later (Borish et al., 1996; EBRD, 1998a) leave the general impression that the banking systems in these countries fit the universal model unchallenged. The table reveals that new legislation introduced an evaluation of borrowers' risk, concepts of risk-weighted assets and risk-weighted capital requirements, defined measures of single creditor and total exposure, including equity ownership and limits on the amount of credit allocated to shareholders and determined supervisory authority.

The second lesson relates to the basic characteristics of the rehabilitation procedures for resolving the bad debt problems of banks and enterprises. The state was heavily involved in banking sector rehabilitation and recapitalisation through the exchange of government bonds for bad debts and without linking the rehabilitation of banks with their privatisation. At the same time, the involvement of the direct banking sector in the rehabilitation, restructuring and privatisation of the enterprise sector was much weaker.

It seems that the theoretical arguments in favour of the universal banking model for CEECs are less important when compared with real life. The same holds for arguments in favour of universal banking based on the level of development of CEECs. More convincing are the observations that the model enters the scene in a manner of a 'Gulliver' or 'neighbour' effect of the EU (specifically as a result of German influences on CEECs), and that the path

Table 8.1: The regulatory framework in Eastern European banking since 1991

	Slovenia	Hungary	Poland	Czech Rep.	Bulgaria	Romania	Croatia
Commercial and investment banking separated	No	Yes	No	No	No	No	No
Limits on equity holdings	Yes	Yes	Yes	Yes	Yes	Yes	Yes
Capital adequacy	8% of risk-weighted assets	8% of risk-weighted assets	8% of risk-weighted assets	8% of risk-weighted assets	8% of risk-weighted assets	8% of risk-weighted assets	8% of risk-weighted assets
Minimum capital	USD 5mn	USD 13.3[1]	No explicit limit	Determined by Central Bank	USD 10 mn	USD 3.5 mn	USD 5mn
Single debtor exposure	25% of guaranteed capital	25% of guaranteed capital	15% of assets	25% of capital	25% of capital	20% of capital	30% of guaranteed capital
Limits to ownership	Yes	Yes	Yes	No	1% of capital	No	Yes
Loan classification	Yes	Proposed	Proposed	Proposed	Proposed	Proposed	Yes
Lending to shareholder	Yes	5% of guaranteed capital	5% of capital	Discretionary	Authorisation required	15% of capital	Yes
Supervision authority	Central Bank	State banking supervision	Central Bank	Central Bank	Central Bank	Central Bank	Central Bank

	Slovenia	Hungary	Poland	Czech Rep.	Bulgaria	Romania	Croatia
Rehabilitation measures	Govt. bonds exchanged for bad loans and bank recap.	Govt. bonds callable on initiation of liquidation procedures	Govt. bonds exchanged for bad loans and bank recap.	Govt. bonds exchanged for bad loans and bank recap.	Govt. bonds and guarantees	Proposed Govt. bonds	Govt. bonds exchanged for bad loans and bank recap.
Bank recap. linked to enterprise restructuring and privatisation	Indirectly	Indirectly	Directly	Indirectly	Directly	No	Indirectly
Bank recap. linked to bank privatisation	No	No	No	No	No	No	No
Bank involvement in enterprise restructuring programmes	Yes	Yes	Yes	No	No	No	Yes
Deposit insurance	Yes	Yes	n.a.	Yes	n.a.	n.a.	Yes

Note:
[1] For commercial banks only.

Source: Thorne (1993) and national sources compiled by the authors.

towards financial universality serves to maximise size and market power, and ultimately generates non-competitive rents. Both would be consistent with the hypothesis of survival of the fittest, but the social implication would be different.

The basic characteristic of banking sector modernisation is therefore universality. As is usual with definitions, universality is not quite a uniform concept. Story and Walter (1997) and Walter (1994) identify four basic types of linkages that have dominated the current debate between the corporate structure and competitive performance in financial services:

1. The fully integrated universal bank, capable of supplying all types of financial services from the same corporate entity: the truly universal, or German-Swiss banking model.
2. The partially integrated financial conglomerate, capable of supplying the same set of services, but with several (such as mortgage banking, leasing and insurance) provided through wholly owned or partially owned subsidiaries: the group universal, or Allfinanz/Bankassurance banking model.
3. The bank subsidiary structure in which an organisation's core is a bank, and a broad range of non-banking financial activities is performed through legally separated subsidiaries: a financial universal, or British banking model.
4. The holding company model, where a holding company owns both banking and non-banking subsidiaries: an ownership universal, or American banking model.

These four versions of universality are the result of different regulatory approaches. The most important distinction is in regard to the possibility for enterprises to be the owners of banks and for banks to have equity stakes in enterprises. These seemingly competing models have entered into the lexicon of reforming economies: the truly universal and partially integrated model through the imitation of EU banking directives and the advice of the IMF and World Bank, the American banking model through the advisory potential of other American institutions. In fact, the universal banking system has become, in one form or another, the typical model in industrial countries. This is true even in countries in which there remains a legal separation between commercial and investment banking activities, as well as legal geographical segmentation, such as in the United States. For reforming countries, the concept of a commercial bank coincides with that of a commercial bank.

Besides detecting differences between the models discussed above, it could also be useful to detect any possible convergence. This convergence may be found along three paths:

- through differentiation regarding risk taking and risk aversion;
- through examining the relationship between banks and the state; and

- in common attitudes toward the expansion of financial universality, which lies behind each of the four models of universal banking.

Such an understanding of convergence has its foundations in the reasonable ground of common Eastern and Western experience, namely that the challenges found in the transition include the restructuring and recapitalisation of insolvent banks, and the reorganising of healthy banks into new institutional categories. Strikingly enough, the second path of convergence is connected with the question of which banking activities should be regulated. Restructuring ideas in the Western world are built around three topics: (1) deposit insurance, (2) competition between banking and non-banking sectors in the provision of financial services, and (3) an interconnection between banks and non-bank businesses. We shall refer to two current and influential proposals of American origin: concepts of narrow banking and core banking.

Litan (1987) tries to equilibrate the benefits from removal with limitations on risks. He discusses two broad approaches for meeting this requirement. Both would allow banking firms to diversify their product and service offerings. The fundamental difference between them is in regard to deposit guarantees. Under the first alternative, bank subsidiaries could operate by collecting insured deposits and re-lending them to customers, while operating parallel affiliates which engage in other financial and non-financial business. Associated risk would be addressed through regulation.

The second alternative is narrow banking. In brief, Litan advocates legislation which would provide for the establishment of financial holding companies. These are a variation of bank holding companies, in which a deposit-taking subsidiary would be required to invest only in reserves, government securities or securities insured by the government against default. Lending by these diversified institutions would be separated from deposit taking, and funded through the uninsured securities market.

Litan's proposal has a different goal. With an eye on the inevitable growing intrusion by banks into activities that were not allowed by American legislation and by intrusion of other firms into banking activities, he envisioned two regulatory responses to this process. The first is an inadequate response to abuses and fraud as they arise. The second is a splitting of the transactions functions from the intermediation functions performed by depositories which belong to highly diversified financial service firms. Three of Litan's conclusions are worth mentioning: (1) a possible contamination of the safety of the banking system due to financial deregulation and product diversification, (2) increasing conglomerate economic and political power, and (3) increasing conflicts of interest. They are relevant for transforming economies as well. If one adds accounting practice and abuses to the first conclusion then unexpected convergence between two seemingly unrelated environments emerges.

The essence of Litan's proposal for narrow banks is as follows. Existing (American) bank holding companies should continue if they are willing to undergo further financial product diversification, and gradually phase in narrow banks. The basic question is how extensively should the government intervene to provide a financial safety net. Suggesting government and government-guaranteed collateral instead of insurance to protect deposits expands but does not exhaust the policy options.

The core bank proposal (Bryan, 1991a) as a part of new social contract addresses the incentive distortions created by the US federal safety net by restricting deposit insurance to a new class of core banks. The overall contract would involve an authorisation of a new kind of financial holding company with no restrictions on what businesses it might own or what businesses may own it. The holding company could have both insured and non-insured subsidiaries.

Banks would be required to be broken up so as to conform to three new legal categories of financial institutions: core banks, money market investment banks, and finance companies. Each would play a distinct role in the economy. In order to transfer the risk to the federal safety net, core banks would be limited to certain traditional banking activities. They would accept deposits in savings accounts, checking accounts, money market accounts, and so on. They would lend to individuals (for home mortgage debt, home equity loans, credit cards, instalment loans, and car loans, including home mortgages, credit cards and small business lending), and to business (for accounts receivable financing, equipment leasing, commercial mortgages, unsecured lines of credit). These activity restrictions would be complemented by regulation of interest rates on core bank deposits, which would be pegged to floating rates on Treasury securities.

The purpose of regulating interest rates would be to prevent destructive competition among banks seeking to attract deposits by bidding up interest rates. In the absence of such competition, core banks would be under less pressure to engage in high-risk lending in order to cover their cost of funds. Regulators could also limit the terms and conditions of loans which could be extended by core banks. Under this proposal, money centre banks, which today offer services beyond those permitted to core banks, would be required to split their operations into two or more entities in order to segregate their core banking operations into a separate corporate compartment. They could continue risky non-core activities based solely on their own financial strength or exit some of the business. Some of these banks could be giant players in the world capital markets – without government guarantees. Non-core services would be conducted through uninsured and largely unregulated money market investment banks and finance companies, subject to disclosure-based regulation by the Security Exchange Commission.

The essence of this proposition is to create core banks that would return to those activities that have proven over time to be relatively safe and where banks have demonstrated advantages over non-banks. Creating safe core banks requires imposing strict controls on what they can do. These regulations would include: pegging interest rates, limiting the size of loans that core banks can extend, and permitting real-estate lending to local developers on strictly regulated terms and conditions.

Money market investment banks would serve corporations, financial institutions and government with a broad array of commercial banking and investment banking products. Their operations would involve trade securities, derivatives and currencies. They would buy, sell, underwrite and distribute corporate debt and equity, and make loans that could be traded on secondary markets. Unlike the core bank, which would be funded with insured deposits, the money market investment bank would be funded with interbank deposits, uninsured CDs and other wholesale funds. Each bank would have unquestioned financial strength founded on its earnings stream, the quality of its assets and its capital base.

Finance companies would provide credit and other banking services that are too risky to be included in the core bank: big corporate loans, financing for highly leveraged transactions and commercial real estate, and large lease transactions for capital equipment and aircraft. Their funding source would be a strong capital base (as much as 15 per cent of their assets). Rating agencies and accounting firms, and not the bank examiners, would be responsible for assessing the quality of the assets. The role of regulators would be to protect affiliated core banks or money market investment banks from being brought down by troubles of the finance company. There would be no safety net beneath these institutions.

Policy options are not exhausted with these two proposals. Tobin (1985) for example takes a similar position in proposing 'segregation' to limit the need for deposit insurance protection and continuous scrutinisation and regulation of assets. Szegö (1993) proposed an organisation of the Eastern European financial system along four, strictly specialised tiers: payments services, lending activities, investments and central banking.

Van Wijnbergen (1994) and Boot and van Wijnbergen (1994) argue that both the need to insure depositors and the need for strong lender regulation and for monitoring managers' investment activities call for transitional separation of deposit-collecting activities from investment activities by creating two types of banks: commercial banks, collecting deposits and lending to the government and other banks, and investment banks, borrowing from the interbank market, and possibly the government. According to their proposal, all one needs to create such a banking system is to (1) forbid the savings (narrow) banks from lending to corporations, (2) forbid commercial banks from taking personal deposits on a significant scale or to refuse deposit insurance to such deposits outside the savings banks, and (3) require the savings (narrow) banks to invest mostly in high-grade assets, which for the time being means government paper, and lending to commercial banks which have a high capital base. In this system the savings (narrow) banks need not be monitored, while monitoring of the investment banks will be curtailed through a higher capital ratio and creditors.

Of course, an essential complement to this system is the development of the interbank market. Also, *The Economist*, 27 August 1994 states:

> The German model may not be suitable for economies that are still making a painful transition from central planning to capitalism. One priority should be to create a stable banking system that wins depositors' trust while allocating credit on the basis of market forces. A second should be to encourage a rapid restructuring of the hugely inefficient industries that central planning has created. And a third should be to promote the development of efficient and competitive capital markets. An unthinking dash for a universal-banking system could make it harder to meet any of these priorities.

AN AMBIGUOUS OUTCOME: EASTERN UNIVERSALITY

Several recent studies (Borish et al., 1996; Anderson and Kegels, 1998) have stressed that the state continues to dominate the banking sector of CEECs. On a balance sheet basis, for example, in five countries (Czech Republic, Poland, Hungary, Slovakia and Slovenia) this dominance accounts for about 60 per cent of total assets and total loans, and about 70 per cent or more of total deposits (Borish et al., 1996, p. 3). According to the same source, the banking sectors of these countries still show regional and/or sectoral segmentation dating back to the earlier period, and are still protected to a varying degree by the state from the pressure of market forces. Due to their size, access to household deposit and traditional client bases, privileges such as implicit state deposit guarantees and sectoral/geographical concentration have provided state banks with a substantial market advantage, and in some cases with direct and indirect subsidisation to offset potential losses. The power of these banks to pass increased costs of intermediation on to the borrowers through higher lending rates remains unchallenged despite their low intermediation rates.

The joint result of the processes is that the size of private banks, measured by their shares in total banking sector resources on a balance sheet basis, is small. The private banks' average assets in Poland, the Czech Republic, Slovakia, Hungary and Slovenia were USD 369 million, compared to USD 2.3 bn for an average state-owned bank in 1995. Average deposits of private banks were USD 149 million and USD 1.4 bn for the state banks. The governments of these five countries also provided nearly USD 13 bn to recapitalise the troubled banks: Slovenia: USD 1.4 bn, Poland: USD 2 bn, Hungary: USD 3.5 bn, and the Czech Republic and Slovakia: USD 6 bn (Borish et al., 1996, p. 27).

It will be instructive now to examine the changes in the balance sheets of West European banks (in the period 1982–86) and of East European banks (after rehabilitation measures were introduced) on a highly aggregate level. From the works of Gardener and Molyneaux (1990), Cherubini et al. (1993) and Maccarinelli et al. (1993) we can draw the following picture of West European banks.

On the assets side, West European banks have experienced an increase in their interbank deposits, compensated for by a decrease in the proportion of loans on their books, as well as by a decrease in cash balances held by the central bank. On the liabilities side, a large fall in the proportion of non-bank deposits, as well as a marginal fall in the holding of interbank deposits, has been compensated for by a substantial increase in borrowing from the central bank, as well as by an increase in bonds and other types of liabilities. The increase in capital and reserves was insignificant. Non-bank deposits constitute more than 50 per cent of banks' liabilities, more than double the size of interbank deposits. Looking at large banks only shows that on the liabilities side, decreases in interbank and non-bank deposits have been compensated for by an increase in borrowing from the central bank as well as by a substantial increase in capital and reserves. On the assets side, securities and other assets are more important investments for large banks than for other types of banks. For savings banks, the assets structure is dominated by loans and securities, and the liabilities structure is dominated by a greater significance of non-bank deposits, although the dependence on interbank and central bank deposits increases as compared to other types of banks.

The picture presented for the balance sheets of CEE banks is vastly different. They have a large amount of non-performing loans from state owned enterprises (SOEs), both inherited from the old system and newly created, and a negligible amount of loans to the emerging private sector. After the introduction of bank rehabilitation measures, commercial banks obtained a large amount of government bonds in exchange for bad loans, in order to improve the quality of both the assets and liabilities sides of the banks' portfolios. Although these rehabilitation measures improved their solvency dramatically, there is still some doubt about the soundness of these banks as they suffer great liquidity problems, an exchange rate–interest rate mismatch and an assets–liabilities maturity mismatch. Despite cleaning up their balance sheet after the legacy of the former system, and despite tightening financial discipline, the bad debt problem is still significant (Table 8.2). Its presence reveals several unwanted developments: sustainability of creditor passivity and weak incentives for banks to cope with it.

Table 8.2: Non-performing loans, 1994–97 (in % of total loans)

Country	1994	1995	1996	1997
Bulgaria	7	13	15	13
Croatia	12	13	11	10
Czech Rep.	34	33	30	29
Hungary	18	10	7	4
Poland	29	21	13	10
Romania	19	38	48	57
Slovak Rep.	30	41	32	33
Slovenia	22	13	14	12

Source: EBRD (1998b, p. 133).

In addition to creditor passivity, the balance sheets also reveal the defensiveness of the CEEC banking sectors. According to Tobin (1982, p. 496), the assets of commercial banks may be divided into two categories: loans and investments, and defensive assets. Defensive assets are assets of very high liquidity and include currency and deposits in the central bank and other banks, and government bills and interbank loans. They cover primary and secondary reserves. The amount by which a bank's net holdings of defensive assets exceeds its required reserves defines its defensive position. In Table 8.3 data for four CEECs are rearranged to present a sectoral breakdown of assets and liabilities. The data are organised so as to extract four sectors: monetary system (cash, central bank, interbank lending), government, corporate sector and households, and to obtain information on investments in equity of non-banks and on own resources of banks. An additional two rows provide estimated data on equity and tradable securities (with the exclusion of central bank and government short-term papers). Table 8.3 also allows additional insights on universality through balance sheet figures.

A recent EBRD survey (1998a, p. 26) concludes that the extensiveness of banking and capital market regulation is far more advanced than the effectiveness of these introduced rules. In other words, the enforcement of rules and regulations seems to be lagging behind the enactment of a sound legal framework, and the methods of risk prevention need to be improved. According to the survey, the main areas in need of improvement and enhancement include the refining of internationally acceptable accounting standards, enhanced enforcement of laws and regulations, and greater improvement of the general legal framework that underpins financial transactions.

Table 8.3: Sectoral breakdown (in % of total assets)

	Poland		Hungary		Czech Rep.		Slovenia	
	96	97	96	97	96	97	96	97
Assets								
Monetary system	26.3	27.4	22.9	26.1	33.5	36.6	29.8	31.2
Government	18.8	20.6	18.6	15.6	6.8	4.4	15.9	15.9
Corporate sector	32.9	33.4	29.5	20.4	46.0	43.4	28.3	27.2
Households	5.6	7.0	4.3	3.2	n.a	n.a	11.5	11.5
Equity and participations	0.0	0.0	2.6	2.8	1.9	0.5	1.2	1.2
Other tradable securities	n.a	n.a	2.6	1.9	6.7	3.8	n.a	n.a
Liabilities								
Monetary system	11.4	15.2	11.5	11.2	26.7	26.1	13.6	10.2
Government	3.0	4.4	4.2	3.8	2.0	1.6	8.4	8.5
Corporate sector	15.5	15.0	15.9	17.3	45.9	47.7	17.1	17.5
Households	24.1	38.9	37.6	33.5			37.0	35.5
Equity	4.1	5.1	9.6	10.2	8.3	8.4	15.8	15.3
Bonds	0.4	0.3	9.8	7.3	3.1	4.0	2.5	2.5
Central Bank's balance sheet as % of commercial banks' balance sheet								
	45.3	46.9	n.a	n.a	24.1	22.0	20.2	28.5
Net position								
Monetary system	9.1	12.2	21.4	14.9	7.4	10.5	16.2	21.0
Government	15.8	20.2	14.4	11.8	4.0	2.8	7.5	8.5
Corporate sector	17.4	11.6	13.6	3.1	0.1	−4.3	11.2	9.9
Households	−18.5	31.9	−33.3	−30.3			−25.5	−24.0

Sources: Calculated from *Annual Report 1997* of National Bank of Poland, *Annual Report* of Hungarian Banking and Capital Market Supervision, Czech NB Banking Supervision 1997 and *Monthly Bulletin* of Bank of Slovenia 6/99, IMF, *International Financial Statistics*, June 1999.

Therefore, the situation found in the banking sector in transforming countries is different from that found in a Western banking sector. The problems faced, and their resolution, indicate that for the foreseeable future the government will play a crucial role in the commercial banking sector in Eastern and Central Europe. Creditor passivity and the relative defensiveness of the banking sector are, of course, in sharp contrast with the expected activities of universal banks. It seems that in CEECs the most important component of the banking sector is involvement in the activities of the central banks and Treasury in the redistribution of resources towards less risky activities.

It could also be a sign of the centralisation of the monetary system. A rough indicator of such a possibility is a comparison of the central bank's and commercial banks' balance sheet totals, as was done in Table 8.4. If this assertion holds, then the state (central bank and Treasury) is deeply involved in risk transformation outside the banking system and the banking system is deeply involved in public finance transactions. Furthermore, judging the banking sector from the perspective of Table 8.3, there is an impression that the banking activities currently being undertaken in the CEECs corresponds much more closely to the concept of a narrow or core bank, rather than the concept of a universal bank. This is despite the presence of legislation that allows for universal banking in each of the CEECs that has been investigated. Nevertheless, the Eastern narrow bank is not necessarily the same as the narrow bank defined by Litan. The banks still maintain a distinct set of idiosyncrasies, based on the unique environment that they find themselves in.

PRELIMINARY CONCLUSIONS: WHAT REMAINS FROM THE UNIVERSAL MODEL?

The financial system is one of the most important elements of the economic system. An established belief prevails that the role of the financial system is to mediate among units with financial surpluses and units with financial deficits. The narrowness of such an understanding neglects the second important task of financial intermediation – the distribution and/or exchange of risks. From the beginning of the 1970s, this second viewpoint has steadily gained ground, as well as a belief that the essence of the financial system or of financial companies is the manner of dealing with risks and the control over risks.

In general, the field of financial services covers collecting deposits, crediting, issuing debtors' and owners' securities, trade in securities, portfolio management, advising, insurance, operations with foreign currency and with derivatives. Units with excess savings can always invest surpluses directly to deficit units so that they may accumulate their securities (ordinary shares, mortgages and other). It is a general characteristic of all modern financial systems, whether they are bank-based or stock market based, that a small part of financial flows runs through this direct channel and that the larger amount of financial flows runs through financial intermediaries.

The modern theory of banking and financial intermediation emphasises that such delegating occurs due to information limitations encountered by potential savers/investors. Thus financial intermediaries are at the same time specialised in producing and providing information services. They have access to the information of debtors, mediate incentives to lenders, and have some control over the debtors, either as lenders and/or as shareholders. A basic limitation for lenders and borrowers, which is solved with the help of intermediaries, is insurance against liquidity risk. And in this context in particular the state has an important role in financial mediating. It offers various forms of insurance to reduce the range of risks faced by economic agents due to information imperfections, regulates the obligatory ways that financial mediators operate, and monitors their activity. This is why financial flows are channelled towards the state (government and central bank) and its direct (budgetary) and indirect (off-budgetary) financial mediation.

The four crucial problems encountered by financial intermediaries and their regulator (the state) are: improving the quality of investments, ensuring capital adequacy, increasing the dependency on floating interest rates on the liabilities side, and the intertwining of balance sheet and off-balance sheet operations. The basic changes occurring in the banking system are shown in Table 8.3. These changes bring new elements into the relationships between the banking, enterprise, households and the government sectors. So, it could be argued that the functioning of transitional banking involves a much greater reliance on government's financial intermediation for both banks and enterprises. The adopted model has been that of universal banking, but due to the specific circumstances of transition, the state plays a greater role than is generally acceptable in a truly universal system. Due to this, Eastern banks operate more along the lines of narrow banks, focusing on government debt rather than lending to the enterprise sector.

The literature on transitional banking almost uniformly acknowledges the privatisation of the still dominating state ownership of banks as the most urgent problem to be solved. But the ownership structure is not the only significant problem. Balance sheet data effectively show that banking sectors of several CEECs intermediate resources to safe havens: to the monetary system (central banks and other banks) and to the government, and that they hold a considerable amount of defensive assets and maintain a defensive position. One possible explanation for such a development is the perception of the state as an ultimate anchorage of stability compared with the risky corporate sector.

We can now approach a conclusion from our discussion on universal, narrow and core banks, on imitation of EEC directives, and from insights into the balance sheets of several CEECs with the help of Figures 8.1 and 8.2, which should provide a bridge across the differences among seemingly competing models. Figure 8.1 translates the universal bank concept to Eastern circumstances, and Figure 8.2 presents the idea of a segmented approach to banking. Both figures are used to present the conflicts of interests which are found within the focus of different proposals. These conflicts are between deposit taking (with implicit government guarantees or explicit deposit insurance schemes), the payments system, the central bank as lender of last resort and risk investments.

TRUE UNIVERSALITY		EASTERN UNIVERSALITY	
Traditional banking activities		*Traditional banking activities*	
	Insured deposits		Insured deposits
Cash and reserves		Forced cash and FX reserves	
	Other funds		Other public funds
Loans (ceilings on amount and lending rates)		Government guaranteed loans	
	Debt		Debt
Securities activities	Capital (amount determined by credit risk, interest rates, exchange rates, other market risks and equity financing)	*Securities activities*	Capital (government-owned)
Government-financed equity		Debt-for-equity swaps	
		Government rehabilitation bonds	

Figure 8.1: Two universalities

REGULATED ACTIVITIES		UNREGULATED ACTIVITIES	
Traditional banking activities	Insured deposits (interest rate ceiling)	*Product differentiation*	Uninsured funds (market-raised funds)
Cash and reserves	Capital (less)	Unregulated investments	
Loans (ceilings of amounts and lending rates)		Equity	Capital (more)
		Securitisation	
Government			

Figure 8.2: Functional separation

As far as reforming countries are concerned, different banking schemes should be drawn depending on net creditor positions of the economy-wide sectors, which are changing significantly. As the EFSAL approach introduced by The World Bank in several CEECs has been designed to support the resolution of the debt overhang problem of enterprises and the portfolio problems of banks (both state-owned) through bank-led activities, it was a natural outcome that all countries reported in Table 8.1 introduced a banking system based on the German universal model, supported heavily by the supervisory and regulatory power of outside bodies. As far as prudential bank regulation and depositor protection is concerned, the German system does not restrict the field of activity of financial institutions. Nor does it attempt to regulate specific financial product markets. Instead, it imposes prudent banking behaviour on all institutions. It is also true that the active monitoring of detailed balance sheet restrictions can be seen as a substitute for the market segmentation of the US system, which incidentally is currently being removed by deregulation processes in the US.

What is left for the reforming economies to do is to observe the changing financial interrelations among economy-wide sectors that are created through rehabilitation and restructuring measures designed to resolve debt overhang problems. These activities (for example, the cleaning of balance sheets as a partial monetary reform) are designed to recapitalise enterprises through self-financing mechanisms, and not through raising outside funds on the domestic capital market, which remains shallow and illiquid in any case. The banking system is left to intermediate as the largest holder and issuer of securities, while households' demand for savings deposits increases and the government becomes a net creditor instead of a net debtor. Spontaneous market segmentation can thus develop in line with the German model. If the opposite is the case, then some variety of segmentation is probable. The messages are two: first, the specific structure of assets holdings and liabilities which arise from restructuring activities influences the 'working' model of banks; and second, the role of the central bank and government operations in intermediation and risk transformation processes is crucial.

NOTES

1. For instance, Bryan (1991b, p. 73) writes: 'As much as 25% of the US banking system –
    representing assets of more than $750 billion – has begun to post such massive loan losses that
    it must focus on collecting loans rather than making them. Healthy banks, shaken by their
    competitors' plight (and worried about more intense scrutiny from bank examiners), are losing
    confidence in their ability to make such loans. This credit crunch has the potential to turn a
    mild recession into a downward economic spiral that feeds on itself.'
2. It is possible in such circumstances to have a bank under rehabilitation with above the required
    capital due to the injection of government bonds, and with complete liquidity dependence on
    the central bank, government deposits or the interbank market.

3. The argument in favour of universal banks says that they achieve better performance due to a superior monitoring and information collection capacity. When a bank takes an equity stake in a firm instead of debt, the firm's leverage ratio is reduced and its risk-taking incentives are altered towards less risk-taking. Having both debt and equity stakes in enterprises, a bank can more easily enforce restructuring of enterprises. The concept of the World Bank's EFSAL approach exercised in reforming economies is based on this (Dervis et al., 1994). On the other hand, knowing that rehabilitated banks are state owned, with unknown prospects for privatisation, building stakes in enterprises could be simply a new wave of nationalisation through debt-for-equity swaps.
4. This is a controversial issue. Leach (1993) writes for the USA: 'The irony is that recent regulation has militated against risk taking in general, and entrepreneurial lending in particular. The Basle Accord, for instance, by requiring no leveraging offsets for government bond holding and reduced levels of capital for mortgage making, biases banks against commercial lending. For the sake of the economy, very different priorities would seem to be in order. It is hard to believe America can become competitive in the next century if ... our banking regulation gives incentives for commercial banks to buy bonds instead of making loans.' Mullins (1993) disagrees with Leach, stating that the cutbacks in loans coincided with the downturn of the economic cycle, suggesting that economic fundamentals, more than Basle standards, were an important causal factor. Nevertheless, due to the fact that banks meet intermediation costs which mutual funds don't, he asks: 'Still, aren't banks in danger of becoming bond mutual funds?'
5. Directives 77/789/EEC and 89/646/EEC (First and Second Banking Directives).
6. Annex to Directive 77/789/EEC.

REFERENCES

Anderson, R.W. and Kegels, C. (1998), *Transitional Banking: Financial Development of Central and Eastern Europe*. Clarendon Press: Oxford.

Boot, A.W. and van Wijnbergen, S. (1994), 'Financial Sector Reform in the Former Soviet Union', Unpublished manuscript.

Borish, M.S., Ding, W. and Noël, M. (1996), *On the Road to EU Accession: Financial Development in Central Europe*. The World Bank: Washington, DC.

Bryan, L.L. (1991a), 'A Blueprint for Financial Reconstruction', *Harvard Business Review*, 69:3, 77–86.

Bryan, L.L. (1991b), *Bankrupt: Restoring the Health and Profitability of Our Banking System*. Harper Business: New York.

Cherubini, U., Ciampolini, M. and DeFelice, G. (1993), 'The Role of Banks as Investors in Securities: Theoretical and Empirical Features in an International Perspective', in *Financial Market Liberalisation and the Role of Banks*, V. Conti and R. Hamaul (eds), 251–76. Cambridge University Press: Cambridge.

Dervis, K., Selowsky, M. and Wallich, C. (1994), *The Transition in Central and Eastern Europe and the Former Soviet Union*. The World Bank: Washington, DC.

EBRD (1998a), *Law in Transition: Advancing Legal Reforms*. European Bank of Reconstruction and Development: London.

EBRD (1998b), *Transition Report 1998: Financial Sector in Transition*. European Bank for Reconstruction and Development: London.

The Economist (1994), 'Central Europe's Model Bank', August 27, 13–14.

Gardener, E.P.M. and Molyneaux, P. (1990), *Changes in Western European Banking: An International Banker's Guide*. Routledge: London.

Goodhart, C.A.E. (1993), 'Can We Improve the Structure of Financial Systems?', *European Economic Review*, 37:3, 269–91.

Goodhart, C.A.E. (1994), 'Banks and the Control of Corporations', *Economic Notes by Monte dei Paschi di Siena*, 23:1, 1–18.

Jones, C. (1993), *Banking and Financial Sectors in East and Central Europe*. Financial Times Business Information: London.

Kaufman, G. and Litan, R.E. (eds) (1993), *Assessing Bank Reform: FDICIA One Year Later*. The Brookings Institute: Washington, DC.

Kregel, J.A. (1992), 'Universal Banks, US Banking Reform and Financial Competition in the EEC', *BNL Quarterly Review*, 45:182, 231–53.

Leach, J. (1993), 'The Future of the Banking Industry', in Kaufman and Litan, 85–89.

Litan, R.E. (1987), *What Should Banks Do?* The Brookings Institute: Washington, DC.

Maccarinelli, M., Marotta, G. and Prosdocimi, M. (1993), 'A Comparative Analysis of the Liabilities Structure in Seven banking Systems', in V. Conti and R. Hamaul (eds), 301–36.

Mullins, D.W. Jr. (1993), 'Capital Standards and the Performance of the US Banking Industry', in Kaufman and Litan, 90–103.

Sacinelli, M. (1992), 'Eastern Europe and the Financial Sector: Where are They Going?', *BNL Quarterly Review*, 45:183, 463–92.

Smith, E.O. (1994), *The German Economy*. Routledge: London.

Steinherr, A. (1993), 'An Innovative Package for Financial Sector Reforms in Eastern Europe', *Journal of Banking and Finance*, 17:5, 1033–57.

Steinherr, A. and Huveneers, C. (1992), 'Universal Banking in the Integrated Marketplace', in *The New European Financial Marketplace*, A. Steinherr (ed.), 49–67. Longman: London.

Stiglitz, J.E. (1985), 'Credit Markets and the Control of Capital', *Journal of Money, Credit and Banking*, 17:2, 133–52.

Story, J. and Walter, I. (1997), *Political Economy of Financial Integration in Europe*. Manchester University Press: Manchester.

Szegö, G.P. (1993), 'Introduction', *Journal of Banking and Finance*, 17:5, 773–5.

Thorne, A.E. (1993), 'Eastern Europe's Experience with Banking Reform: Is There a Role for Banks in the Transition?', *Journal of Banking and Finance*, 17:5, 959–1000.

Tobin, J. (1982), 'The Commercial Banking Firm: A Simple Model', *Scandinavian Journal of Economics*, 84:4, 495–530.

Tobin, J. (1985), 'Financial Innovation and Deregulation in Perspective', *Bank of Japan Monetary and Economic Studies*, 3:2, 9–29.

Walter, I. (1994), 'Efficiency, Stability and Competitiveness of Universal Banking: Lessons from the German Experience', in *Restructuring Japan's Financial Markets*, I. Walter and T. Hiraki (eds), Business One Irwin: New York.

van Wijnbergen, S. (1994), 'Banking Regulation and Fraud in Eastern Europe: An Argument for Narrow Banking?', Unpublished manuscript.

Zysman, J. (1983), *Governments, Markets and Growth: Financial Systems and the Politics of Industrial Change*. Cornell University Press: Ithaca, NY and London.

PART IV

Conclusion

9. The New Pragmatism and a New Paradigm: The Transformed Role of the State

David Green and Karl Petrick

POLICY PERSPECTIVE

The central aim of the financial sector reforms in each of the three countries studied in detail has been to help enable them to promote financial stability and create a reasonably efficient, market-oriented financial infrastructure. This aim has been pursued both as part of the wider project of creating a capitalist economy and so that each country may meet the conditions for accession to the European Union.

Shared aims have not led, however, to the adoption of similar policies. The governments of each of the three countries studied here have chosen to pursue quite different paths of financial sector and banking reform. The Czech Republic began by relying on domestic private investors and mass privatisation. This was relatively unsuccessful and was followed by the Czech government beginning to sell majority stakes in large banks to foreign strategic investors. In Hungary a much earlier decision was taken to seek foreign strategic investors with the result that the majority of Hungary's banking activity is now foreign owned and the banking system, as a whole, is reasonably compliant with EU norms. However, this has been a far from painless process and a period of 'state desertion' proved very costly. In contrast, Slovenia has remained relatively closed to foreign investors throughout the 1990s and the pace of financial sector reform in this small, stable country has been slow. As all three countries have many positive achievements in the transition process as a whole, these variations provide useful material for illuminating the policy choices available.

MAJOR POLICY CONCLUSIONS

The research and analysis presented in the foregoing chapters suggest several policy conclusions. Three major themes for future policy direction may be identified (see Figure 9.1). These are, first, that the state has a major role to play in creating and maintaining a reasonably effective financial sector. In turn, this financial sector needs to include a number of healthy commercial banks. This is necessary, as experience has shown that capital markets are not an effective substitute in practice, in the transitional economies, for financial intermediation. These commercial banks, both domestic and foreign owned, need to be supervised by an effective domestic supervisory authority operating within the context of the internationally agreed Basle rules. The adoption of these rules and appropriate domestic legislation is a necessary but not sufficient condition for the creation of an effective financial sector. Each of these major policy conclusions is discussed in turn.

The Role of the State and the Dangers of 'State Desertion'

It is, apparently, paradoxical to argue that state institutions and authorities need to play a major role in the creation of a private-sector-led banking and financial system. In the transitional economies, the state needs not just to retreat from economic life but to have its remaining, proper powers highly focused so that it can play an essential modernising and regulatory role. This conclusion is a considerable variation from the findings of some other recent work in the field. For example, Anderson and Kegels (1998) make facilitating the retreat of the state one of the main goals of financial policy-making in transition economies.[1] In summarising their well-researched study of transition banking, they argue that there should be four general goals for financial policy-making in transition economies. In their view these should be:

- assuring a stable financial environment;
- enhancing the quality of enterprise governance;
- promoting the liquidity of real and financial asset markets, and
- facilitating the retreat of the state.[2]

It is argued here that this perspective generates policy errors. Of course, there is heated agreement on the desirability of a stable financial environment and the better governance of enterprises. However, the focus on market liquidity and facilitating the retreat of the state is misplaced. As Steinherr (1997) has argued persuasively 'The political, economic and organisational pre-requisites for an efficient capital market exceed by far what seems possible in east European countries.'[3] Reform efforts should instead be directed at creating an honest, stable and reasonably efficient banking industry. The evidence presented in this book suggests that Geoffrey Hodgson was correct to argue that 'There is no robust theoretical basis for the advice given to economies in transition that markets will emerge spontaneously.'[4] Rather, it is the case that

---

The state has a major role to play in creating and maintaining a reasonably effective financial sector

- State institutions and authorities need to play a major role in the creation of a private-enterprise-led banking and financial system.
- 'State desertion' is a significant danger and has led to a significant accumulation of major problems in the financial sectors of two of the three economies studied. Attempting to introduce a free capital market by legislation and privatisation alone is not, in practice, a solution to the problem of 'monobanking'.

In practice, effective commercial banks are needed; capital markets are not an effective substitute

- Commercial banks in the transitional economies have a major role to play. Strengthening their ability to play an effective role in the process of financial intermediation and the allocation of capital is a crucial ingredient in successful economic development.
- Attempting to skip over the creation of effective privately owned banks and jump straight to a free capital market has proved unsuccessful.
- Strategic foreign investors have the capacity to play a central role in creating a sound financial infrastructure in the associated countries if properly selected.

International rules need to be accompanied by the operation of an effective domestic bank supervisor

- The transplantation of EU rules and the *acquis communautaire* combined with the implementation of the Basle Committee's 'Core Principles of Effective Banking Supervision' are necessary but insufficient for the creation of a stable, efficient financial infrastructure.
- Building the professional capacity of the state agencies charged with banking supervision within an internationally acceptable regulatory framework is a key aspect of creating a functioning, 'normal' financial system.

Figure 9.1: Themes for future policy direction

the proposition that free capital markets, unburdened by highly regulated financial intermediaries, would provide an efficient, stable financial system in the transition has been comprehensively disproved.

So too has 'the idea that all that is needed to achieve efficiency is to move any and all enterprises from the public to the private sector' been proven fallacious.[5] It is not the case, as Jeffrey Sachs has argued that 'markets spring up as soon as central planning bureaucrats vacate the field'.[6] Instead, experience has shown that it is essential to ensure that state agencies play a carefully specified, focused role in developing as well as in supervising the financial system. This has been graphically illustrated by the experience of Hungary as is detailed in the foregoing chapters by Karl Petrick and István Ábel.

Of course, the old financial system where the state was the main borrower, intermediary and lender needed to be unequivocally shattered in order to facilitate the development of a modern capitalist economy. Ensuring the retreat of the state from the financial system has proved to be a necessary, but far from a sufficient, condition for the achievement of this goal. Far from dealing with the overwhelming dominance of the state being the central issue of the transition, the problems of state desertion and inappropriate focus have proved to be central. As Ellman (1997) noted:

> Another surprise has been the importance of the banking sector and of financial fragility ... banks play a very important role in the transformation. They provide (or fail to provide) the payments transmission system, their bad loans can burden the state budget (as in Hungary) or precipitate a deep economic crisis (as in Bulgaria), they can play a positive role in the work out of overdue loans (as in Poland), and poor supervision and regulation of their activities may permit spectacular banking collapses with negative economic consequences (as in the Baltic states and the Czech Republic).[7]

One conclusion to be drawn from this analysis is that reformers may most usefully look to the lessons drawn from the experiences of developing economies in reforming their financial sectors, rather than the advanced economies, for inspiration. Following this line of reasoning leads to placing greater weight on the importance of the prevention of financial crises and the stabilisation of the economy rather than pursuing more apparently ambitious policy options. After all, the reality in the transitional economies to date has been that '*banking crises have been numerous*'.[8] They have also been economically damaging.

The regular incidence of such crises suggests that the perspective that the World Bank has advanced in recent years regarding reforming the state in developing countries has much to commend it. The World Bank has advanced the argument that one critical building block for economic success is the creation of a focused, capable state.[9] The research presented here supports the World Bank's contention that initiatives are needed along the following lines:

- Higher standards of competence and integrity of bank management, as well as effective management controls.
- More transparency and adequate information on the soundness of banks.
- Public financial safety nets that boost confidence in the financial system but also limit induced distortions, such as explicit or implicit government guarantees that encourage excessive risk-taking.
- Effective regulatory and supervisory oversight for controlling risk and limiting the adverse impact of official safety nets.

- Transparent ownership structure that enhances competitive behaviour, and limits on connected lending.[10]

Commercial Banks Are Still Needed

The countries aiming for European union membership in the early years of the twenty-first century have made remarkable progress in reforming their financial systems. The appropriate legislation for a reasonably sound, normal banking system is largely in place. The critical tasks for the first few years of the century are to build up the capacity of privately owned banks and other financial institutions so that they can carry out business effectively and efficiently, within a regulatory and supervisory framework which is appropriately targeted and efficiently conducted.

The outcome of this process is a matter of great concern to the citizens of the associated countries of Central and Eastern Europe, and to the European Union as a whole. A corrupt, insider dominated 'crony' or 'Mafia-style' banking system will have deeply negative effects on the rest of the economy and society more widely. Conversely, a normal financial system will provide many positive benefits while being subject to all the familiar risks which have led to the development of supervision and regulation and attempts to ensure that capitalism's fluctuations are not too extreme. However, designing policy initiatives to create a normally functioning financial system have proved far from straightforward.

One of the most widely employed strategies, that of 'insider privatisation', has failed. As the Transition Report of the European Bank for Reconstruction put it 'the insider privatisation that has been widespread cannot be recommended. Rather, greater emphasis should be placed on attracting strategic investors, both foreign and domestic'.[11] Nor is it the case, as some have hoped, that securities markets can simply supersede banks. The deep-seated process of disintermediation internationally does not imply that the Central and Eastern European economies can simply jump from the situation where the state acted as 'the key depositor, credit controller and customer for lending'[12] to one in which securities markets handle all decisions on credit.

The EBRD's 1998 study on these issues found that:

> Recent experience documents the importance of well-designed and vigorously enforced regulation for the operation of both banks and securities markets. Deep and liquid markets develop only when enterprises issuing publicly traded securities are subject to disclosure, auditing and accounting requirements that support the information environment for financial transactions.[13]

Furthermore the authors of the EBRD study observed 'stock- and bond-market capitalisation and liquidity are even less adequate than bank finance'.

The research presented in the foregoing chapters is consistent with the conclusion of the EBRD report that:

> Strengthening the performance of banks in transition economies, however, remains a vitally important task. Over the medium term, their financial systems are likely to remain primarily bank based and the performance of their banks will be an important determinant of how rapidly their economies grow and how stable they will be.[14]

Furthermore, the experience of Hungary with the extensive role played by foreign-owned commercial banks indicates that strategic foreign investors can play a very positive role in the creation of a normal banking system.

The Transplantation of International and European Standards is Necessary But Not Sufficient: Bank Supervisors Play a Crucial Role

A major finding of the research presented in this book is that banks will continue to play a vital role in the financial system of the transitional economies. As this will continue to be the case for some time, the effective supervision of the financial system will also be essential. Poor supervision has frequently played a significant role in the generation of banking crises and wider financial collapses. In Caprio and Klingbiel's study of banking insolvency in 29 countries, poor supervision and regulation was cited as an important explanatory factor in 26 of the maximum of 29 possible occasions. The importance of supervision is underlined by the fact that poor supervision was found to be more significant than any one of recession, deficient bank management or a significant deterioration in the terms of trade.[15] The microeconomic causation of many macroeconomic problems is increasingly recognised. Hawkins and Turner's review of banking crises and subsequent restructuring in 23 emerging economies underlines the significance of microeconomic failings as well as the more familiar macroeconomic and system-related causes.[16]

The specific legal framework within which intervention takes place is also significant. For example, 'Hungarian law tends to encourage the financial reorganisation of insolvent industrial enterprises, rather than liquidation. By contrast, laws in the Czech Republic tilt more towards liquidation of enterprises when their current liabilities cannot be met, regardless of their longer-term prospects'.[17] The detail of both the framework and the practice of banking supervision is, therefore, increasingly under the spotlight.

Furthermore, the wide scope of banking supervision has made reform a vexed issue. The list of tasks facing supervisors is extensive and includes:

1. Issuing banking licences. This involves taking decisions about what is 'fit and proper' and what class of institutions can engage in banking (most importantly links between banking and industry).

2. Certifying minimum managerial competence.
3. Certifying that minimum capital requirements are fulfilled (application of banking Basle rules).
4. Permitting bank mergers and acquisitions.
5. Taking measures to prevent fraudulent transactions and money laundering.
6. Ensuring that bank management operates within supervisory guidelines on credit concentration and foreign exchange exposure.
7. Ensuring that contracts entered into are legal.[18]

This list is just as pertinent to the development of the regulation and supervision of the financial system in the transitional economies of Central and Eastern Europe as it is elsewhere. Banking supervision has been one of the issues most effectively tackled in a global context. In both the advanced economies and the developing world, it has become increasingly widely recognised that the goal of the authorities is to promote conditions in which markets can function effectively and, in the case of financial markets, impart a stabilising rather than destabilising impulse.

In this connection, Andrew Crockett, general manager of the Bank for International Settlements, has contended that there are three central requirements for the operation of effective bank supervision: 'transparency, norms or standards of conduct, and appropriate incentives'.[19] However, it is not the case that one can simply move away from discretion and operate through rules that are automatically enforced through the operation of quantitative lending ratios, for example. In fact, effective supervision involving the exercise of judgement within a framework rather than the automatic application of rules has become more necessary despite the great success of the wide adoption of the Basle Accords. As Andrew Crockett said in 1998:

> The prime requirement for the prudent conduct of business is a proper understanding of the measurement and pricing of risk, and a set of systems and controls that is capable of monitoring and controlling risk. This means that the former quantitative tools of enforcing prudential norms are no longer adequate. What is required is the capacity to judge the overall management capacity and control environment in a supervised institution.
>
> This implies an increasingly subtle approach to supervision. As markets have become more integrated, and the activities of banks have become more complex, it is harder to foster prudent behaviour only through the adoption of administrative ratios and controls. An assessment of a financial intermediary must be based on how it manages and measures all the risks to which it is exposed. The supervisory profession is therefore in the process of becoming quite a bit more demanding.[20]

Crockett's argument presented here supports our contention that the simple transplantation of the rules and regulations of the European Union and the adoption of the internationally agreed accords on banking will prove insufficient for the development of an effective financial sector. Instead, legislative reform must be accompanied with a drive to build up the capacities of institutions. This must include building the capacity of both the privately owned banks and other financial intermediaries and the publicly accountable supervisory agency. The old system, in which politics as mediated through the Communist Party or its equivalent such as the Hungarian Socialist Workers' Party was primarily responsible for resource allocation and undermined the development of any proper framework of political accountability. It is entirely understandable that frustration at the failures and corruption of this system led to the adoption of a renewed capitalist economic framework.

It is unrealistic to think that the transitional economies can jump to best market practice as found in the United States and other advanced industrial countries. The ability of economists to simply assume away institutions as if they were a veil for markets is wrong. In any case, as Crockett has argued 'we are dealing with a deep seated set of market failures'.[21] Once again, the approach taken by the World Bank in the late 1990s to building the capability of state and private sector institutions is helpful. As the Bank argues 'Building the institutions for a capable public sector is essential ... Evidence across a range of countries has shown that well-functioning bureaucracies can promote growth and reduce poverty'.[22]

The World Bank has found that the three essential building blocks are:

1. Strong central capacity for formulating and co-ordinating policy.
2. Efficient and effective delivery systems.
3. Motivated and capable staff.

There are challenges in all three areas pertinent to banking supervision in the transitional economies. As the World Bank has concluded 'most countries have a long way to go to build the institutional capability needed to respond effectively to the many demands of transition'.[23] Furthermore, as Bonin et al. (1998) have correctly argued, 'The failure to establish a functioning independent banking sector has serious macroeconomic implications.'

An uncontentious recommendation of Bonin et al. is that 'Bank regulatory agencies should be independent of the government and protected from political pressures'.[24] The question is how is this to be achieved. Central banks are inevitably concerned with major macro economic decisions. In recent years, much of the institutional reform effort in the advanced industrial countries has concentrated on the type and degree of independence and protection from direct political pressures, which the Central Bank is to be afforded. One way of conceptualising this is to give the Central Bank operational independence, while the government should define goals.

A further complication is presented by the question of whether the supervisory agency should be in the Central Bank. Experience in the European Union on this is mixed, with some countries choosing to supervise banks from within the Central Bank and others choosing to have a separate supervisory agency. There is a significant gap in this area at European Union level with a significant unfinished agenda which is bound to be problematic as the European banking industry is transformed by competitive pressures.[25] There is certainly no template within the European Union for the transitional economies to follow. Practice is changing rapidly. For example, the Labour government has transformed the position in the UK since 1997. Policy changes included making the Bank of England operationally independent from government, stripping the Bank of its supervisory powers and creating a new, single financial supervisory authority independent of both the Central Bank and the Treasury.

Overall, the research presented here supports the separation of banking supervision from the Central Bank. A critical reason for this is that such separation enables the supervisory agency to concentrate on its tasks. Such a focus is consistent with the World Bank's experience of seeking to establish satisfactory banking arrangements in developing countries. In the World Bank's framework, banking supervision is set to remain in the core public sector. This means that the key tasks are to:

1. Ensure clarity of purpose;
2. Improve compliance with rules;
3. Strengthen voice mechanisms.

To this list should be added that the supervisory agency needs to be transparent and properly accountable. Supervisors need to be well trained and there has been much progress in this regard in recent years. They also need to be reasonably paid and to enjoy proper status, as this will contribute to developing a culture of integrity. This is particularly important in the transitional economies, as there are many displaced agents looking for new sources of rent. Every possible step needs to be taken to move away from an economy dominated by rent-seeking towards a productive economy where people are paid for producing goods and services or for forgoing immediate consumption on a modest scale.

Here banking supervision can contribute not just by helping to produce a sound financial infrastructure but also by reducing moral hazard in the financial system by adopting relatively minor reforms in the deposit insurance system. These can be restructured so that they meet their goals of avoiding calamitous financial collapse, while not giving rash or criminal investors a free ride. There are measures that may be taken in order to help ensure this, such as regulations allowing a single claim per depositor, with each claim receiving a significant, though small, percentage less than the deposit lost; with refunds to be made over a period of time rather than immediately, and with a total limit on payouts. Such mechanisms take away much, and in practice probably all, the moral hazard faced.

As Begg and Altunbas demonstrated in Chapter 2, the potential for contagion in the financial system plus the collision of national political interests leads to a significantly enhanced risk of financial fragility. The emerging European Union system does not have a blueprint to copy or adapt – instead there are separate, competing systems within the European polity as present. Furthermore, existing arrangements have yet to be tested by a major financial crisis or unforeseen economic shock.

Experience in the transitional economies suggests that significant progress can be made in creating a viable banking system. As Matoušek and Taci show in Chapter 4, remarkable progress has been made in the case of the Czech Republic. While it is true that by the end of the 1990s progress was still needed in the areas of consolidated accounts, supervision and capital adequacy in other areas significant changes had been successfully implemented. Furthermore, a successful learning-by-doing process was in operation.

PREPARING FOR ACCESSION TO THE EUROPEAN UNION

In conclusion, three main challenges confront those who wish to see an effective financial system in operation in the transitional economies. The first is to refocus the state on its proper tasks. The second is to build up banking institutions so that they can play their role as part of the economic infrastructure. The third is to design and operate a regulatory and supervisory system, which is compatible with the *acquis communautaire* and the broader international system of banking supervision.

The European Union's *Agenda 2000* made it quite clear that countries entering the EU must have a functioning market economy as well as the capacity to cope with competitive pressures and market forces within the Union.[26] The transplantation of appropriate legislation is largely complete and much of the regulatory system has been designed. Appropriate rules help shape good policy and foster positive business outcomes. But, on their own, they will never ensure that the financial infrastructure works effectively. This conclusion is further reinforced by Tison's study of the transitional rules (Chapter 3). He also points out (p. 57) that EU prudential standards do not always correspond exactly with those espoused in the Core Principles.

What is needed now is to breathe life into the commercial banks and ensure that the supervisory authority operates in a competent, subtle and effective way. Progressive macroeconomic change depends on effective microeconomic institution building and operation.

NOTES

1. Anderson, Ronald W. and Chantal Kegels (1998), *Transition Banking: Financial Development of Central and Eastern Europe*, Clarendon Press, Oxford, UK and Oxford University Press, New York, p. 259.
2. Ibid., p. 259.
3. Alfred Steinherr (1997), 'Banking Reforms in Eastern European Countries', *Oxford Economic Papers*, Vol. 13, No. 2, p. 110.
4. Hodgson, Geoffrey M. (1998), 'Institutions and the Viability of Macroeconomics: Some Perspectives on the Transformation Process in Post-Communist Economies', *Journal for Institutional Innovation, Development and Transition*, Vol. 2, p. 14.
5. Spulber, Nicolas (1997), *Redefining the State: Privatisation and Welfare Reform in Industrial and Transitional Economies*, Cambridge University Press, Cambridge, UK and New York, p. 85.
6. Sachs, Jeffrey D. (1993), *Poland's Jump to a Market Economy*, Harvard University Press, Cambridge, MA, p. xxi.
7. Ellman, Michael (1997), 'The Political Economy of Transformation', *Oxford Economic Papers*, Vol. 13, No. 2, p. 27.
8. Lavigne, Marie (1999), *The Economics of Transition*, Macmillan, London UK, second edn, p. 189.
9. World Bank (1997), *Annual Report*, The World Bank, Washington, DC.
10. World Bank (1999), *Global Economic Prospects and the Developing Countries: Beyond Financial Crisis*, The World Bank, Washington, DC.
11. European Bank for Reconstruction and Development (1998), *Transition Report 1998*, European Bank for Reconstruction and Development, London.
12. Green, David M.A. and Karl Petrick (1999), 'The Eastward Expansion of the European Union and the Transformation of the Financial System', *Review of Radical Political Economics*, Vol. 31, No. 3.
13. European Bank for Reconstruction and Development (1998), *Transition Report 1998*: Financial sector in transition, EBRD, London, p. 103.
14. Ibid.
15. Caprio, Gerard Jr and Daniela Klingebiel (1996), *Bank Insolvency: Bad Luck, Bad Policy or Bad Banking?*, World Bank Conference on Development Economics, The World Bank, Washington, DC, p. 91.
16. Hawkins, John and Philip Turner (1999), *Bank Restructuring in Practice*, BIS Policy Paper No. 6, Bank for International Settlements, Basle.
17. Ibid. pp. 33–4.
18. Steinherr, Alfred (1997), 'Banking Reforms in Eastern European Countries', *Oxford Economic Papers*, Vol. 13, No. 2, p. 110.
19. Crockett, Andrew (1998), *Banking Supervision and Financial Stability*, Group of Thirty, Washington, DC, p. 10.
20. Ibid., p. 20.
21. Ibid., p. 10.
22. World Bank (1997), *World Development Report: The State in a Changing World*, Oxford University Press, Oxford, New York, p. 80.
23. Ibid., p. 86.
24. Ibid., p. 13.
25. Begg, Iain and David Green (1996), 'Banking supervision in Europe and economic and monetary union', *Journal of European Public Policy*, Vol. 3, No. 3, pp. 381–401.
26. European Commission (1997), *Agenda 2000, Communication of the Commission*, European Commission, Strasbourg.

Index